Powerful Places
in Ireland

Powerful Places
in Ireland

Elyn Aviva &
Gary White

Powerful Places in Ireland

by

Elyn Aviva & Gary White

Copyright © 2011 by Pilgrims Process, Inc.

http://www.PowerfulPlaces.com

The authors and publisher have made every effort to ensure the accuracy of the information in this book at the time of publication. However, they cannot accept any responsibility for any loss, injury, or inconvenience resulting from the use of information contained in this book.

ISBN: 978-0-9835516-5-2

Library of Congress Control Number:

2011946233

Set in Adobe Caslon Pro 10 pt. and Gil Sans Light 10 pt., with display in Adobe Caslon Pro in various sizes. Cover and title set in Reliq Std and Briso Pro.

Cover photo: Athgreany Stone Circle (Piper's Stones) by Elyn Aviva. Photos on pp. 9, 30, 36, and 94 by Michael Fox.

Contents

A Note About QR Codes

Throughout this book you will notice strange square boxes filled with tiny rectangles of various sizes. These boxes are QR codes (quick response codes) that link to websites. To read these codes you need to have a QR code reader installed on your smart phone or tablet and you need an internet connection. You can find the app in the app store for your device if one is not already installed.

When you have the app installed start it up and aim the camera at this QR code:

You should see the Powerful Places website appear on the device. You can move about that website and see what we have to offer and how to order our books in various formats.

Every URL reference in this book has a QR code near it to allow you to easily and quickly go to the websites we recommend. These will provide additional information, photos, videos, and other resources to enrich your reading experience. Let us know if the QR codes make a positive contribution to your experience in *Powerful Places in Ireland*.

The URLs were active when this book went to press. However, the internet changes every day and it is inevitable that some of the references will be out of date or no longer active when you view them.

Acknowledgments

Gratitude to our mentors and teachers, including Ferran Blasco Aguasca, Mara Freeman, Sig Lonegren, Anne Parker, R. J. Stewart, and Dominique Susani. Gratitude to all the earth-mystery writers and researchers, including Paul Devereux, Tom Graves, and Nigel Pennick, who have opened the way for so many others. Gratitude to our friends and consultants, including Mike Croghan and Martin Byrne, for their comments and corrections, and especially to Michael Fox, Howard Goldbaum, and Nora Judge for their invaluable assistance. Gratitude to each other for patience, tolerance, and enthusiasm. Gratitude to the land, the stones, the trees, the water, and the temples of Ireland, which are an ongoing source of inspiration.

For those interested in following up with our mentors we offer the following websites with QR codes for each:

Ferran Blasco Aguasca: http://www.zahoriart.com/

Mara Freeman: http://www.chalicecentre.net/

Sig Lonegren: http://www.geomancy.org/

Anne Parker: http://www.latitudewithattitude.com/

R. J. Stewart: http://www.rjstewart.org/

Dominique Susani: http://www.sacredgeometryarts.com/

Introduction to Powerful Places Guidebooks

Over the years we have traveled to a number of unusual places, drawn by curiosity, lured by possibility. Gradually we realized that although many of these sites were interesting, some of them were much more—they were powerful. These were places where we felt something out of the ordinary, ranging from a shiver up the spine to an unexpected sense of serenity. Sometimes we had a strong intimation that we had entered a "thin place" where the veil between this world and the "other realm" was more easily parted.

In this guidebook we describe some of the powerful places we have found in Ireland and invite you to experience them for yourself. We don't know what you will feel when visiting these sites. We have observed that one person may bask in the energy of a particular site; another may feel nothing at all; and a third may want to leave as quickly as possible.

How did we choose these particular locations? We talked with people; we did research to discover powerful places that were not likely to be on every tourist's itinerary; we made extended visits to Ireland; and we paid attention to what we experienced at different sites. We traveled with and consulted with expert guides. We then chose a variety of powerful places to include in this guidebook. We make no claims to be exhaustive; instead, we are selective.

Each chapter includes at least one brief, personal account by Elyn of a visit to a particular powerful place. This is followed by information about the site, along with suggestions for experiencing the place, quotations in grey boxes, and numerous photos and graphics. There are directions on how to get there, other places to experience, and additional resources. The guidebook concludes with an afterword, a glossary, a bibliography, and an index.

Powerful Places in Ireland is intended as an invitation to experience powerful places in Ireland. We hope that it's the beginning of a relationship between you and Ireland—and our guidebook series. We look forward to hearing from you.

Powerful Places

The way a powerful place feels can take many forms, and it can be subtle or very strong, positive or otherwise. For example, during one visit inside a large, earth-covered passage grave in Ireland, Elyn felt increasingly uncomfortable and shaky but, against her better judgment, she stayed to listen to our guide. Afterwards, Elyn learned that several people had left immediately because they felt so ill at ease—but others thought the cairn was a wonderful place. A friend who visited the site at another time remarked on the exquisite rose fragrance that permeated the chamber during her meditation.

In an isolated monastery in the mountains of Spain, we (Gary and Elyn) were shown into an abandoned chapel. Instantly, we both felt an incredibly unconditional loving presence. Our companion, a sensitive, intuitive woman, looked at us in puzzlement. She thought the energy in the room was nothing special.

Our experiences have differed on subsequent visits to the same site. Sometimes the explanation is simple: a large, noisy tour group has just trampled through the site, oblivious to what was there. Other times the answer isn't so obvious. Perhaps it has something to do with being there at a different time of year or during a different phase of the moon—or in a different state of mind.

Experiences can never be repeated, whether it's your first taste of a chocolate gelato cone on a sunny day in Rome, or your first kiss, or your first visit to the Grand Canyon. To paraphrase the Greek philosopher Heraclitus, "No one ever steps into the same river twice, for it's not the same river and they are not the same person." This is equally true of powerful places.

What Makes a Place Powerful?

In powerful places we experience an interaction between the energies of the place itself, the human activities at that location (offerings, ceremonies, constructions such as stone circles or temples), and our own openness to experience what is happening at that moment. The land itself has underground water lines, faults or cracks in the earth (sometimes called fire lines), energy vortices, "blind" springs, and so on, which our ancestors were able to sense and utilize. An old Gaulish word, *wouivre*, refers to snakes that glide, to rivers that snake through the landscape, and to telluric currents that snake underground from the depths of the terrestrial strata.

Sergio Berti, an Italian geobiophysical analyst, says "powerful places" produce a measurable effect on the body. They affect the sympathetic component of the autonomous nervous system. An increase in sympathetic activity is linked to action, optimism, and readiness to fight; A decrease is linked to relaxation, slower breathing, and the predominance of the mind over body. An underground fault may reduce sympathetic activity; granite may stimulate sympathetic activity; and metallic minerals may stimulate activity or not, depending on the type.

Experienced dowsers using rods or pendulums can locate these underground features with great accuracy. If they couldn't, oil exploration and well-digging companies wouldn't waste their money on hiring them.

Our ancestors utilized these energies and their knowledge of geometry (circles, triangles, pyramid shapes, etc.) to construct sacred places. For example,

"We don't understand how dowsing works, but we do understand that it can be worked to produce usable results, and we also understand how it can be worked. In that sense dowsing can be said to be a technology, though it can't be scientific." Tom Graves, p. 22.

an alignment of standing stones may have been placed to draw off energy from a destabilizing underground fault; a circle of stones may have been built to utilize the energy of an underground spring. The altar of a twelfth-century church may have been carefully placed over the crossing of underground water and fire lines. In addition, the ancient Master Builders used their knowledge of astronomy to orient some of these powerful places toward important seasonal events like the winter solstice.

Experiencing a Powerful Place

How do you experience a powerful place? The brief answer is: by centering, grounding, and being present to a site in whatever way works for you. Feeling the subtle energies that are present in a place requires sensitivity and intuition. It is a bit like tuning a radio dial to a particular frequency. Although some people are naturally gifted in sensing these energies, others need to be taught. We didn't feel much at powerful places until we started studying with geomancers and dowsers. Detailed instruction in dowsing and sensing earth energies is outside the scope of this guidebook, but we will give suggestions for how you can "attune" yourself to the powerful places we describe.

We encourage you to listen carefully to your own inner guidance as you open yourself to what may be available to you at a particular place on a particular day, at a particular time of day, with the particular predisposition you bring to that moment. You must use your own judgment to determine what is good or not good for you. Trust your feelings—and enjoy the mystery.

Much of the time we humans oper-

"To our civilized view, places are just commodities, to be bought and sold like any other commodity; but in the pagan view, probably best typified by that of the American Indians, places can have a sacredness, a spiritual importance, that seems to bear no relation to the more physical characteristics of the place." Graves, p. 5-6.

ate on "automatic," hardly registering where we are or what we feel. Visiting a powerful place is an opportunity to be intentional and alert. In order to fully experience a powerful place, it is important to be aware of your surroundings and of

"There is a sane and balanced ground for a thoughtful and rational agnostic to be open to the idea that consciousness and awareness pervades the universe, that it may be as or even more fundamental than material physicality, that there's no such thing as dead, unconscious matter; that we live in a psychophysical universe with interiority and exteriority, with an innerness, an inner life as well as its outer manifestation." Terry Patten, Lesson 4, Evolving Wisdom, spring 2011.

changes in yourself in response to the environment.

We suggest an acronym, **BLESSING**, to help remember how to prepare to enter a powerful place—whether it is a forest, a church, or a stone circle. **BLESSING** stands for: **B**reathe slowly and regularly, paying attention to your breath moving in and out. If you have a breathing practice, now is the time to do it. **L**ook and **L**isten within: what are you sensing internally? How do you feel? **E**stablish yourself in your location, perhaps by orienting to the seven directions (east, south, west, north, above, below, and the center within; or, before you, behind you, to your right, to your left, above, below, and the center within). **S**ense your surroundings, opening your five (or six) senses to what is around you. **S**tate your **IN**tention to respect this place, to experience what is present. **G**ive gratitude for this opportunity.

Mara Freeman suggests the acronym **ECOLOGY** to remember how to approach a stone circle. It can, of course, be modified to apply to powerful places in general. "**E**" stands for **E**ntry, which means enter by first circling the site in a clockwise (sunwise) direction. "**C**" is for **C**entering yourself. This is often best accomplished by touching one of the stones or an entryway. "**O**" stands for **O**ffering, which can be a bit of grain, milk, a strand of hair, saliva, etc. This shows that you come in good faith. The best offerings

> "The nature of sacred art is to connect us directly to our highest being, our purest potential. And that is the purpose of working with the Earth energies. The 'art of the stones' or the art of working with the Earth energies as I understand it, is not just about dowsing rods or pendulums, not about water veins or underground faults. Those are the external aspects. The art of the Master Builders is a spiritual art: it enables us to experience that sacredness that we are, that infinite space of bliss." Ferran Blasco Aguasca.

are biodegradable so they don't linger in the environment or build up over time. "**L**" is for **L**istening. Listen to the sounds around you: birds, wind, wild creatures, and other sounds of nature. "**O**" stands for **O**pening up your inner and outer senses. "**G**" is for **G**ratitude to the place, the Earth, all of life, and Nature. "**Y**" is for **Y**ou: you should leave a place just as you found it. Take nothing and leave nothing. You can see the result of people not observing this injunction at many popular sacred sites: trees damaged by people taking pieces of their bark or carving on them; sites littered with paper wrappers and trash; melted wax dripped over ancient stones. Observe **ECOLOGY**: the Earth and future visitors will thank you.

Before entering a church, temple, or tumulus, place your hand lightly on the column or stone to the right of the entryway. Pause a moment to attune yourself (come into energetic harmony) with the place. Then step over (not on) the threshold.

You might want to bring some narrow silk or cotton ribbons that will biodegrade and perhaps some oatcakes to leave as offerings at particular sacred sites. You also might want to have some empty bottles for collecting water at holy wells.

Powerful Places in Ireland

Magic is afoot in Ireland—not that we have seen faeries peeking out from behind tree trunks during our visits to the Emerald Isle. No, nothing as obvious as that. Rather, the land itself exudes an indescribable but palpable power. It's greener than one would imagine. It's mistier, more mysterious. Sacred wells abound, often sheltered by trees, their branches dangling with offerings. Immense, elaborately carved Celtic crosses stand tall in abandoned cemeteries, and rounded, paired hills, referred to as the Goddess's breasts, nurture the landscape.

Hereditary custodians still look after some of Ireland's holy wells, and unseen guardians still watch over ruined sanctuaries and megalithic sites. Watching the River Boyne flow around the bend, or walking on the soft, giving ground, we sense a feminine presence permeating the landscape. A shiver of expectancy flows through us. What waits to be discovered?

Over the millennia, the Irish have managed to keep alive the spirit of the land, to tell stories situated in the landscape—epics and legends filled with vibrant words and stunning images. Warrior queens, giant heroes, a youth's transformation from son to seed to salmon, fearless monks, fearsome faeries, demigods, valiant ocean journeys—myths morph with history and meld with the land itself. Each wave of legendary invaders battled the previous, and gifted bards created an oral history of war and raids, filled with acts of bravery, deception, and divine intervention.

Because so many ancient place-names have remained in continuous use in Ireland, it is easy to map myth onto mountain, legend onto stone. For example, you can follow a trail around Ireland that replicates the *Táin Bó Cúailnge*, the mythic *Cattle Raid of Cooley* that supposedly took place 2500 years ago. Numerous dolmens are named after

Gráinne and Diarmuid, a love-crossed duo whose flight across Ireland is described in the epic tale, "The Pursuit of Diarmuid and Gráinne." As you explore the powerful places on the Emerald Isle, "soften" your vision so you can experience the "double-exposure" that overlays the contemporary Ireland with millennia of mythic imagination.

Kinds of Powerful Places

"A sacred space is a *temenos*, a Greek word meaning an enclosure that makes it possible to enter into a relationship with a greater reality. Entering into sacred space, one crosses a threshold and moves from *chronos*, human time and space, into *kairos*, eternal time." Hale, p. xiii.

Location, Location, Location

A powerful place does not exist in isolation from its surroundings. Ancient people often constructed several (or numerous) sites within a relatively close distance to each other. These sites often have a visual (and probably energetic) relationship to each other and to prominent natural features such as hilltops, gaps between hills, etc. This phenomenon is called "intervisibility," and the landscapes themselves are called ritual landscapes.

Examples of prominent ritual landscapes occur around the Calanais Stones in Scotland, the megaliths at Carnac in Brittany, and Stonehenge in England, to name a few. In Ireland, dolmens dot the ridges around northern Co. Sligo and the Bricklieve Mountains in the south. Standing in the low lands and looking around, you feel yourself surrounded by a protective circle of sacred constructions. In the Boyne Valley, numerous mounds and passage graves are intervisible. There is much speculation about the purpose of these landscapes, but it is increasingly clear that they were created intentionally.

Megalithic sites in the Boyne Valley

Not only were sacred sites constructed with an awareness of the energies of the earth and in relationship to each other and to surrounding natural features, they were also often built to interact with solar, lunar, or stellar events. Just as churches used to be constructed so that the altar was in the east, facing the rising sun and signifying the resurrected Christ, so were many megalithic sites designed to take advantage of recurring astronomical events.

For example, the light of the setting winter solstice sun shines into the entry passageway of Maeshowe, a site described in *Powerful Places in Scotland*. The Newgrange passage mound in Co. Meath is the location of a spectacular winter solstice event. On a clear morning the light from the rising sun enters through the roof box and pierces the 19 m (62 ft) long corridor, reaching toward the rear interior wall (see p. 38). At other megalithic sites, such as stone circles, it may be more difficult to prove which, or how many, astronomical events were being marked.

Holy Islands, Mountains, and Caves

Because of the natural geography of Ireland, numerous tiny islands dot narrow lakes and rivers, and others are located a relatively short distance off the coasts. "No man is an island," but living on one can give you the sense that you are set apart, isolated from the mainstream of life by the ebb and flow of tides. Combine these bits of land with Irish monasticism, and you have a match made if not in Heaven, at least in the minds of monks

> "According to traditional thinking, islands are inherently sacred, being places cut off by water from unwanted physical and psychic influences." Pennick, *Celtic Sacred Landscapes*, p. 105.

seeking to escape from the mundane world. The ecclesiastic buildings on St Patrick's Purgatory, a popular pilgrimage shrine, stand on a tiny island that barely rises above the lapping of the waves of Lough Derg (see p. 222). The now-abandoned beehive huts on craggy Skellig Michael, 10 km (6 mi) off the southwest tip of Ireland, are striking testimony to the devotion and hardship of such enforced isolation (see p. 190).

Mountains are often the focus of folklore and legends, probably because their hard-to-access peaks are that much closer to the heavens. They provide panoramic views, making humans feel less important but paradoxically more brave and powerful because they have reached the summit. The gods are often reported to have appeared on mountains, and many mountaintop altars are dedicated to deities. Dangerous to climb, places where the weather is fierce, the winds strong, mountains are often sacred not only to the Sky God but to the Earth Mother. In west Co. Mayo, the holy mountain of Croagh Patrick was originally home of the pagan mother goddess. Later it became the site of St Patrick's 40-day Lenten retreat, during which he managed to get rid of all the (nonexistent) snakes in Ireland (see p. 222). In the southwest, Mount Brandon (St Brendan's

Mountain) still beckons to Catholic pilgrims, just as it beckoned to pre-Christian ones, millennia ago (see p. 195).

A cave is an opening into the earth, an entrance into the Underworld, a journey into the womb of the Great Mother. Caves offer us darkness, mystery, danger, death, rebirth, initiation, and transformation. They are the realm of the Sidhe—the faeries—

Cave of the Cats

and of the mythic Tuatha Dé Danann, who disappeared into "the Hollow Hills." What else lurks within? The ancient goddess of the land? A sleeping hero? Is it a place of oracular wisdom, of healing dreams or nightmares? A subterranean, otherworldly kingdom, filled with treasures and guarded by dragons?

The Cave of the Cats in Co. Roscommon (p. 287) has an awesome reputation. Female werewolves and terrifying wild pigs are said to issue out of its mouth, and the Morrigan, Celtic goddess of death, destruction, and passion, is said to reside within. Many Irish caves have their own legends and mythic associations, woven into a complex tapestry over the years. Awareness of the uniqueness and archetypal nature of each cave enriches the journey into the earth and within yourself.

12

Healing Springs and Rivers

Our bodies are approximately 60% water: it is literally life giving. We also use water for cleansing, purification, and transformation. Water is a central part of baptismal rites around the world. Rivers and streams, and the lands they nourish, are vital for life and important for transportation of goods—and raiders.

A river is not just a conduit of water. The fresh-flowing, abundant River Boyne with its fertile banks is the embodiment of the goddess Bóand or Bóinne. There are many tales about this gracious goddess, also known as the White Cow, whose abundant milk forms the stars in the Milky Way. Important megalithic sites were constructed at the bend in the River Boyne (see p. 34).

Water is also associated with healing, especially when it flows up from the ground or out of the side of a hill. Spring water comes from the realm of the unseen and brings some of that mysterious realm up into the light. Some holy wells (natural springs with buildings over or walls surrounding them) are believed to heal eye problems, others address "female" issues, still others are purported to ameliorate skin diseases or nervous conditions. Some holy wells may grant wishes of other kinds or impart wisdom. Visiting a holy well is an opportunity to interact directly with the sacred by taking it into your mouth and swallowing, or by dipping your hands in the flowing waters.

> "Celtic sacred waters are associated with the three archetypes of light: the sun, the eye and consciousness. When we use sacred waters, we commune with these archetypes, which manifest themselves to us as deities, legends, traditions and folk practices." Pennick, *Celtic Sacred Landscapes*, p. 63.

Miraculous wells are numerous in Ireland and have been in use continuously for millennia. At one time these wells may have had resident *anima loci* or were dedicated to particular pagan deities. Now Christianized, many sacred springs are associated with saints or the Virgin Mary. People continue to visit them, seeking healing that they have not found through more conventional means (see index).

Trees

Trees provide humans with fruits and nuts, with fuel, with wood for boats, shelter, furniture, weapons, and coffins. But trees are much more than objects for human use. Trees are vital to the wellbeing of the planet, helping to maintain the stability of the climate. They "inhale" carbon dioxide and release much-needed oxygen into the environment. They hold the soil in place and exchange nutrients with it. They provide home and haven for animals, insects, and birds.

At the symbolic level, a tree is an *axis mundi* (a cosmic axis) uniting the underworld, this world, and the heavens. Its roots are in the earth, its trunk in the air, and its branches reach toward the sky. Different trees have different mythic associations. Yggdrasil is the ancient ash tree that Norse mythology describes as an immense "world tree," complete with dragons entwining in its roots. Other examples of symbol-laden trees include the Trees of Life and Knowledge in the Garden of Eden, the Christmas evergreen, and the Yule log.

Trees were often linked with particular deities, but they were also thought to have their own resident spirits. Individual trees might be the

Mara Freeman tell us that in Celtic times, "trees not only provided earthly sustenance: they were regarded as living, magical beings who bestowed blessings from the Otherworld. Wood from the nine sacred trees kindled the need-fire that brought back the sun to earth on May Eve; tree names formed the letters of the Ogham alphabet which made potent spells when carved on staves of yew; rowan protected the byre; ash lent power to the spear's flight." http://www.chalicecentre.net/celtictreeoflife.htm

Nigel Pennick reminds us that "The wild wood is the place in which we can restore our conscious link with our inner instincts by contacting the 'wild man' within all of us. When we are supported by the elemental powers of the wood, a rediscovery of forgotten things can take place." (Celtic Sacred Landscapes, p. 24). Killarney National Park (see p. 178) is one such place.

source of great wisdom or inspiration. Living for hundreds of years, they become imbued with a kind of "personality." Greeks and Celts worshipped in sacred groves called *nemetoi* or *nemeton*. The sacred yew and oak trees are found at many sites in Ireland (see p. 208, p. 298). In Ireland, thorn trees have a special place in the mythic landscape. They are associated with the faery folk and are often found near holy wells and megalithic sites (see p. 113). Legends warn of the harm in cutting them down or disturbing them.

Faery tree, Hill of Tara

Stones

Stone: enduring, eternal—or at least closer to ageless than frail human flesh. Meditate on a stone and eons of geological time unfold before you. Perhaps part of the allure of the megaliths is this contact with what seems like eternity. It is also contact with a part of ourselves, for we, too, are made out of minerals. Dust to dust, rock of ages, we come from the earth and return to it.

But there's more to the attraction of the megaliths. We often find that the stones are not just inert building blocks used in sacred constructions. They seem to have their own energies, their own "personalities." Perhaps we are anthropomorphizing the stones, seeing faces and meaningful shapes in the random wear patterns of millennia. Perhaps not. Perhaps the stones were selected precisely because of their appearance. Some stones definitely have a "masculine" feel, others a "feminine" sensibility. Some seem to be standing guard or to hold a particular mystery.

We ponder about the meaning of ornately carved slabs found inside passage chambers or decorated kerbstones arranged around a large burial mound. We puzzle over the purpose of these constructions, often called tombs because of the remains found within. Calling Newgrange a passage grave, however, is like calling Westminster Cathedral a tomb, just because people are buried inside.

A number of researchers report strange electro-magnetic phenomena at the megaliths. Dowsers often discover underground lines of energy or water threading beneath the stones. Psychics may experience strange guardian-like figures or shadowy reenactments of ancient rites. Modern researchers have discovered that many chambers appear to have a particular resonance that enhances the sound of the voice and drumming, making it both louder and more mysterious. The enigmatic stones reveal and hide their purpose with the changing of the day, the turning of the seasons.

Stone circles, table-like dolmens, immense earth-covered cairns, their interior walls covered with mysterious symbols—when you find one that calls to you, draw near, breathing slowly, contemplating the slow breath of stone. Perhaps sing to it, or hum, or chant, and see if it replies. See what you discover as the minerals in your bones and skin and hair respond to the minerals that make up these silent monoliths. Take your time. Slow down.

> "Singing brings a holy place into vibration, as if it were a tuning fork being struck. In these journeys the tuning fork was also my body, set into motion in a new way. I discovered that the ancients built their temples according to ratios of sacred geometry, universal principles that exist in numbers, shapes, and musical intervals and in the proportions that compose our bodies." Hale, p. xvii.

y've been there for millennia. They don't divulge their
:ets quickly—and never to the casual tourist.

Some Historical Background

It is important to have a context for what you see, so
we are providing an abbreviated overview of Irish history.
Some of it is factual, some mythic. In Ireland, it can be hard
to tell the difference.

"We live in the present moment of the past." TS Eliot.

Ireland is the third largest island
in Europe, separated from neighboring Great Britain to the east
by the Irish Sea. Covered with ice until more than 9500
years ago, the first inhabitants of the Emerald Isle appear
to have arrived around 7500 BCE (Before Christian Era).
Navigable rivers, a central plain surrounded by low-lying
mountains, a mild climate, once heavily forested with oak,
pine, and elm—Ireland was a desirable place to be, judging
by the waves of im-
migrants and invaders
that laid claim to the
land.

According to leg-
ends, poems, and
stories recorded in
the eleventh-century
Book of Invasions, the

"Ever since the first people arrived on
its shores, Ireland in its entirety had been
regarded as a female deity, identified
by many names, including Banba, Fódla,
and Ériu. From Ériu, the modern Eire is
a conscious derivation. To pagans and
Christians alike, Ériu-the-Island was a living divinity...." Dames, p. 34.

original settlers of Ireland were descended from Noah.
They were followed by a series of invaders, their mythic
exploits etched deeply onto the Irish landscape and into
the Irish imagination. These included the Partholónians
(from Greece); the Formorians (AKA Fomorians), giant,
demonic, and malevolent; and the Nemedians (battling
the Formorians, they later fled to northern Europe and
Greece). The fourth wave of legendary invasions included

three groups: the Fir Bolg (perhaps descendents of the Nemedians who had fled to Greece); the bronze- and magic-working Tuatha Dé Danann (the People of the Goddess Danu, who later retreated "into the Hollow Hills" to become the Sidhe or faery people); followed at last by the arrival of the iron-working Milesians (Scythians, perhaps, arriving from Asia Minor, or arriving via Spanish Galicia).

According to archeologists, in Co. Mayo we find the remains of wheat and barley fields worked between 3500-3000 BCE by Neolithic farmers, and we find the earliest megalithic sites. The Bronze Age, a period of beautiful gold work, began around 2000 BCE. It is during this period that the impressive passage mound at Newgrange was built.

In the Late Bronze Age, Ireland was probably part of a networking maritime culture that included what we now know as Britain, France, Spain, and Portugal. This was followed by the Iron Age, associated with cultural change and the arrival of people commonly identified as the Celts. However, there is uncertainty about who the Celts were or where they came from, although we do know that they didn't call themselves Celts. They appear to have arrived sporadically between the eighth and first centu-

"Keltoi is the Greek term meaning barbarian, or foreigner. The name was first ascribed to the Gauls and the European tribes, who would most likely not have recognized what it meant, and would not have used it to describe themselves. We have continued to know them—those people who are loosely defined by their language, religion, art and culture—as the Celts." Delyth, p. 68.

ries BCE. Modern historians suggest there was no actual invasion of Ireland but rather the bloodless transfer of ideas and material culture.

Never conquered by Rome, Ireland remained a patchwork of bellicose tribes until the seventh or eighth century CE, when the High King of Ireland became a more or less recognized force, presiding from Meath and the Hill of Tara over the other four traditional kingdoms: Connacht (west), Leinster (east), Munster (south), and Ulster (north).

By then, other important changes in Ireland had already taken place. In the fifth century, the Christian missionary Palladius arrived, soon followed by St Patrick (or possibly several St Patricks). The indigenous Druid tradition gradually melded into a learned monastic culture, giving Ireland its nickname, "Island of Saints and Scholars." Ireland's monks became famous for scholarship, which preserved Greek and Latin learning, and for far-traveling missionaries, including St Columba (Colmcille), who founded a monastery on Iona in 653. By the ninth century, the monastic way of life was threatened by Viking raids and endemic warfare.

Anglo-Norman knights invaded from England in 1169 at the behest of Dermot McMurrough, deposed king of Leinster (p. 224), and in 1172 the Pope affirmed King Henry II of England's lordship over Ireland. Two immediate results were that the Irish Catholic Church was taken over by Rome, and Gaelic Brehon Law was supplanted by Norman feudal law. Another result was the social, political, and economic marginalization of the native Irish. With much backing and forthing, the English Crown gained and maintained control of Ireland over the centuries. In an attempt to keep the Anglo-Normans from assimilating, the 1366 Statutes of Kilkenny forbade, among other things, marriage between Anglo-Normans and Irish.

Despite repeated attempts to re-establish Irish independence, in the sixteenth century Ireland suffered nearly complete conquest by England. Deep sectarian divisions developed between Catholics and Protestant Dissenters, both deprived of numerous rites and privileges, including religious practice, and Anglicans. In the seventeenth century, England began taking native Irish land and "planting" foreigners in Ulster in the so-called Plantations. In 1649, the Englishman Oliver Cromwell brutally "pacified" Ireland. This colonization (or usurpation) was followed in 1690 by the decisive defeat of Catholic and pro-Irish William II by Protestant and pro-English William of Orange at the Battle of the Boyne. The 1695 Penal Laws continued the process of disenfranchising the Catholic Irish and Presbyterians, restricting land ownership, education, intermarriage, holding political office, and so on.

Ireland had been a Gaelic-speaking nation; now English became the language of those in power. Poverty, disenfranchisement, famine in 1740, and the Great (Potato) Famine in the 1840s led to the death or dispersal of part of the native population. In the late nineteenth century and early twentieth century, Irish nationalism (mostly Catholic) began to regain strength, leading, after the failed Easter Uprising of 1916, to the Anglo-Irish treaty in 1921. This was followed by civil war, which ended in 1923. Ireland split into the predominantly Catholic Republic of Ireland, which makes up almost five-sixths of the island landmass, and the predominantly Protestant Northern Ireland, which is part of the United Kingdom.

In 1937 a new constitution declared complete independence from Britain and changed the country's name to Eire. That was not the end of the fighting, however, for Northern Ireland continued to suffer internal violence between the Unionists and the Nationalists. This ethno-political conflict was known as "the Troubles." The Good Friday Agreement of 1998, however, brought a sense of hope for self-government for the North.

The Republic of Ireland joined the European Union in 1973. During the 1990s it became known as the "Celtic

Tiger," surging fast forward in economic development. Unfortunately, the global downturn and crisis of recent years has been devastating to the nation.

This brief overview doesn't begin to adequately describe Ireland or the Irish. Nobel-prize-winning writers (George Bernard Shaw, William Butler Yeats, Samuel Beckett, Seamus Heaney), award-winning musicians and dancers (think "Riverdance" and spontaneous traditional music sessions in pubs), world-renowned philosophers and scientists, breath-taking scenery, diversity of heritage sites, fantastic horse-racing, fishing, Gaelic sports, Irish whiskey, Guinness stout, world-class cuisine—the list goes on and on. *Powerful Places in Ireland* is not a general guidebook for Ireland, however; it's a guidebook devoted to powerful places in Ireland. So we'll leave the many other attractions of Ireland for you discover on your own.

Traveling in Ireland

We have divided Ireland into three large areas because it works well to base yourself in each of these regions and explore from a central location. For example, from Dublin you can make day trips to the Boyne Valley in the north and to Glendalough and Kildare in the south. If you fly into Shannon Airport, you can easily explore The Burren to the north or head south to Lough Gur and Killarney National Park. From Sligo you can make day trips north to Co. Donegal and Northern Ireland and south to Co. Roscommon.

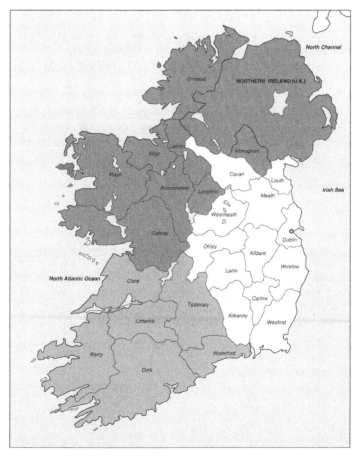

Traveling by train, bus, and airline, you can reach a number of the larger towns in Ireland. However, in order to visit most of the places we describe, you will need to either rent a car **(remember: drive on the left)** or rent a car and driver. The distances between sites aren't large but many of the roads are narrow and driving tends to be slow.

Detailed maps such as the Discovery Series are quite useful. In this guidebook we provide degrees, minutes, and seconds coordinates, which can be translated into GPS or decimal format using online converters. One that does multiple conversions and maps the spot on a Google map is http://boulter.com/gps. It is very helpful to bring or rent a Sat-Nav (GPS) device, although it may not have up-to-date maps, or it may fail to indicate that a bridge is out or a road is under construction. Remember: it is a useful but fallible tool.

If possible, do not leave valuables in your car when parked at apparently isolated sites such as Monasterboice, Dowth, and Fourknocks, and probably other places as well. An increasing number of break-ins and thefts have been reported at those sites.

Bring a flashlight for peering into megalithic sites. A candle (with a protective sleeve so it doesn't drip) is excellent for walking into caves since it illuminates more fully—but bring a flashlight as well. A compass is useful for orienting yourself in ritual landscapes.

Ireland is often damp and rainy, so be prepared with a large umbrella, an impermeable and warm rain jacket, and "wellies" (high rubber boots). Wellies are easily purchased in Irish garden supply shops or department stores. You will be grateful for the protection to your feet and pant legs when slogging through a damp meadow. When in doubt, put on your wellies.

A number of sites in Ireland are oriented toward specific astronomical events. For example, Newgrange and Dowth are oriented to the winter solstice; Loughcrew to the spring and autumn equinoxes; and Beltane Circle in Co. Donegal to Bealtaine (1 May). Your journey will be enriched if you plan to experience some of these sites at those times.

Double-check opening hours for managed sites. They are subject to change, especially off season.

The stories and legends of Ireland's powerful places are a vital part of the experience. Some places (Tara, Roscommon) may not look like much, but with a knowledgeable guide they come to life. Because of this, we suggest several guides whom we know from personal experience to be "in resonance" with powerful places.

Additional Resources

Websites

There is a plethora of excellent websites for powerful places in Ireland. They don't always agree with each other, and they have their own, sometimes idiosyncratic interpretations (not surprisingly, since most megalithic sites are from a period before written history). Here is a partial list, in no particular order:

Two academic websites: http://www.archaeology.ie/ and http://www.heritagecouncil.ie/

24

http://www.heritageireland.ie/ (Office of Public Works website)

Michael Fox's several websites, including http://www.newgrange.com and http://www.knowth.com/

Howard Goldbaum's http://www.voicesfromthedawn.com (under construction in 2011 but partially available)

Tom FourWinds' http://www.megalithomania.com

Martin Byrne's http://www.carrowmore.com and http://www.carrowkeel.com

Anthony Weir's http://www.irishmegaliths.org.uk

Anthony Murphy's http://www.mythicalireland.com/

Ken Williams' http://www.shadowsandstone.com

Philip Powell's http://www.megalithicmonumentsofireland.com

Brian T. McElherron's http://irishantiquities.bravehost.com

Guides

Although we don't usually recommend guides, we have found the following people extremely helpful, knowledgeable, and attuned to powerful places. Check their websites for areas of expertise. They are listed in alphabetical order.

Martin Byrne at http://www.carrowkeel.com/ and http://www.carrowmore.com   (See QR code, p. 24)

Mike Croghan at http://www.rathcroghantours.com

Michael Fox at http://www.boynevalleytours.com

Mara Freeman at http://www.celticspiritjourneys.com

Nora Judge and Martin Dier at http://www.nativespirit-tours.com and http://www.taracelebrations.org

John Willmott at http://www.celticways.com/

A new information hub for guides: http://www.Sacred-SiteTours.info

Names and Numbers

We usually provide Gaelic and English names for locations. We also follow the convention of referring to Irish counties as "Co." —for example, "Co. Meath." Determining the age of megalithic sites is not an exact science. As a result, sources sometimes give different dates. Even determining the number of stones or the size of a megalithic site can sometimes be difficult. We have done our best to resolve such differences, but some are irresolvable.

Ireland has changed to the metric system but not completely. We provide both metric and English measure units. Kilometers are abbreviated as km; miles as mi; meters as m; feet as ft.

To call the Republic of Ireland from outside the country, dial your own country's international access numbers, followed by 353 (Ireland's country code). For example, here is how to call the Brú na Bóinne Visitor Center, (0)41 988 0300. From the US, dial 011 353 41 988 0300. Do not dial the initial (0). When dialing from within the Republic, dial 041 988 0300. The country code for Northern Ireland is 44.

Midlands (Including Dublin) and Southeast

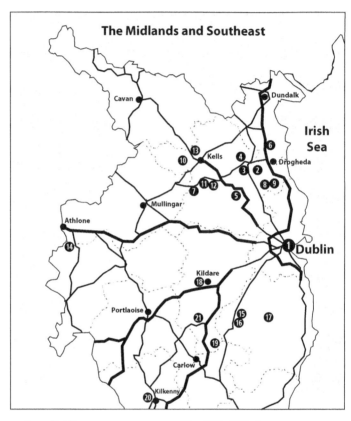

1.	Dublin	12.	Hill of Ward
2.	Brú na Bóinne	13.	St Ciarán's Well
3.	Lady Well, Slane Castle	14.	Clonmacnoise
4.	Hill of Slane	15.	Piper's Stones
5.	Hill of Tara	16.	Castleruddery Stone Circle
6.	Monasterboice	17.	Glendalough Monastic Site
7.	Rathmore Church	18.	St Brigid Holy Wells
8.	Balgeeth Sheela-na-gig	19.	Brownshill Dolmen
9.	Fourknocks	20.	Kilkenny
10.	Loughcrew	21.	Moone High Cross
11.	Tlachtga		

Midlands

Dublin (N53 20 42 W6 16 03)

*Who would have thought that a museum could be a power-
ful place? The National Museum of Ireland – Archaeology in
Dublin dispels all doubts. It's because of the gold. Objects include
breathtaking jewelry and a miniature ship, complete with tiny
golden oars. All that glitters isn't gold, but gold does glitter. And
lots of gold glitters even more. Gold really* does *resemble con-
densed sunlight—a brilliant fragment of the sun, fallen to earth
to our astonishment and delight—but instead of falling from
the sky, it has been harvested from the earth. The quantity of
gold (case after case filled with handcrafted treasures); the size of
individual pieces (necklaces as thick as rope and earplugs larger
than silver dollars); the antiquity of the pieces, some more than
3000 years old; and the consummate mastery of the long-dead
artisans fills me with awe. Who could possibly have worn that
huge twisted gold torque that ends in a spiral? It's big enough
for a horse! And on what occasion? The golden artwork opens
a window into the past, but I see through the glass but dimly.
(Elyn)*

Ireland's capital sits astride the River Liffey and looks
seaward to Dublin Bay and south to the Wicklow Mountains. If you like big cities, Dublin is an excellent base from
which to take day trips to the Boyne Valley to the northwest and to Counties Kildare and Wicklow to the south.
Numerous organized tours leave from Dublin and travel as
far as the west of Ireland and the Cliffs of Moher.

Ha'penny Bridge over the River Liffey

Dublin has much to recommend it: great shopping, traditional ("trad") music, museums and galleries—and the Guinness Brewery tour. If you are interested in Irish history, politics, art, architecture, theater, public gardens, pubs, or literature, Dublin has a great deal to offer. A hop-on, hop-off tourist bus is an effective way to familiarize yourself with the city. Most guidebooks do a fine job of describing Dublin, so we will focus on the National Museum, Trinity College Library, and St Audoen's Church.

The National Museum

We recommend beginning and ending your journey to powerful places in Ireland with a visit to the National Museum – Archaeology. The museum contains an impressive collection of artifacts dating from the Neolithic to the twentieth century, including important early Christian material. Many of the sites we describe in this guidebook have yielded archeological finds that are on display. Seeing them before you travel around Ireland will give you a general impression; seeing them after you return is eye-opening.

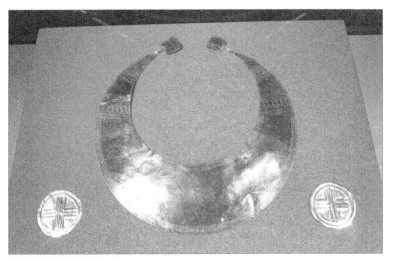

Prehistoric gold work in the collection at the National Museum

The exhibition "Kingship and Sacrifice" includes sensitively displayed bog bodies (if you are squeamish, it is best to avoid them) and material related to sovereignty and kingship during the Iron Age. Royal regalia, weapons, votive deposits are included, as is a replica of the impressive Gundestrup Cauldron, found in a Danish bog. This stunning basin includes images of Celtic deities, including Cernunnos, the Horned God, sitting in a yogic pose, and scenes of kingship. We describe several royal sites in this guidebook, so seeing this exhibit may enrich your experience at those places. http://www.museum.ie/en/exhibition-list/archaeology-and-ethnography-permanent-exhibitions.aspx

On display are numerous objects decorated with "Celtic" designs. What we often think of as Irish "Celtic" art (complex interlace patterns, zoomorphs, curvilinear designs, and so on) is actually a mixture of Germanic, Mediterranean, Eastern, Roman, Anglo-Saxon, and Scandinavian artistic influences. This doesn't diminish the skill and creativity of the people who created these beautiful and enduring artistic works; it simply puts them in a broader context.

Trinity College Old Library

Trinity College has much to offer. Don't miss the Treasury of the Old Library, where several magnificent illuminated manuscripts are on display. The most richly decorated is the *Book of Kells,* probably the work of monks from Iona

who fled to Kells in 806 CE after a Viking raid. *The Book of Durrow,* created around 700 CE, and the *Book of Armagh* (807 CE) are also on display. The fascinating exhibit "Turning Darkness into Light" places the Irish illuminated manuscripts in a context and provides interesting information on their production. On our guidebook journey around Ireland, we will visit several important monastic settlements that were famous centers of learning and where illuminated manuscripts were copied.

Page from the Book of Kells

There are also some awesome trees on the grounds of Trinity College, including the largest Oregon maple in the world (http://www.pbase.com/photokohn/image/3630891).

St Audoen's Church

There are two St Audoen churches side by side on the corner of Bridge Street: a large nineteenth-century Catho-

Old St Audoen's Church

lic one and, next to it, a small Church of Ireland (Protestant) church built around 1190. The older St Audoen's is a national monument, the earliest surviving medieval church in Dublin. It was founded by the Anglo-Normans and dedicated to St Audoen of Rouen in France. Although it is open for tourists, on Sunday it is still used for worship—as it has been for 800 years. Excellent displays show how the church building changed over the centuries.

The guided tour is quite informative, although guides provide somewhat different information. On one visit we were shown an engraved stone slab kept in the main porch. It is an early Celtic gravestone, documented to have been in the church since before 1309. It is called "the Lucky Stone" and was supposed to bring good luck, especially to merchants and traders who rubbed it. The stone was stolen on various occasions but always found its way back to the church. Once, enemies tried to destroy it, but when the masons tried to cut it up, the stone

The "Lucky Stone"

groaned. Frightened, they returned it to St Audoen's. When is a stone not "just" a stone? When it grants good luck, returned "home" when stolen, and cries out when threatened. This is an example of ancient traditions about sacred stones being incorporated into a Christian setting.

On another occasion, our guide described how people had been buried in layers in the floor in the chapel. A descendent could stand on the family grave marker and know it would be theirs as well. This custom reminded us of the burial practices at certain megalithic sites, where human remains were deposited layer upon layer, removed and reburied, century after century. Perhaps the megalithic practices morphed over time and instead of group burial in a cairn, families were buried together under a church pavement.

The area around St Audoen's is a quiet oasis in the midst of the big city. It's a good place to spend some time, contemplating your journey into magical Ireland.

Brú na Bóinne, Co. Meath

Our guidebook said that the passage tomb at Dowth was closed, so the mound was not worth visiting. The guidebook was right (the passage is closed) and wrong (Dowth is worth visiting). One August afternoon we joined a group that gathered there for an autumn equinox ceremony. We walked slowly through the bright, wet grass that surrounded the ancient mound. Dowth seemed asleep, perhaps dreaming of the time 5000 years ago when farmer-folk flocked to her ample sides to witness the light of the setting winter sun piercing her stone-lined passageway. It seemed to me that as we stood upon her flank, honoring the balance of day and night, Dowth began to stir, waking briefly from deep slumber. (Elyn)

Newgrange, Knowth, and Dowth are huge man-made mounds located close together in the Boyne Valley (Brú na Bóinne) near a great loop of the River Boyne. Within each mound are carefully constructed stone passage graves; they

The great looop of the River Boyne

also served as ceremonial venues. The mounds are the best-known archeological complex in Ireland and a UNESCO World Heritage Site. The complex also includes a number of smaller mounds, henges, and standing stones.

Brú na Bóinne's fertile soil supported Neolithic farmers beginning around 3800 BCE. By about 3300 BCE—700 years before the Egyptian pyramids and 1000 years before Stonehenge—these farmers began constructing megalithic monuments. They had sophisticated expertise in engineering, geology, art, and astronomy, which they put to use in their constructions.

Newgrange, Knowth, and Dowth are each constructed in their own ritual landscape, but they are intervisible. From the top of Dowth you

The River Boyne is named after the goddess Bóand or Bóinne (Illuminated or White Cow). One can imagine the foam-specked waters of the Boyne resembling nourishing milk. In Gaelic, the Milky Way is called *Bealach na Bó Finne* or *Bothar na Bó Finne*: the Important Road (or Way) of the White Cow.

Intervisibility of Knowth and Newgrange

can see Newgrange and, if you stood on top of Newgrange, you could see Dowth. Knowth is visible from the back of Newgrange as well. Three or possibly more satellite tombs stretch from Newgrange towards nearby Dowth. Although we don't know what this meant to the megalith builders, we can assume that this intervisibility was important.

These huge man-made mounds are constructed from alternating layers of earth and stone, with carefully engineered interior stone passages that end in chambers. Large kerbstones, laid end to end, surround and stabilize the mounds. Many of them are elaborately carved. At its height as a ceremonial center and cemetery complex, there may have been as many as 700 decorated stones in Brú na Bóinne.

The only way to visit Newgrange and Knowth is by an OPW (Office of Public Works) guided tour from Brú na Bóinne Visitor Center, located on the south side of the

> "Brú na Bóinne was more than simply a location where burials took place; it was most likely a center of ceremony and ritual. The decorated kerbstones may be evidence that processions around the mounds took place. Special events may have taken place at certain times of the year." Eogan, p. 11.

Boyne River near Donore (see p. 42 for details). Dowth, however, is directly accessible to visitors who walk or drive to the site (see p. 43).

Newgrange N 53 41.686 W6 26 48

High on a ridge in the middle of the Boyne Valley, Newgrange is the best known of the three mounds. Its unique triple-spiral kerbstone is emblematic of Irish megalithic art. Newgrange was probably constructed around 3200 BCE and continued to be the focus of religious activity into the late Neolithic and early Bronze Age. At one point, it was thought (or imagined) to be the burial mound of the legendary kings of Tara. Romano-British votive objects were buried there between the first and fourth centuries CE, indicating its ongoing importance as a ritual center.

The squashed-oval diameter of the surrounding kerb varies from 79 m (260 ft) northwest-southeast and 85 m (280 ft) northeast-southwest, though these figures depend on who is holding the tape measure. It is 11 m (36 ft) high. A partial circle of standing stones surrounds it. Newgrange has one interior passage tomb, which ends in a cruciform, a shape that also resembles the human body with outstretched arms. Large, chiseled basins that once held cremated remains are located on the floor in each of the three side recesses. Paul Devereux (2001, p. 86) believes that the interior of Newgrange was deliberately constructed to produce acoustic effects, complete with acoustical "hot spots."

Newgrange's reconstructed façade of white quartz interspersed with dark, egg-shaped granite stones may or may not be accurate but it is impressive. One can imagine the sunlight glinting off the white surface, making it shine like a beacon. It is interesting and probably important that the glittering quartz remains cool to the touch, while the darker granite absorbs the sun's rays. Newgrange is awesome today; it must have been even more compelling 5000 years ago, when it was the site of ceremonies and ritual.

The OPW guided tour permits you to enter the 19 m (62 ft) long passage for a short time. On a clear morning around the winter solstice, sunlight streams through a roof-box opening above the entrance and penetrates the passage, coming to rest on the back wall of the rear chamber. Or at least it used to. Subtle shifts in the position of the earth and sun now cause the light to fall a little short of its intended target. A triple-spiral design is carved into the side wall of the rear recess, and it is possible that the morning sunlight was reflected (by a polished stone?) onto the triple spiral. An annual lottery provides access to the interior for the

The white quartz façade of Newgrange

winter solstice sunrise around 21 December (http://www.knowth.com/newgrange-solstice-lottery.htm).

Although Newgrange is called a passage tomb, presumably because bone and cremains (cremated remains) were found inside the chambers, it is obvious that it was not just a place of burial. It was used for cyclical ceremonies of great importance. Some writers speculate that Newgrange was used for rituals related to childbirth or fertility. Perhaps the numerous stone balls, phallic-shaped objects, and large basins found in the chambers relate to this.

> "This womb-like function of the inner chambers of cairns ... is illustrated in mythology by the association of so many of them with a particular goddess." Meehan, p. 260.

A huge body of mythology swirls around Newgrange. One story tells how the Dagda (father god of the Tuatha Dé Danann) mated with the great goddess Bóinne, who lived at Brú na Bóinne. Nine months later (magically time had stopped, so it only seemed like a day), she gave birth to a son, Aenghus Óg—Aenghus the Young. Perhaps the winter solstice light penetrating deep into the passage was a visual representation of this mythic sexual union.

A later legend describes Newgrange as the "Fairy Dwelling" where the great Irish hero Cúchulainn was born. The god Lugh (the Shining One) "visited" his mother, Dechtire, on her wedding night, after which she was informed she would bear his child. She retired to Brú na Bóinne and, nine months later, gave birth to Cúchulainn.

These legends demonstrate that Newgrange has continued to have a powerful hold on the mythic imagination for millennia. It is still a powerful place, drawing thousands of visitors throughout the year who bring a mixture of curiosity, awe, and reverence.

Although it is impossible to experience the site as it once was, especially on an OPW guided tour, consciously center yourself and be present (see p. 4). Walk around the outside of the mound in a circular direction, following the line of the standing stones. When it is your group's turn to enter the mound, you will cross behind the triple-spiral kerbstone and over the threshold into the narrow, dark passageway. What do you feel? Is it like entering a cave? A birth canal? As the passage opens into the main chamber, how do you experience this expansion? Your guide will use lighting to recreate the winter solstice sunrise light entering the darkness and illuminating the passageway. What do you experience? If you have a chance to hum or tone in the passage, notice if the quality of the sound or the volume shifts because of the acoustical qualities of the space.

A great link for a panoramic view of Newgrange: http://www.voicesfromthedawn.com/ and search for Newgrange.

Knowth

Located about a kilometer (0.6 mi) away on a bluff high above the Boyne, Knowth is larger and older than Newgrange. It lacks Newgrange's quartz-fronted façade and visitors are not permitted inside the main passage tomb, but it has other attractions. Archeological evidence indicates it was first a settlement, but by 3300 BCE construction was begun on what would become one main mound with two passage tombs opening to the east and west, roughly in line with the equinox sunrises and sunsets, and eighteen satellite tombs. Today, the grass-covered cairns, surrounded by kerbstones, resemble a cluster of enormous mushrooms.

The main mound at Knowth is the biggest in Brú na Bóinne. It is 85 m (279 ft) in diameter, nearly 10 m (33 ft)

Knowth

high, and includes over 300 decorated stones, making it the largest collection of rock art at a single site in Europe. It has a kerb of 127 contiguous stones, many of them ornately carved with motifs whose meaning has yet to be deciphered.

Knowth was utilized from Neolithic times until about 1400 CE. At some point it was turned into a fortification, and in the 800s it was the seat of the kings of northern Brega. They knew a powerful place when they found it, even if by then the entrances into the mound had been long forgotten. At the end of the twelfth century, the Normans used the mound as a motte.

The OPW guided visit to the site explains in detail its transformation over the centuries. Although you can't enter the passage graves, Knowth is an impressive, though heavily reconstructed, site.

Getting There

To visit Newgrange and Knowth you must go to the Brú na Bóinne Visitor Center. Entrance is only from the Visitor Center, and a strictly limited number of tickets are available daily for specific time slots. You buy your ticket(s), then

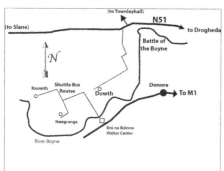

cross the footbridge over the river to the north side at the appointed time. You then get on a shuttle bus that takes you to one or the other monument. http://www. meath.ie/tourism/ heritage/heritag- esites/newgrange/

Go early in summer to avoid long queues. Allow three hours minimum for the visit to both Knowth and Newgrange. The Visitor Center has excellent exhibits and a well-stocked bookstore, as well as a reconstruction of the entrance and interior of Newgrange. http:// www.heritageireland.ie/en/midlandseastcoast/ brunaboinnevisitorcentrenewgrangeandknowth/

It can be confusing to drive to the Visitor Center. Do not trust your GPS to get it right. The Brú na Bóinne Visitor Center is 2 km (1.2 mi) west of Donore Village on the south side of the River Boyne. The route from the east (M1 and Drogheda) is via Donore. From the west (N2 and Slane) take the turn on the N2 2 km south of Slane sign-

posted Brú na Bóinne (Newgrange). It is advisable to check the latest directions and opening hours from OPW (Office of Public Works), which is in charge of the Center. http://www.heritageireland.ie/en/media/ Directions.pdf

Day tours are available from Dublin to the Boyne Valley. Bus Éireann busses run from Dublin to Drogheda to Brú na Bóinne (see heritageireland link above). Michael Fox leads tours of the Boyne Valley and beyond. He is attuned to earth energies and the mysteries of the sites, as well as being very knowledgeable and a great travel companion. Check out his website http://www.BoyneValleyTours.com and his informative Facebook Boyne Valley Tours.

Dowth N53 42 13 W6 27 01

Unlike at Knowth and Newgrange, a visitor to Dowth does not have to take a guided tour. This means that once you find your way there, you can experience the site at your own rhythm. You can meditate, do ritual, perhaps have a

East side of Dowth

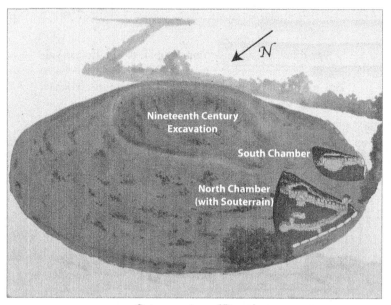

Cutaway view of Dowth

picnic under the huge sycamore tree on the south side of the tumulus. Although it is only a kilometer from Newgrange, Dowth is no longer "managed" and is not much publicized, so it is rarely visited. Bring a flashlight to help you see into the passages.

Park your car by the gate and walk up the trail past the now-closed ticket shed. Dowth is just beyond. The grass-covered mound is 85 m (279 ft) in diameter, with 115 kerbstones, a few of which are still visible. As you walk around, you'll notice entrances on the west to two interior tombs known as North and South Dowth. The more northerly has an 8 m (26 ft) long passage that opens into a cross-shaped chamber with an annex and a corbelled roof. It appears to be aligned with Samhain (Halloween) sunset and includes impressive megalithic carvings. A large basin stone, 1.4 m by 1 m, (approx. 4.5 ft by 3 ft), occupies most of the floor of the main chamber. At one time, you could enter the passage by

Martin Dier says, "Dowth has found its own healing [after depredation by treasure hunters]. Through the stability of time, the mound has found its own settling point and balance."

climbing down an iron ladder, but now there is no access. An early medieval souterrain leads off from the passage, its purpose uncertain. Souterrains may have been used for storage or concealment of goods, for temporary refuge, or perhaps for dream incubation and ritual.

The shorter, more southerly passage leads to a pear-shaped chamber. The winter solstice light that penetrates Newgrange in the morning reaches this passage at sunset. The Gaelic name for Dowth, Dubhadh, means darkness; perhaps it refers to the darkness of the longest night of the year. The light of the setting sun enters the chamber and lights up carvings in a side recess on the right as well as carvings in the main chamber. Note the cup markings in the kerbstone in front; they may represent the path of the setting solstice sun. (To see Dowth at winter sunset, go to http://www.knowth.com/dowth-sunsets.htm.)

If you climb up the mound and the weather conditions are right, you can see Newgrange and Knowth, the Hill of

Closed entrance to the north chamber and souterrain of Dowth

Slane, and Tara. The grass-covered crater at the top is the scar that remains from nineteenth-century treasure hunters or perhaps stone quarrying. On the east side of the mound is a "faery" tree (a lone thorn tree) and a fence, guarding a row of kerbstones with interesting carvings visible if the sunlight (or your flashlight) falls at the right angle. Kerbstone K51 has a series of what looks like sun signs, but no one knows what they really mean. There are also two standing stones in the field, and our companions described them as the focus of powerful earth energies. Although the standing stones appear short, the soil surface is now 1 m (3 ft) higher than it used to be.

Archaeologist and tour guide Martin Dier showed us around Dowth. His enthusiasm helped us to see not a mound desecrated by quarrying and treasure hunting but a powerful sacro-religious space. According to Martin, part of the delight of Dowth is that it hasn't been reconstructed like Newgrange and Knowth. He told us, "We're seeing Dowth the way it's looked for hundreds of years. We couldn't have that if it was excavated and 'under control.' It's sort of the 'wild sister' of the Boyne Valley.'"

The grass-covered tumulus with its gated entry is no longer open for tourists, but that's a good thing. You are free to wander, to imagine what it might have looked like millennia before, and to experience the energies that run strong beneath the land. This power is still palpable: after all, people are still drawn to Dowth to conduct ceremonies, just as they have for more than 5000 years.

Getting There

Dowth is off N51, 3 km (2 mi) east of Newgrange, on the north side of the Boyne River. Or, you can take N51 west from Drogheda, then take the first left after the turn for the site of the Battle of the Boyne. You'll find a small sign on the left, just after Netterville House and Dowth castle.

It is also possible to walk to Dowth from the Brú na Bóinne Visitor Center—approximately 2 km (a little over 1 mi)—but the path is only open when the Visitor Center is open.

Contact Martin.Dier@gmail.com or Martin Dier and Nora Judge at http://www.nativespirittours. com/ for private tours of Dowth and surrounding areas. To participate in seasonal celebrations in the area, contact http://www.taracelebrations.org/

More to Experience

The Boyne Valley also includes a number of other sites worth seeing, including Duleek, with its 300-year-old lime tree and medieval abbey.

The Newgrange Boyne Walk is a river walk, 1.8 km (1 mi) each way, that follows along the Boyne River on the south side of the river. It starts about 1 km from the Brú na Bóinne Visitor Centre towards the N2. The walk begins at the Boyne Currach Centre and ends at a small carpark. There is place to park on a wide grass margin near the Currach Centre or continue to the other end of the walk and park in the designated carpark. For photos, go to http://www.facebook.com/album.php?aid=40319&l= 470d83cac6&id=146045948768290.

Another walking route goes from Navan toward Slane (http://www.meath.ie/Tourism/SportsandActivities/Walking/WalkingRoutes/CanalRiverand-HillWalks/).

You can base yourself in the Boyne Valley and use that as a center from which to explore the region. Possible locations include the town of Drogheda, with its rich medieval heritage and lively arts scene; Trim, a pleasant market town, with its impressive medieval castle; or Slane, an attractive village on the Boyne, near the Slane Castle and Hill of Slane (p. 53).

Lady Well at Slane Castle, Hill of Slane, and Hill of Tara

Lady Well N53 42 35 W6 33 20

Since time immemorial (what a lovely, vague phrase, covering all sorts of forgetfulness) people have come to Lady Well, located on the banks of the River Boyne in the wooded grounds of Slane Castle. One day a year, 15 August, the water is believed to become especially charged and be able to cure maladies. I sat on a bench beside the stone-encircled hole, sheltered by low-lying tree limbs. Except for the babbling of the fresh-flowing spring, the place was quiet. Hidden in the woods is the ruined hermitage of St Erc. Listening intently to the stillness, I imagined I heard the gentle footsteps of the hermit plodding up the path. I imagined I saw him approach the well and bend down, scooping up the life-filled waters in his palms, and drinking deep. (Elyn)

Lady Well is in a secluded, wooded spot in the 1500-acre Slane Castle estate, next to the River Boyne. Hidden in the dense woods behind Lady Well is the ruined hermitage of St Erc, an early convert of St Patrick. The Hill of Slane overlooks the castle. It was here that St Patrick purportedly lit the Paschal fire in direct challenge to the High King (see p. 54). The elegant eighteenth-century Slane Castle can be toured and is a fashionable location for weddings (http://www.slanecastle.ie/). The natural amphitheater beside Slane Castle holds 80,000 spectators and is a popular rock concert venue.

Slane Castle

Lady Well has been a sacred site for millennia, long before St Erc established his nearby hermitage in the fifth century. According to Irish mythology, Lady Well was probably the well blessed by Dian Cécht, the Celtic god of healing: "He blessed a well called Slane, located to the west of Magh Tuireadh and east of Loch Arboch, where the Tuatha Dé could bathe in when wounded; they became healed and continued fighting. It would heal any wound but decapitation" (http://en.wikipedia.org/wiki/Dian_Cecht, retrieved Jan. 22, 2011). Later the well was Christianized, presumably by St Erc, whose abode was nearby.

We don't know if there was a particular date associated with visiting this holy well when it was pagan, but beginning sometime in the Christian era, folks flocked to Lady Well on 15 August, the Day of the Assumption of the Virgin Mary into Heaven. They partook of its healing waters, mixing water with mud and nearby laurel leaves to form a healing poultice. But times change and customs fade, and beginning in the mid 1950s, Lady Well lay abandoned.

Over the years, it devolved into a neglected muddy hole, lost in the midst of overgrown brush and laurel trees.

Then something happened. Alex Mount Charles, son of Lord Henry Mount Charles, 8th Marquess Conyngham, and heir to Slane Castle, wanted to give something back to the Slane community. He had the trees cut back around the well and surrounded it with rounded rocks and stabilizing cement. In 2008 he reinstated the annual fête, which now includes duck races, hot air balloons, antique cars, children's games, food vendors, and purveyors of religious souvenirs. Funds raised are donated to Slane Village development (http://www.ladywellfete.

Gary and Alex Mount Charles at Lady Well

com/). Alex Mount Charles also has plans to open a path to what is known as St Erc's hermitage, currently hidden in the woods. The ruined hermitage was built in the fifteenth to sixteenth centuries, over 1000 years later than the saint, but near it is an earlier dwelling.

We were able to arrange an interview with Alex. He met us at the castle and led us down the hill to Lady Well, sharing his deep affection for the place. He told us that he frequently walks down to the well to experience the peacefulness that surrounds it. Although he was born in England, he, like every member of his family, was christened with water from Lady Well. Much to the surprise of the English vicar, his father brought to Alex's baptism a plastic bottle filled with water from the holy well. The water was added to the baptismal font.

The Spanish chestnut tree

You can visit Lady Well during the fête or when the castle is open for tours. Alex also told us it might be possible to arrange to visit at other times (see p. 53). After you have entered the castle grounds, head down the path that leads straight from the castle to the impressive 300-year-old Spanish chestnut tree standing alone in the park. Its outer limbs are dead and bleached, as is much of the huge trunk, but the rest of it is full of exuberant growth and (depending on the season) a large number of chestnuts. It is a commanding presence.

Take the trail to the right of the tree, which leads down the hill into the natural amphitheater. When the trail ends, continue into the woods, walking parallel to the River Boyne. You'll soon reach Lady Well.

Ask permission from the tree to draw near. Then walk around it in a spiraling, clockwise manner. Remember that trees, like other beings, have an energy field around them. See if you can sense it as you approach. If this sage old chestnut tree welcomes you, you may find it has great wisdom to share.

Lady Well is fed by a spring that issues from the nearby cliff-face. From there, water flows down to the Boyne. En route, the stream disappears from view several times, hidden beneath grass-covered "stepping stones." Lady Well is the last place where the water surfaces before flowing into the river. Large stones have been carefully positioned under the rim of the well so that you can sit on the edge and draw up the water.

Sit on the nearby bench or at the edge of the well. Take time to center yourself. What do you feel? Do you sense a shift in the atmosphere, perhaps notice a faint flowery fragrance? Who might the Lady be that inhabits Lady Well? Perhaps you will see energy rising from the well like heat waves in summer. Perhaps you will see something as you stare at your reflection in the waters. You may want to leave an offering or a bit of

Rags or clooties are often found tied to tree branches near sacred wells in Celtic lands. "Clootie," from Scottish Gaelic for "strip of cloth," is a frequently used term for these strips of cloth or ribbon. In Ireland, however, the term is not widely used and "rag well" or "rag tree" is preferred.

cloth tied to a nearby tree. Once, the trees around the well were covered with strips of cloth that had been dipped into the healing waters and left behind to enhance the hoped-for cure.

Getting There

Slane Village stands at the crossroads of N2 (Dublin-Monaghan highway) and N51 (Drogheda-Navan road).

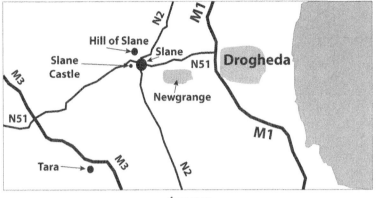

Area map

Slane Castle is about a kilometer upstream from the village. The Hill of Slane is a short drive or a fifteen-minute walk north from the crossroads in Slane Village. Visiting Lady Well: You can visit Lady Well when Slane Castle is open for tours, Sunday through Thursday, May through August. There is a fee to tour inside the castle but not to visit the grounds, and Alex says you can wander down to the well.

 Outside these times, you will need to contact enquiries@slanecastle.ie. They might or might not be able to accommodate your visit. Click on the Lady Well Slane map at http://www.boynevalleytours.com/places-to-visit.htm for an aerial view.

Hill of Slane N53 42 54 W6 32 45

The 158 m (518 ft) high Hill of Slane is just a kilometer or so north of Slane Village and 15 km (9 mi) north of the Hill of Tara. It was the site of a famous conflagration, the fiery contest between a foreign Christian missionary and native Irish pagans in 433 CE (Christian Era). At that time, Ireland was a country of warring tribes, led by kings and united, more or less, under a High King. Religious leaders called Druids provided guidance to the kings and performed important rituals. Into this pagan world came St Patrick, sent if not by God then by the nearest thing on earth: the Pope in Rome.

At the spring equinox, the ruling High King always lit a fire on the Hill of Tara, the religious-political center of Ireland. Then the flames would be lit around Ireland. In 433 CE, High King Laoghaire gave the command that no one, on pain of death, was to light a hilltop fire before he lit his. Enter St Patrick, who saw the opportunity to make an inflammatory statement. He climbed up to the top of the Hill of Slane— though some claim he climbed Brú na Bóinne or Knowth— and stole the show, lighting his Paschal fire before that of the High King. The enraged king knew this was a direct challenge to his authority. He rode to Slane, or maybe he had Patrick brought to Tara, and a confrontation took place.

> There is some scholarly debate whether Patrick ever existed—and whether he was perhaps an amalgam of two saints, not one.

Legend says that the King Laoghaire's irate Druids demanded the fire of Christianity be extinguished that very night or else they feared it would burn forever. They challenged St Patrick to magical battle but could not defeat him. Impressed, the king permitted his followers to become converts if they so chose. At least one did: St Erc (p. 55). St Patrick rewarded St Erc by naming him bishop of Slane, and on the now-Christianized Hill of Slane he established a school. A local church still holds an annual fire ceremony on the hill to commemorate the event. The Hill of Slane holds a legendary place in the history of Irish Christianity, symbolizing the victory of the new religion over the old ways.

Over the centuries a unique Celtic Christianity developed, influenced by Irish traditions, the Desert Fathers, and Egyptian Coptic Christianity. This new faith embraced isolated, ascetic monastic life such as found on Skellig Michael, a craggy, desolate island 10 km (6 mi) off the southwest shore of Ireland. Celtic Christianity encouraged far-flung missionary activities and maintained a close relationship with the natural world. It lasted at least until the twelfth century, when Norman England and Rome-administered Catholicism conquered the Emerald Isle. It was never completely extinguished, and in recent decades it has experienced a renascence.

For years there has been speculation about the connection between early Ireland and Egypt. In 2006 the eighth-century *Faddan More Psaltery* was found in an Irish bog. Papyrus fragments found inside the book's cover support the connection between early Irish monastic traditions and the Egyptian Coptic church. http://www.seandalaiocht. com/1/post/2010/09/papy-rus-fragments-found-with-ancient-irish-bog-book.html, retrieved 24 January, 2011.

The Hill of Slane has other claims to fame than Patrick's Paschal flame. The so-called motte on the western side, inaccessible and hidden in the trees, is said to be the remains of the 1170s fortification of Richard le Flemyng of Flanders. In fact, it is probably the burial mound of the Fir Bolg king Sláine, who legend claims is buried there. An ongoing archeological survey should soon provide additional information about the mound and nearby barrow. (Contact Michael Fox at http://BoyneValleyTours.com for more information.)

A ruined Franciscan church and college from the sixteenth century can be visited on the Hill of Slane. St Erc's original foundation and his remains may lie to the south of the present church, or possibly in the ruined "mortuary house" in the graveyard. Tradition says that the two gable ends, with large upright rectangle stone end-blocks, are what remains of Erc's shrine. These standing stones may be

Ruined Franciscan church on the Hill of Slane

the remains of a megalithic construction that was Christianized—as was the Hill of Slane. As late as the twentieth century, the shrine was visited as part of local burial rites.

The Hill of Slane is intervisible with Newgrange and Knowth, about 5 km (3 mi) to the east. On a clear day you can see Drogheda, the Irish Sea, and the Wicklow Mountains to the south.

According to Anthony Murphy, "Slane sits on an extraordinary 135-mile equinox alignment stretching from Millmount in the east as far as Croagh Patrick in the west, passing through the town of Kells and the impressive monument complex at Cruachan Ai (Rathcroghen, see p. 283). We call this Saint Patrick's "Equinox Journey." The near-equinox alignment involves watching the sunset around 23 March from Millmount, overlooking the Boyne in Drogheda. This sunset falls behind the Hill of Slane. An observer looking at this equinoctial sunset is unwittingly looking also in the direction of Croagh Patrick in County

Mayo. Thus, two sites closely associated with Saint Patrick are in a near-equinox alignment." http://www.mythicalireland.com/ancientsites/slane/index.html, Jan. 22, 2011.

Take time to stroll around the ruins, perhaps climb the church tower and look out at the distant sacred sites. Contemplate the location of the hill and its history. Regardless of whether Patrick actually lit the Paschal flame on the Hill of Slane, alignments place it on important lines of power. What do you feel? What do you discover?

Getting There

Slane Village stands at the crossroads of N2 (Dublin-Monaghan highway) and N51 (Drogheda-Navan road). The Hill of Slane is a short drive or a fifteen-minute walk north from the crossroads in Slane Village.

You can view a historic-trail walking map from Slane at www.discoverireland.ie/historictowns.

Hill of Tara (Teamhair na Rí)
N53 34 51 W6 36 34

The fame of the Hill of Tara ("The Hill of Kings") spreads wide and deep through Irish history. WB Yeats called it "the most consecrated spot in Ireland." In Gaelic, Tara is Teamhair, and the name may refer to the burial mound of Tea, ancestor queen and goddess of the Celts, who died on Tara and made it sacred soil. Or it may come from the same root as the Greek *temenos*, meaning sanctuary.

58

Tara probably first came into use around 3500 BCE. Some 130 monuments, including barrows, Neolithic tombs, and circular Iron Age forts, have been identified in the immediate area. It has been a sacred location for millennia, a veritable cemetery of the renowned. Most of the sites remain unexcavated, although unscientific digs in the nineteenth century left parts of the area pockmarked and disfigured.

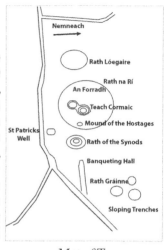

Map of Tara

Although the Hill of Tara is only 91 m (300 ft) high, you can see 40% of Ireland from its summit. On a clear day you can see the glimmering white quartz façade of Newgrange from the so-called "Banquet Hall." It was from the Hill of Tara that King Laoghaire, purported to be buried upright in armor in a ring fort on the hill, saw the Pascal fire that Patrick may have lit on the Hill of Slane.

Early Irish sagas describe Tara as the home of the god Lug, that great master-of-all-trades. Its greatest prestige was during the time of the Celtic

"Ancient sources say that the great [Samhain] gatherings at Tara, called *Feis Teamhrach* in Irish, were first held by the Ard Ri Ollamh Fodhla in the year 1317 BC. The *Feis* was held every three years and exercised both legislative and judicial power. In attendance were the High King's elite band of warriors, Na Fianna Eireann, and the Chieftains with their Bards, the Druids, Brehons (Judges) and people." http://www.iol.ie/~histpub/child1/places.html, 22 January, 2011.

High Kings of Ireland, and legendary kings Cormac Mac Airt and Conaire Mór were inaugurated on the hill, along with 142 other kings over the centuries. Legend reports that the royal contender for kingship

Lai Fáil, the "Stone of Destiny"

had to be accepted by the Lai Fáil, the "Stone of Destiny," the standing stone erected on the hill. If the Stone of Destiny approved, it would screech out the successful candidate's name.

Seventh-century documents describe the battles between dynasties to claim kingship of Tara and hence kingship over the whole of Ireland. Tara continued to be the nominal seat of kingship until it was abandoned in 1022.

Although Tara was no longer the seat of power in Ireland, in 1843 Daniel O'Connell "the Liberator" chose the site for a major speech promoting Roman Catholic emancipation. Some 750,000 people came to Tara to hear him speak. Like the nearby Hill of Slane, with which it is linked, the Hill of Tara continues to carry a powerful emotional charge. Unfortunately, the mythic importance of Tara has not protected it from desecration. The Rath of the Synods ring fort was devastated in the early twentieth century by a group called the British Israelites. They had hoped to find the Ark of the Covenant.

Many consider the Hill of Tara a "must-see," but there isn't as much to see as you might expect. It's a gentle hill, undulating with grass-covered

> "Tradition demanded that a sacred marriage take place between the new king and the goddess, who held the fertility of the land in her power. ... Nowhere was this ritual more celebrated than at Tara. And there was no sovereignty goddess more powerful or more celebrated than the great Maebh." Meehan, p. 271.

depressions and elevations of ringforts, barrows, and misguided digs. Signs give fanciful labels based on the fevered imagination of nineteenth-century excavators. It may be romantic to think that one is seeing the remains of the Royal Palace, the Royal Banquet Hall, the Royal Enclosure, or Gráinne's Fort, but is it accurate? In most cases, no.

A knowledgeable guide like Nora Judge (http://www.nativespirittours.com) will enhance your experience of Tara. Nora took us to several less-well-known sites, provided an archaeological and historical context for Tara, and regaled us with legends. (Ask Nora about the connection between the High King and horses.)

The Well of Tara

The area around Tara has many wells, both domestic and sacred, and we visited one holy well with many names: the Well of Tara, the Well of the White Cow, King Cormac's Well, and St Patrick's Well. According to RAS Macalister, writing in 1918, it was also known as Liaig Dail Duib Duirb, Tuath Linde, Tipra Bo Finde, and Topur Tuirme Gland. "Liaig" relates to the Irish Gaelic word for "physician" and probably indicates a healing spring; Tipra Bo Finde refers to the sacred white cow. Derc Dub refers to "black eye" and may describe the dark waters. The fourth name, Topur Tuirme, refers to land and "the well of the numbering of clans." Macalister claimed that it was well-worship that created Tara as a sacred place. At any rate, it

The Well of Tara

is clear that the well of Tara was sacred long before it was called St Patrick's Well.

There is nothing overtly Christian about the Well of Tara, no statue of Mary or of any saint, including Patrick. It is located along the Kells to Dublin road, one of the five ancient roads that met at Tara. This holy well has a very special atmosphere that is worth experiencing. Take your time at the well, sensing into the space, the place, the stone-lined waters.

The Tech Mídchúarta

The Tech Mídchúarta (the misnamed "Banquet Hall") is a ceremonial avenue, constructed between the fifth and eighth centuries CE. High banks on either side isolate you

Nora Judge describes Tara as a powerful place of death and rebirth, of energies that exacerbate anger and enhance joy. She says it is both a place of violence and battle—and of healing. Ancient documents describe generous feasts held at Tara, demonstrative of ample hospitality. The Knights Hospitallers established an outpost at Tara to give aid to pilgrims. Personal communication, October 2011.

The Tech Mídchúarta

from the outside world, creating an almost subterranean entryway to Tara. Gaps (perhaps a total of seven) provide glimpses of the tombs of ancestors, which legends claim to have been kings and queens. Center yourself and be present to your surroundings and you may begin to feel their presence, especially if you are there around Halloween/Samhain.

The Mound of the Hostages

This fancifully named passage grave was built around 3000 BCE, the same time as the massive mounds at Brú na Bóinne. Its name refers to the much-later Celtic practice of exchanging hostages with neighboring kingdoms. The mound is 21 m (70 ft) in diameter and 2.7 m (9 ft) high. Once it held over 200 Neolithic cremations and forty buri-

Tara is the site of both the Well of the White Cow and the Well of the Calf. In addition, the Hill of the Cow (perhaps an ancient dolmen) once stood in the field where the wells are located. We learned about the White Cow goddess Bóinne at Brú na Bóinne. We meet her again at Tara. Imbolc is known as the "season of the cow," and the Mound of the Hostages on the Hill of Tara is oriented to the rising sun on Imbolc.

The Mound of the Hostages

als from the Bronze Age, proof of its continued importance as a sacred site. Two beautiful gold torcs dating around 2000 BCE were also found in the mound and are now at the National Museum, Dublin. One complete skeleton of a young man was found with a dagger and a bead necklace

The Irish Celtic solar year is cyclical, with eight divisions. It is based on four astronomical events associated with important rituals and myths: the summer and winter solstices (approximately 21 June and 21 December) and the spring and autumn equinoxes (approximately 22 March and 22 September). In between are the four cross-quarter days (which were/are fire festivals), each of which also has its mythic associations and ceremonies. The "day" begins in the evening before the date given. The astronomical cross-quarter days are Samhain (1 November or, more accurately, 5-10 November), the beginning of the year and the beginning of winter; Imbolc (1 February or, more accurately, 2-7 February); Bealtaine or Beltane (1 May or, more accurately, 4-10 May), which was the beginning of summer; and Lughnasa (1 August or more accurately, 3-10 August). Many of these days have been transformed into Christian holidays (Halloween, Christmas, Candlemas or St Brigid Day, Easter, Mayday, and St John the Baptist Eve).

of jet, amber, bronze, and Egyptian faience, testimony to far-flung trade routes.

The mound has many associations with the moon, including an interior wall carving of thirteen spirals, perhaps representing an early moon calendar. The Lia Fáil standing stone ("The Stone of Destiny") was originally placed in front of the passageway, and its shadow would have fallen on the interior carvings on the left. The Stone of Destiny was moved to the top of the hill in 1824 to become a memorial to those who died in the 1798 rebellion against the British.

The passage is oriented toward the rising sun on the astronomical cross-quarter days of Samhain (between 5-10 November) and Imbolc (between 2-7 February). Legend and archaeology come together, for both indicate that Tara was important at the beginning of winter and at the beginning of spring. How appropriate that both dates should be marked in this sacred landscape of death and rebirth.

Sheela-na-gig

To the north, just below the hill, are the decommissioned nineteenth-century church of St Patrick and a weather-worn statue of the saint, a visual reminder of who won the contest between Tara and Slane. In the church cemetery an almost obliterated, tenth-century carving is barely visible on a large upright slab referred to as St Adamnán's Pillar. It is thought to be a Sheela-na-gig (see p. 77), but the details of the carving are hard to discern, and it might once have had horns, thus associating it with the Celtic horned god Cernunnos or Herne.

Sheela-na-gigs are usually thought to be associated with sexuality, but Nora Judge says that some midwives in Ireland carry small, hidden Sheela figures as a talisman for safe deliveries. She suggests that their skeletal appearance and hanging breasts could represent a woman who has just given birth but whose milk has not yet come in.

The Sheela-na-gig
More to Experience

The Hill of Tara's modern popularity may soon be its downfall. Already it feels like a theme park, not a sacred site, and the situation will grow worse now that it is easily accessible from M3 motorway. There's talk of replacing the discrete interpretive center and limiting access, as at Brú na Bóinne.

But all is not yet lost. Wander off the well-trod path and find the faery hawthorn tree, dripping with rags and ribbons, on the west slope of the Hill of Tara. It's a fine place to meditate. See if you can feel the power of this place, location of so many burials and celebrations, center of sovereignty for so many centuries. What is it about Tara that generates so much importance? Is there power innate within the land? If so, what is it? Or does the power come from the human pageant that has taken place upon it? Or can the two be separated?

The faery hawthorn tree

It is also worthwhile contemplating the relationship of stones and kingship. Arthur proved he was the awaited king by pulling a sword from a stone; the High Kings had to be approved by the screeching Lia Fáil. Ponder the polarities of masculine and female power, the phallic Stone of Destiny and the sovereignty goddess Medb/Tea, both considered vital to validate the High King.

You might also spend some time at Ráith Gráinne, legendary site of the beginning and end of the love story of Gráinne, daughter of King Cormac Ma Airt, and Diarmuid. We'll be learning more about them when we reach Kesh Corran in Co. Sligo (see p. 277).

 The coffee shop/café, gift shops, interpretive center in the church, and bookstore at the base of the Hill of Tara are pleasant places to visit (http://www.heritageireland.ie/en/MidlandsEastCoast/HillofTara/).

Getting There

Tara is 12 km (7.5 mi) south of Navan on R147; it can be reached via exit 7 (to Skryne) off M3, the new motorway from Dublin.

Additional Resources

Michael Fox's tours: www.BoyneValleyTours.com

Nora Judge: http://www.nativespirittours.com/

Hill of Tara/M3 development controversy: http://www.m3motorway.ie/Archaeology/Tara/

Some more background on Tara: http://www.iol.ie/~histpub/child1/places.html

For some background on early monasticism: http://www.historyworld.net/wrldhis/PlainTextHistories.asp?ParagraphID=dgk

Monasterboice, Rathmore Church, Balgeeth Sheela-na-gig, Fourknocks

Monasterboice, Co. Louth N53 46 39 W6 25 03

The Round Tower

I wasn't interested in visiting Monasterboice, famous for its two high crosses. I'd already seen a number of high crosses in several museums, so why see more? They were impressive art objects, but "been there, done that." However, our guide, Michael, declared Monasterboice was one of his favorite places and insisted that we visit it. I'm glad he did and that we did. It's one thing to see Irish high crosses (real or replica) in a museum or displayed inside an abandoned church—it's quite another to see high crosses where they were first placed and where they have stood for a thousand years. Standing next to the mammoth South Cross in the cemetery at Monasterboice, I felt tiny and ephemeral. I suppose that was the original intention. (Elyn)

Monasterboice, Clonmacnoise (see p. 105), and Glendalough (see p. 121) are three iconic examples of early monastic settlements in Ireland. Of the three, Monasterboice is the smallest and least developed, but that doesn't mean it is the least worth visiting.

From a distance, the first you see of Monasterboice is a tall round tower, jagged at the top, missing its original conical roof. The 28 m (92 ft) high tower pokes up above the surrounding countryside, announcing, "Here is Monasterboice." Yet its original purpose was not just to be a beacon and a belfry: the unique Irish round towers, associated with monastic complexes, were probably also built to

West face of Muiredach's Cross

shelter inhabitants and valuables during Viking raids; they also served as status symbols.

Their doorways are always high—up to 4 m (13 ft)—above the ground. Entry is only possible by ladder, which could be drawn up in times of danger. Unfortunately, that strategy did not prevent Monasterboice's tower from being burned in 1097, along with the monastery's library and other treasures. Before being burnt, the tower was probably 33 m (108 ft) high. (The tallest surviving round tower is at Kilmacduagh, Co. Galway; it is 34.3 m [112 ft] tall.)

St Bhuithe (died 521 CE) founded Monasterboice, hence the name, derived from Mainistir Bhuithe. It was a dual foundation with both monks and nuns. A similar arrangement occurred in a number of other major ecclesiastical centers, including Kildare (see p. 128) and Clonmacnoise (see p. 105).

The oldest monuments that survive are the three high crosses and the round tower, which date from the tenth century. Little is known about the monastery. After the Cistercian abbey at nearby Mellifont was established in 1142, Monasterboice was abandoned. A parish church was established on the site in the thirteenth century, and the remains of two small churches can still be seen.

> The cross itself is not a uniquely Christian symbol. It is found worldwide, often referring to the cardinal directions, or to the dualities of earth/feminine (horizontal) and spiritual/masculine (vertical), or to the four elements (earth, air, fire, water), or to the four spatial dimensions (height, width, depth, and breadth)—you get the idea. The cross as a Christian symbol representing the pole and crossbar of the crucifixion developed slowly. It only began to be widely depicted after the fourth century CE, when Christianity became the official religion of the Roman Empire.

High crosses are found in both Britain and Ireland, but they are more numerous—and much more finely carved—in Ireland. Over 300 survive in Ireland. Along with their height, a distinctive feature is the ringed crosshead. The decorated ring or wheel that surrounds the center of the cross supports the weight of the center and the extended arms. It also brings a touch of Celtic spirituality to the Christian form, reminding us of the

> "The symbolic structure of the fully developed wheel-head Celtic cross can be seen as representative of the axis mundi or cosmic axis. ... the cosmos is conceived as having several 'circles' or levels, which can be visualized as if they were stacked one on top of the other along an axis." Pennick, *The Celtic Cross*, p. 75.

cycles of seasons and of the cycle of life, death, and rebirth, and of unity and perfection. The sunwheel was and is a protective sigil (a symbol created for a magical purpose), and sacred signs are often inscribed within a circle as magical talismans. Crichton Miller hypothesizes that the Celtic (wheeled) cross could have served as a navigational instrument (http://www.viewzone.com/crichton.html).

East face of Muiredach's Cross

The circled head of the Celtic cross also has similarities to the chrismon, sometimes found carved over church doorways or on altars. A chrismon is a circle inside of which are an "X" and superimposed "P," standing for chi/rho, the first two letters in the Greek spelling of Christ; within the crossbars of the "X" are the alpha (α) and omega (ω), the first and last letters in the Greek alphabet, standing for Christ as "the beginning and the end."

Irish high crosses were carved between the eighth and twelfth centuries. Early crosses were decorated with simple geometrical reliefs, but in the ninth and tenth centuries, sculptors introduced biblical scenes meant to be "read" in a particular order, usually from the ground up. Interlaces, geometrical motifs, and entangled creatures often enliven the sides. It is probable that high crosses were originally colored or brightly painted. Although the scenes carved on the high crosses may have been edifying sermons in stone, similar to the "sermons in glass" found in stained-glass windows, the high crosses were also status symbols for the monasteries and their patrons.

Monasterboice has three high crosses, two

What we often think of as "Celtic" art—entwining vines, knots, interlacing geometrical motifs, zoomorphs, etc.—is derived from the style found across northern Europe, Germany, Scandinavia, and Anglo-Saxon England.

of which are quite impressive. The South or Muiredach's Cross is 5.5 m (17 ft 8 in) high and is one of the most beautiful in Ireland, a true national treasure. It is probably named after the abbot Muiredach mac Domhnaill, who died in 923 CE and is commemorated

According to Nigel Pennick, the image of Christ on the east face of Muiredach's Cross is "based on the iconography of the resurrected Egyptian god, Osiris. Christ is holding a cross and *Irminsul*-staff in the Osirian position, and on his head is an eagle that resembles the crown of Egyptian gods and pharaohs" *(The Celtic Cross,* pp. 86-87). Pennick interprets the figure to the left of Christ as Pan with his pipes, the harp-playing figure on the right as either King David or Apollo.

on the base. Carved from a single block of sandstone attached to a pyramidal base, the cross features a decorative sandstone capstone.

The surface of Muiredach's Cross is covered with ornate designs based on an underlying geometrical grid. It has been suggested that the skilled stone carvers were presenting the geometry matrix that underlies reality. Detailed figural sculptures of biblical stories (both Old and New Testaments) decorate the cross on the east and west sides; geometric and interlace ornamentations are carved on the

narrower north and south sides. A series of zodiacal figures adorn the base. The charming capstone is a tiny roofed building or miniature oratory, perhaps representing a reliquary. It includes a depiction of St Paul and St Anthony in the (Egyptian) desert.

Detail of east face of Muiredach's Cross

The east face of Muiredach's Cross, as is usual for high crosses, focuses on images from the Old Testament. It begins at the base with a scene from the Garden of Eden, then moves up to Cain and Abel, David and Goliath, Moses, and the Magi. Within the wheeled center and extending through

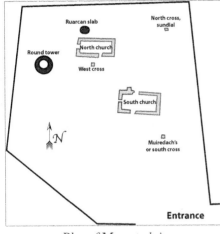

Plan of Monasterboice

both arms is Christ at the Last Judgment.

The west face is devoted, more or less, to the Passion of Christ, beginning at the base (above the inscription and some charming Celtic-style cats) with his arrest at Gethsemane and continuing upward to his crucifixion, complete with mocking soldiers, and then his resurrection. On the north side, under the outstretched cross-arm, is a depiction of the Hand of God *(Dextera Dei)* with a nimbus of power behind it, above intertwining vines with human heads.

The West Cross or Tall Cross stands near the north church and the round tower. It is 7 m (23 ft) high, the tallest high cross in Ireland or anywhere else. It also is covered with biblical scenes, but they are badly eroded. On the east side of the crosshead is a carving of David killing a lion with a hurley stick (something like a hockey stick) and ball, the earliest depiction of the game in Ireland. The west side includes another crucifixion scene. The North Cross, which has been heavily reconstructed, stands to the north, next to what remains of an old stone sundial.

Even though the church was in ruins by the late seventeenth century, the cemetery is still in use today. Fresh flowers adorned several graves when we were there. As is usual in Irish cemeteries, many of the tombstones list a number of family members. We admired one headstone, engraved at the top with the inscription "Judith Leonard, died 1887" and at the bottom with "Sr Mary Priscilla Leonard, died in

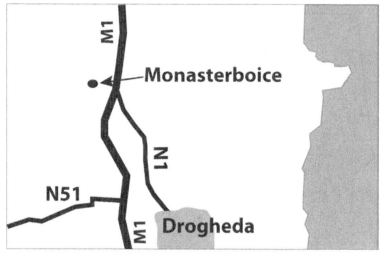

Area map

Australia in 1967." In between, a number of deceased family members were listed. These "multiple listings" seemed to provide continuity with the megalithic burial practices in which numerous remains were interred in the same location over the generations.

Monasterboice is in a delightful rural setting, surrounded by a low stone wall and numerous trees. It is neither neglected nor over-developed. Visiting Monasterboice is like discovering a new friend—but one that you feel you have known for a long, long time, and one that you look forwarded to seeing again.

Getting There

Monasterboice is approximately 8 km (5 mi) northwest of Drogheda off M1 (Drogheda-Dundalk). Take minor road to west off M1 and follow signposts. No entry fee.

More Resources

For more on high crosses, see http://www.megalithicireland.com/High%20Cross%20Home.htm.

For more on round towers, see http://archiseek.com/2010/round-tower-monasterboice-co-louth/.

Rathmore (St Lawrence) Church, Co. Meath
N53 38 49 W6 51 48

You can see the ruined church in the distance across the field, behind a fence, sheltered by towering trees. Don't hesitate. Park the car near the signpost. Open the gate. Walk boldly past the grazing cattle, avoiding squishy, fragrant cow patties if you can. Open another gate. Getting there is half the pleasure. Breezes waft through the arched stone windows. Mystery abounds. (Elyn)

The name Rathmore comes from An Ráth Mhór (Big Ring Fort), so one would suppose there must be a ring fort nearby, although there doesn't appear to be. Perhaps the nearby castle or deserted medieval village was constructed on top of it. Rathmore church was built by Sir Thomas Plunkett in the first half of the fifteenth century. A tomb with moss-covered effigies of Sir Thomas and his wife Mary Cruice is in the sacristy. The church has two towers:

Approaching Rathmore

one was a bell tower; the other was the living quarters for the priest.

A 36 cm (14 in) diameter stone labyrinth was found in the rubble in 1931 and mounted on the interior wall near the

The labyrinth

doorway. Its original purpose and location are not known, but perhaps it was a corbel, high up on one of the walls. The labyrinth has the standard eleven-circuit design found in medieval churches throughout Europe. The path is raised and can be traced by hand.

To the north of the church stands a much-damaged cross, erected in 1519 by Sir Christopher Plunkett. It has carvings of St Lawrence, St Patrick, an abbess, and veg-

The churhyard at Rathmore

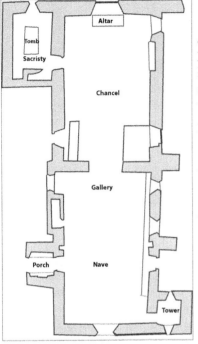

Floor plan of the church

etation. We're told that a large stone known as St Lawrence's stone, a peculiar stone with a hole through the center, was recently removed from the foot of the Hill of Tlachtga (see p. 93) and placed at the entrance of Rathmore Church.

Rathmore church is a lovely ruin, long on atmosphere and short on tourists.

Getting There

Rathmore is 5 km (3 mi) outside Athboy on N51 to Navan, to the west of M3.

For more on labyrinths in Ireland, see http://www.labyrinthos.net/irelandlabs.html.

Balgeeth or Ardcath Sheela-na-gig, Co. Meath N53 36 14 W6 24 44

The grey, black-specked Sheela is set into a low, vegetation-topped stone wall at the entrance to a private farmhouse and dairy farm. For several hundred years or more (nobody knows how long), the carving was hidden inside a gatepost and forgotten. But not too long ago a milk collection truck ran into the gatepost and the long-hidden Sheela was revealed. She was reinstated facing out, mortared into

The Sheela-na-gig

the whitewashed stone wall to the right of the driveway.

The carving is 20 cm (8 in) by 38 cm (15 in). The figure has a large round head, big egg-shaped eyes, a sweet smile, and no neck. Her skeletal arms end in hands that hold open her vulva. She has long thin legs with feet pointing to her right.

Sheela-na-gigs are stylized carvings of naked, often skeletal women, clutching their vulvas. There is much disagreement about the origins and significance of Sheela-na-gigs. Some claim they are pre-Christian fertility symbols; others claim the so-called "exhibitionist" figures are Christian representations of lust. They occur in European churches built after the twelfth century (or sometimes earlier) and occasionally in secular buildings as well—usually above a window, or high up on a wall. In recent centuries they have often been defaced, hidden, or destroyed.

The present farmer moved into the farmhouse awhile ago. His young wife used to wipe the carving down a bit to highlight various features and take care of it. Within the year, she became pregnant and gave birth to triplets, even though there was no history of triplets on either side of the family. Since then, she has kept her distance from—and her hands off—the evocative carving.

The name Sheela-na-gig is from the Irish language, but the exact meaning is uncertain. According to Jack Robert's annotated map, "It is often rendered in Irish as *Sile na gCioch*. *Sheela* or *Sile* means femininity but it also means a special kind if woman, a hag or spiritual woman and also related to the word for a spirit or fairy in Irish, the *Sidhe* (pronounced 'shee')."

According to Jack Roberts, one of many researchers on the topic, Celtic gods and goddesses were often depicted as ugly to appear more impressive and other-worldly. He also suggests that a skeletal female image that focuses on the vulva, rather than on a full belly and breasts, is likely to symbolize death, life, and regeneration. Irish midwives often carry Sheelas as good-luck talismans. Interestingly, some of the Sheela figures are known in local folklore by the names of particular saints.

It is good manners to park your car, go up to the farmhouse door, and ask permission to see the Sheela. With luck, you'll even meet the three triplets (born around 1999-2000) who may, or may not, have been the result of Sheela's fertile blessing.

Fertility symbol? Good luck talisman? Apotropaic images meant to turn away the "evil eye"? A warning against lust? A celebration of the goddess? We leave it to you to decide.

For more on Sheela-na-gigs, see Anthony Weir's website, http://www.beyond-the-pale.org.uk; or go to http://www.newgrange.eu/stonelight15.htm, http://www.knowth.com/sheela-na-gig.htm, or http://www.irelands-sheelanagigs.org.

Getting There

Balgeeth Sheela-na-gig: Approximately 1 km from Ardcath village in the townland of Balgeeth. From Ardcath village travel west/southwest past the old churchyard and go through the next intersection. The second farmhouse has a whitewashed stone wall topped by a hedgerow. The carving is not visible from the road. The Balgeeth Sheela is less than 5 km (3 mi) from Fourknocks and just 4 km (2.5 mi) from N2 at R152 when heading north to Duleek.

Fourknocks, Co. Meath
N53 35 49 W6 19 29

This 4500-year-old passage-tomb cemetery and prehistoric complex is located on a hill above the village of Naul, southeast of Newgrange. Fourknocks I (Na Fuarchnoic or "The Cold Hills") is under guardianship of the State and can be entered; the other monuments are on privately owned land. It appears that the individual tombs in the complex were inter-related. Gabriel Clooney describes the gradual "twinning" of Fourknocks I and II over millennia, during which time they were transformed into complementary ritual settings. For example, the passageway in Fourknocks I goes upward, but that in Fourknocks II, 50 m (164 ft) to the east, goes downward.

The passageway of Fourknocks I opens to the northeast. The chambered cairn can be entered if you go with a guide, or you can arrange to get the key by following the instructions signposted at the entrance to the path to Fourknocks. We highly recommend visiting the site with a knowledgeable guide (Michael Fox for example). If you go on your own, be sure to bring a flashlight. And be careful of your head: there is a low iron bar above the entrance.

Entrance to Fourknocks I

The site was excavated in the early 1950s and reconstructed with a concrete domed ceiling, which has undoubtedly changed the energies of the place. Nowadays, concrete is rarely used for reconstruction. The mound was re-grassed on the outside so that it would look like it had before the excavation. You can climb to the top of the cairn and enjoy the view. Fourknocks is 16 km (10 mi) southeast of the Boyne Valley and 17.7 km (11 mi) east of Tara.

The 5 m (17 ft) long passage leads into a large, circular chamber that is 5.5 m (18 ft) by 6.4 m (21 ft). The chamber has three recesses, giving it a kind of bloated cruciform shape. Geometrical patterns decorate twelve stones, with zigzags predominating. Notice the zigzags over the lintels: were they used to identify different tribes or families? Are they star maps? Anthony Murphy in his book *Islands of the Setting Sun* thinks so. One of the orthostats (interior standing stones), to the left of the entrance, is thought by some to represent a face.

Bone fragments from approximately 60 individuals were found in the passage and the three side recesses, dating

82

both from Neolithic times and later re-use during the Bronze Age. Cremains and unburned skulls and long bones were discovered, carefully positioned, sometimes with associated small stones. Grave goods including stone and bone pendants and beads, chalk marbles, pins (including a stunning antler pin), flints, and stone balls were also found.

Approach a sacred site as you would a stranger you would like to meet. Be polite and attentive. Ask to get acquainted; wait for an invitation to draw closer; and give thanks for being invited to enter—if you are. Act courteously. Express appreciation when you leave.

The roof was partially corbelled, the center probably closed off by a wooden roof with timber supports. It is hard to see how a chamber open to the sky would be consistent with the use of the mound as a grave. Another theory is that the roof was left open as a star observatory. Martin Brennan, writing in *The Stones of Time*, believes the zigzags on some of the stones represent Cassiopeia, the W-shaped constellation, which was visible from Fourknocks during

Carved lintel stone in the interior of Fourknocks I

Anthony Murphy and Richard Moore believe there is a link between Fourknocks and the constellation Cygnus. They believe that the cairn is oriented toward the rising place of Deneb, the star in Cygnus's "tail." They cite abundant mythological and archeological evidence supporting the significance of swans in the region, including the flock of whooping swans that wintered and continue to winter around nearby Newgrange. *Island of the Setting Sun* and http://www.mythicalireland.com/ancientsites/fourknocks, retrieved 24 January, 2011.

the Neolithic. Obviously, there is much to be discovered.

If you enter Fourknocks I, be conscious of the energies you feel. Does it feel good to you? Weird? Welcoming? Unwelcoming? As is true at all sacred sites, it is important that you first ask permission to

enter. If it is given, then enter. Stay aware, pay attention, and take care of yourself. For better or for worse, Fourknocks can be a very powerful place.

Getting There

Fourknocks is southeast of Newgrange. From Naul, the site is reached via R108 (to Drogheda) to the north, taking the first turn to the west. Or, you can get there via R122 (to Garristown/Oldtown) to the west, taking the first turn to the north. It is signposted. You get the key from Mr Fintan White [(0)1 835 4722] a mile or so down the road. A deposit is required, and it must be returned by 6 pm.

More to Experience

Old Mellifont Abbey

Old Mellifont Abbey (not New Mellifont in Collon), Co. Louth, was the first Cistercian house in Ireland, founded on the banks of the River Mattock in 1142 with four Irish and nine French monks. The Cistercians were a reform movement and, like their rule, their architecture is austere. The name means "Honey Fountain" and may refer to the beauty of the surroundings—or to the reputation of the monks

for creating "sweetness" out of hardship. http://www.
heritageireland.ie/en/midlandseastcoast/OldMelli-
fontAbbey/. Old Mellifont Abbey is 10 km (6 mi) west of
Drogheda by N51, R168, and a minor road west of Tullyal-
len. Open access year around; fee from May through September for guided tours of the Abbey and Chapter House.

The National Museum of Ireland Sheelas

The National Museum of Ireland – Archaeology (Dublin) has a collection of Sheela-na-gigs. They have either
been prudishly hidden away or are being carefully maintained in storage: it all depends on your perspective. If you
ask at the main desk, you may be given permission to see
them. We did and we were. The carvings are intriguing, but
they are also out of context, which transforms them from
powerful presences into interesting artifacts. If it is very
important for you to see the Sheelas, it is best to call in
advance [(0)1 677 7444].

Ardcath

Ardcath (Irish *Ard Cath* means "height of the battle")
is a hamlet in Co. Meath, Ireland, with two interesting
churches. Ardcath's medieval church, dedicated to St Mary
the Blessed Virgin, is an evocative ruin in the middle of Ardcath village. The cemetery is still in use. The "new" (a mere
150 years old) parish church has recently undergone a
complete restoration and is quite attractive. (Contact
Michael Fox, www.BoyneValleyTours.com, for more
information on both.) Ardcath is close to Fourknocks
and worth a stop if you are in the vicinity.

Faughert

Faughert, Co. Louth, is one of the legendary birthplaces
of the Goddess/Saint Brigid and the site of one of her many
holy wells (see p. 127). It has recently been significantly restored. Faughert is north of Dundalk, near Proleek Dolmen.
For more information, go to http://www.dundalkonline.

net/index.php?id=stbrigid or http://www.discoverireland.
ie/Search-Results/Details.aspx?touristItemID=49965.

The Sliabh Foy Loop

Near Faughert, in the hills outside Carlingford, Co.
Louth, you can visit "The Sliabh Foy Loop," a protected
area for flora, fauna, wild animals, and leprechauns. Kevin
Woods, a local man and one of founders of the group that
lobbied the EU for biodiversity protection for the Cooley
Mountains, states that "there are only 236 leprechauns still
living in Ireland on the Foy mountain at Slate Rock. He
believes that this place is of the spirit world." The epic *Táin
Bó Cuailnge (The Cattle Raid of Cooley,* see p. 291) takes
place in the Cooley Mountains. Carlingford is a good base
from which to explore the Cooley Peninsula. http://www.
irishcentral.com/travel/Leprechauns-are-now-protected-
under-new-European-law---SEE-VIDEOS-117791804.
html.

Additional Resources

Guides for Fourknocks: Michael Fox (www.BoyneVal-
leyTours.com and Anthony Murphy (www.mythicalIre-
land.com) (see QR codes on p. 84 and p. 24).

Guides for the area: http://www.nativespirittours.com/
and www.BoyneValleyTours.com (see QR code on p. 84
and p. 26).

Loughcrew (Sliabh na Caillí); Tlachtga, Hill of Ward; and St Ciarán's Well, Co. Meath

Loughcrew (Sliabh na Caillí or Slieve na Cailliagh) N53 44 40 W7 06 51

We gathered in front of Cairn T at Sliabh na Caillí in the chill damp September dawn, hoping that the rising sun would pierce the clouds and light the interior of the cairn. For millennia, the rising equinox sun has sent a beam into the passage grave, illuminating the numerous enigmatic carvings on the backstone of the rear chamber. I listened to women drumming in a nearby ruined passage grave. I hoped their chant would part the clouds, but it was not to be. Soon a dozen or more people huddled inside Cairn T while outside the darkness gradually turned to light. I climbed over the sillstone into the rear recess of the chamber and shone my flashlight on the ancient symbols carved on the wall. Reverently, I touched an eight-lobed shape enclosed in a circle. That was enough. It was more than enough. (Elyn)

Loughcrew Megalithic Cemetery is also known as Sliabh na Caillí, Slieve na Cailliagh, the Hill of the Hag, the Cairn of the Witch, the Mountain of the Sorceress, the Witches Hops—you get the idea. Loughcrew, also the name of the local township, is one of the four largest megalithic cemeteries in Ireland. More than thirty chambered cairns, many with interior stone carvings, are spread over a ridge of three hills. The interior passage graves are usually described as constructed of limestone, but their composition includes sandstone, a coarse greywacke called gritstone, and conglomerate. The stones were either left by glaciers or taken from local outcrops. The area has a variety of monuments, including stone circles, henges, standing stones, Iron Age forts, and the remains of a cursus (a ceremonial entrance way).

Built between 3500 and 3300 BCE, the Loughcrew cairns are contemporary with Brú na Bóinne, but they are much less reconstructed and have not been comprehensively excavated. Although less famous than Brú na Bóinne, Loughcrew is worth visiting because of the lack of touristic infrastructure, the number of cairns in proximity, and the stunning 360° views over undulating farmland and quiet lakes. Most important of all, you can spend time inside Cairn T without a guide. It is a very powerful place.

The Loughcrew cairns spread over Cairnbane (Carnbane) East and Cairnbane (Carnbane) West. Cairnbane (from *carn*, meaning pile or heap) West include cairns A through L; Cairnbane East includes cairns R through W. The cairns on Cairnbane West may not be visited because the owner does not allow public access to his land. Cairn L is oriented toward Imbolc sunrise, like the Mound of the Hostages at Tara (http://www.carrowkeel.com/sites/loughcrew/cairnl.html).

Cairn T, AKA The Hag's Cairn, is the largest on Cairnbane East and can be entered if you get the key in advance

"Passage tombs may have been as much beacons in the landscape as windows to the sky. Some scholars think they served as conspicuous markers defining tribal territories. ... The cairns might also have been designed to represent different stages of life or death." McCann, p. 44.

or if the OPW guide has opened it. Oriented slightly south of east, it is 37 m (120 ft) in diameter and 113 m (369 ft) in circumference. At the end of the narrow passageway is a 3 m (10 ft) high domed chamber with corbelled roof and three side chambers or recesses, also with corbelled roofs. Fragments of charred bones, charcoal, and a bronze pin were found during the original excavation. Several of the uprights in the passageway and in the inner chamber are decorated with geometric patterns, including circles and zigzags, and flower and sun motifs. Most impressive is the ornately carved backstone of the rear chamber, which can be lit by a beam of sunlight during spring and fall equinox sunrises.

"At the time the cairns were in use they must have been profoundly sacred. As the only permanent monuments of the community, they may have served many of the functions we now assign to communal structures. They might not only have contained and commemorated the dead, but also have been the age's equivalent of our libraries, civic centers, theaters, and assembly grounds." McMann, p. 44.

On the north side of Cairn T is the Hag's Chair, a massive kerbstone shaped into a bench. It has barely discernable carvings on the front side. A cross was carved into the seat, perhaps in the eighteenth century, when it might have served as an altar during secret outdoor Masses (pub-

Approaching Cairn T with a smaller, ruined cairn in the foreground

The Hag's Chair

lic Catholic ritual was forbidden). The chair-like stone has been called Ollamh Fodhla's Seat, after the mythic poet who was the first lawgiver of Ireland. It is also known as the Seat of the Cailleach, and folklore asserts that you can sit there and make a wish—but only one. Traditions claim that Queen Tailte or Queen Medb (Maeve) sat on it and proclaimed laws, or that the old hag, the "Cailleach Beara," sat on it.

The word "Cailleach" (KAL-y-ach) comes from "old veiled one"; *caille* means veil or caul. Why veiled? She is veiled in mystery. The Cailleach was the ancient ancestral goddess found throughout Ireland and Scotland, and each tribe had its Cailleach. She was often associated with the sovereignty of the land. Numerous mountain ranges and large hills are said to have been formed when she accidently dropped rocks out of her apron.

She has similarities to the Hindu goddess Kali, another powerful transformative "dark" divinity. The Cailleach represents death and rebirth, transformation and winter, in contrast to Brigid, Celtic goddess of healing, creative inspiration, eternal flame, and springtime. The Cailleach and Brigid are understood to be in an ongoing struggle, paired goddesses who traded places twice a year. The Cailleach's time is said to begin at Samhain (1 November) and end on Imbolc (1 February), while Brigid rules the rest of the year.

Medieval monks who wrote down local stories turned this powerful goddess of death and rebirth into a sad hag. Later the word Cailleach came to mean "nun": one who takes the veil. Later still, it degenerated in common usage to mean "old bag."

"[Cailleach Bhéarra, the hag/mother-goddess] constitutes, in popular tradition, an overarching female matrix of sovereignty and fertile power that is as vast and as untameable as the wild, wide landscape, and that is yet as nurturing and as intimately fruitful for human beings and for human existence as are the services of the [midwife, wise-woman, and keening-woman]..." Ó Crualaoich, p. 28-29.

There are those who say the Cailleach can still be found inside Cairn T, if you know how to seek her. For 4000 years the Cailleach, the winter earth goddess, has been associated with this place, and although her power may have diminished with the passing of millennia, it is still palpable. Perhaps Cairn T is "recharged" twice each year with the entrance of the beam of light at the equinoxes.

You don't have to be a worshipper of the goddess to feel the powerful earth energies that surge up inside the cairn. Before entering, remember BLESSING and ECOLOGY (see p. 4). Center yourself and make an offering, in whatever form you consider appropriate, to the earth energies, personified or otherwise, that reside in the hill; or simply set your intention to experience this powerful ceremonial site. Enter slowly, noticing how it feels to move deeper into the passage and into the central chamber. Notice the different energies in the different side chambers. Contemplate

The entry into Cairn T

the numerous carved symbols. Perhaps one will draw your attention. If so, remember it, sketch it, photograph it. If you chant or drum inside, notice the shifting energy and atmosphere. Perhaps you will even sense the presence of the Cailleach.

Getting There

In the summer, OPW has been setting up a portacabin in the parking lot. Unobtrusive guides come with you to open Cairn T, or you might find one sitting in a lawn chair in front of the cairn. If it is early morning on the spring or autumn equinox, an OPW guide will be waiting at the cairn with the key. The OPW schedule may change, so check first by contacting Brú na Bóinne Visitor Center, (0)41 988 0300, or the site phone at Loughcrew, (0)49 854 1240, or http://www.heritageireland.ie/en/

There's a legend that the wind would give wisdom or information to the Cailleach on Loughcrew, and she would then fly to Tara to tell the High King. For more on the Cailleach, http://en.wikipedia.org/wiki/Cailleach.

 midlandseastcoast/Loughcrew/.

 If you are visiting at a different time, you will need to get the key from the nearby Loughcrew

Gardens coffee shop (€50 deposit). The coffee shop is an excellent place for breakfast and light meals.

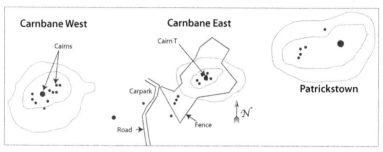

Loughcrew site plan

Please note: the unpaved path to Cairnbane East and Cairn T goes up and around the side of the hill. It is steep and the grass is slippery. Wear appropriate shoes and take care.

To get to Loughcrew Gardens and coffee shop (and the key): in brief, take M3 northwards from Dublin and get off near Kells at junction 10 to R163 in the direction of Oldcastle. Ignore the turning to Oldcastle and continue

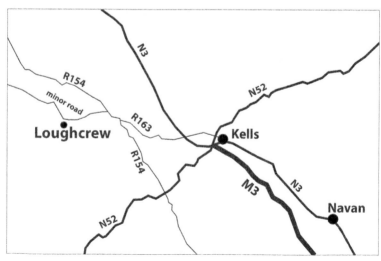

Area map

in the direction of Loughcrew, where you will find Lough-crew Gardens and coffee shop. (Note: Google maps are not necessarily up-to-date.) To visit the cairns en route to Loughcrew House & Gardens: 3 km (2 mi) before reaching the Loughcrew Gardens coffee shop, a brown sign indicates a turn to the right, to the cairns. Continue along the very narrow road for about 1 km (.6 mi) until you reach the parking lot. The way to both Cairnbane East and West is signposted in the parking lot at the base of the hills.

Tlachtga, Hill of Ward N53 37 32 W6 53 18

Located in a corner formed by crossroads, Tlachtga is a jumble of four badly deteriorated concentric earthen rings leading up to a central high point marked with a surveyor's cement pillar. Despite the disarray and damage caused by nearly a millennium of neglect, the place still holds power. Legends swirl around it, and it is associated with the "thin time" of Samhain. While Gary and Michael dowsed the rings, I stood in the center getting a nasty headache from the powerful vortex that spun up and out around me. I wondered if the legends of ghosts were an effort to put a face or form on the highly charged energies that spread out in waves from the Hill of Ward. (Elyn)

Tlachtga (pronounced "Clocktah") is a very important Iron Age earthwork located near the summit of the Hill of Ward. Nobody knows how old it is: two millennia? More? Less? For centuries it has been associated with Samhain, the Celtic New Year that begins on the eve of 31 October. It is rumored that all the Druids of Ireland gathered at Tlachtga to celebrate Samhain with an elaborate fire ceremony and offerings.

Tlachtga on the Hill of Ward

Tlachtga was probably a local fertility goddess. Later her story became entangled with other legends, and she was said to be the daughter of the sorcerer (or Druid) Mug Ruith (or Roith) of Valentia Island in west Munster. Tlachtga and Mug Ruith purportedly flew to Italy, where they met the legendary Simon Magus and had something to do with beheading John the Baptist. Later, Simon Magus' sons raped Tlachtga. After giving birth to triplets, she was buried in the barrow mound at the top of the Hill of Ward. This garbled legend is probably a mythic way of reporting that Tlachtga was an ancient fertility goddess who was supplanted by invading sun-worshippers, with an additional Christian subtext.

Today Tlachtga is an unimposing place, its grass- and weed-covered banks slumped and broken, its ditches filled in over the centuries from erosion and neglect. According to John Gilroy, however, Tlachtga in its heyday was a striking site. About 149 m (489 ft) in diameter at its outer bank, its four concentric earthen banks were once as high as

> "The fires on Samhain at Tlachtga were the public celebration of the victory of light, while the relighting of the household fire marked the domestic celebration of the feast." Gilroy, p. 111.

2 m (6 ft), and the corresponding ditches would have been just as deep. The outer of the four banks may have been topped with a wooden palisade, the inner banks perhaps topped with wicker fencing. Very few ring forts had four banks around them, so this is clear indication of Tlachtga's importance. If Gilroy's reconstruction is accurate, Tlachtga would have been impressive: four high, concentric barriers surrounding a central ritual complex near the top of the hill.

The entrance was in the north-north-west, through a well-guarded doorway. The area inside the inner bank is not particularly large, and no one knows what kind of building was constructed there, but presumably this was the location for important ceremonies. Near the center are a flat-topped barrow burial (Tlachtga's tomb?) and a toppled standing stone. This ancient barrow is proof that this location has been sacred for a long time.

Location, location, location. Tlachtga is built on a hill with an impressive view over its surroundings, including

Tlachtga as it might have originally appeared, according to John Gilroy

96

Tara, 19 km (12 mi) to the east, the Hill of Slane to the north, and the cairns at Loughcrew to the northwest. In addition, holy wells and ring forts surround it. The former is further evidence of the sanctity of the area, the latter of its political importance.

Most of what we know about the importance of Tlachtga is speculative and legendary. It is documented, however, that on the night of Samhain all fires in Ireland had to be extinguished until the Winter Fires of Tlachtga were kindled—thus defeating the powers of darkness again. Only after the successful rekindling of the flame did the king on Tara begin the Samhain feasting.

> "The tendency to situate these structures on eminencies and hilltops, as well as with practical defensive purposes in mind, reflects a desire to stress the social importance attributed to them ... A proximity to the sky and the power beyond is symbolically suggested in the siting of Tlachtga." Gilroy, p. 50.

Samhain, the beginning of the Celtic new year on the eve of 31 October, is the great festival of the dead. The "lighter" half of the year, which began on 1 May at Bealtaine, is ending, and the "darker" half beginning. Winter is drawing

Modern pagan ceremony on Tlachtga

"The Winter Fires were kindled at Tlachtga in an elaborate ceremony, in which the gods were appeased. It seems to have been a fertility festival as well as being a festival of the dead. All ancient peoples engaged in the practice of ancestor worship and the ghosts of the dead needed to be appeased and were likely to be encountered by the living [on Samhain]." Gilroy, p. 107.

close; the days are getting shorter and shorter. Traditionally, Samhain marked the time when the crops had been gathered in and excess livestock slaughtered, their bones tossed into a large bonfire kindled especially for that night. (The word bonfire comes from "bone fire.")

Samhain was a time of drawing inward and waiting, and doing what one could to ensure that the days would grow longer again. It was a liminal time, a time "in-between," when the boundaries between the world of the living and the realm of the dead became permeable.

The days around 1 November were clearly important to Neolithic peoples; they constructed various passage mounds to mark the date. At Cairn L at Loughcrew the Samhain sunrise illuminates a standing stone in the chamber of the cairn (see p. 87); at Tara, the Mound of the Hostages is also aligned with the Samhain sunrise (see p. 62).

It was a time of offerings to the ancestors. Many of us celebrate Halloween, and that modern holiday draws a number of its practices from this pagan festival—still celebrated at Tlachtga on 31 October by modern "Druids."

When we went to Tlachtga, we knew very little about the site, except that it was associated with Samhain and hence with the spirits of the dead. We wondered what the land would have to tell us. Gary and Michael dowsed the site. Gary "got"

"The sacred sites, as we have seen, are on node-points of the energy-matrix; and the structures at those sites were built where and how they are, and with the extraordinary properties they show, not through analysis and logical systems, but because the builders understood and obeyed that 'something' beyond them, through dreams, through divination, through 'coincidence', through feelings." Graves, 173.

that it was a place of power and domination, of energetic protective magic. Michael dowsed the energies in the banks and found that the energy continued unbroken over the gaps. Elyn felt so queasy from the powerful vortex in the center that she left the area as soon as possible. Later she wondered if the vortex was part of the "protective magic" that Gary had dowsed: powerful earth energies that made one feel ill.

> "Water-lines, blind springs and the like aren't real, physical 'things' at all: they are ways of defining and describing the apparent lines and points on the surface that coincide with certain kinds of definable water-flows below. You could call them a 'constructed reality,' an imaginary reality, in the same way that the image on a radar screen or television screen is a reconstruction of reality." Graves, p. 25.

Was Tlachtga chosen for the Samhain celebrations because the ancient builders experienced its geomantic energies, or did the Samhain festivals enhance those energies? We also wondered whether the earth energies were magnified by the earthwork constructions or whether the concentric rings were placed where they were to take advantage of the pre-existing energies radiating out from the central vortex.

> "...these mysterious stones and mounds and circles were built to do something. It does seem they were expressions of a kind of magickal technology that relied upon something within the mind of the individual to make it work. Something that mankind has, over the millennia, lost touch with, and that is intimately connected with time and other-dimensional awareness." Richardson, p. 122.

It is also possible that some of the eeriness of the Hill of Ward is due to a more recent, identifiable source: the energetic "residue" left by Oliver Cromwell's brutal troops, who based themselves at the site. Perhaps they were drawn to the site because of the unpleasant energies. If you visit Tlachtga, let us know what you think and feel.

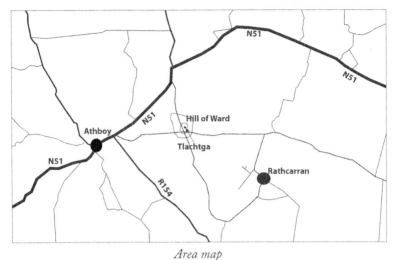

Area map

Getting There

Hill of Ward (Tlachtga): 2 km (1.2 mi) east of Athboy, a short distance off N51 (Athboy-Navan), on a minor road, at the crown of the hill, next to waterworks. Signposted. It's at a crossroads between Athboy (2 km to the west) and Rathcarran (4 km to the south), and 6 km south of Ford-stown (R164). From the road, it is hard to see the Hill of Ward because it is hidden behind trees. Look for the large round water-works, marked with a white gate and "Keep Out" sign. To the left of the stop sign is a set of stone steps and a fence. Climb over them and walk up the

Entrance to the Hill of Ward

hill toward the highest point—a concrete surveyor's marker. That will bring you to the center of the earthworks and the place where Elyn felt a powerful vortex.

St Ciarán's (St Kieran's) Well, Castlekeeran
N53 44 20 W6 57 31

We parked the car by the side of the road, crossed a small footbridge, and walked over to a bubbling spring shaded by a tree. St Ciarán's Well was deserted, but I saw a wet footprint on the stone ledge and smelled the pungent scent of just-burnt sage. There was no one there, no sign of a smudge stick. The fragrance faded gradually but returned just before we left. (Elyn)

Each holy well is different. Each exists in a particular locale with particular mythic and historical associations. Although holy wells are often associated with the sun,

St Ciarán's Well

The "hoary ash tree" in an 1849 photo

consciousness, and the eye—and hence are often thought to cure vision problems—each well has its own unique ambience and associated rituals. (For more holy wells, see index.)

St Ciarán's Well (anglicized as St Kieran) is located on a pretty hillside, its grassy slope broken by patches of grey-white limestone. This water-eroded bedrock forms a series of wells, fed by a spring that comes bubbling out of the hillside. The water in each spring is supposedly beneficial for a particular ailment. There is a "blessed drinking" well, good for throat ailments, shaded by a tree; a well for back ailments (limestone slabs form a kind of seat in the well); a well for warts, stomachaches, and toothaches; and another for feet and ankles.

> "At the same time there is another force or agency, which I suppose we could call 'angelic interference,' which tends to bring out-of-balance Yin and Yang into equilibrium. It is this quality which, when associated with a well, for example, makes it into a holy well, for the water of such a well will tend to re-balance the energies in people, making them whole." Graves, 137-138.

Near the top of the hill is a century-old shrine in the shape of an early Irish oratory. Below it on the hillside is a rag- and offering-covered tree. When we were

> "Up to 3,000 holy wells have been recorded in Ireland. Many of them will by now have been abandoned or forgotten... More surprising, perhaps, is the fact that so many of them are still 'active' in the sense that they are still visited.... Furthermore, a large number that had faded into insignificance ... are being 'resurrected'..." Healy, p. 19.

there, it was laden with socks, underwear, hankies, a baby "onesie," rosaries, and torn strips of cloth. In 1849, a "hoary ash tree of surpassing size and beauty" had stood beside the "blessed drinking" well.

St Ciarán (not to be confused with St Ciarán of Clonmacnoise, p. 105) was a medieval Irish monk who died in 770 CE. He founded a nearby monastery and his name is associated with this holy well. Although legend claims that the well was created at St Ciarán's command, it is much more likely that it was originally a pagan site and later Christianized.

As with many holy wells, the Patron Day (Saint's Day) is the first Sunday of August, a date that links it to the Celtic feast of Lughnasa, the harvest festival. St Ciarán was given many of the attributes of the Celtic god Lugh—including Lughnasa as his saint's day. People come and celebrate at the holy well, performing the particular "patron" or "pattern" of ritual associated with it. The healing powers of the water are supposed to be strongest then. It is said that with luck you may see the three

The bridge to the wells and shrine

> "In Celtic belief, natural waters—springs, streams, rivers, ponds, and lakes—are ensouled with indwelling spirits which must be acknowledged and nurtured. ... Water from holy wells ... comes directly from the waters that exist unseen beneath the earth, the mysterious chthonic realms of Annwyn. We have a personal relationship with the origin, literally drawing our water from the source."
> Pennick, *Celtic Sacred Landscapes*, p. 63.

otherworldly fish that swim across the well at midnight.

Fresh-running water issuing from a hillside: how miraculous that must have seemed! Today, one's first thought might be whether the spring water is safe to drink; we leave that to your discretion. Whether you drink the water or not, take time to experience the atmosphere of St Ciarán's Well. It is filled with hopes and prayers, some of them visible as they dangle from the rag trees. Perhaps you can sense the "devi" or resident spirit of the waters who was here long before St Ciarán came.

Getting There

St Ciarán's Well is 3 km (2 mi) west of Kells. Take R163 west past the Spire of Lloyd on right. This "folly tower" looks like a lighthouse and has amazing views across to Tara and Loughcrew. A little farther on, turn right on a minor road at the sign to Castlekeeran High Cross. Follow

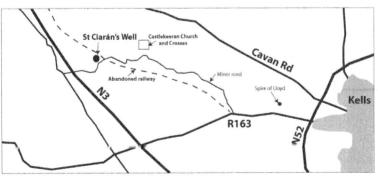

Area map

this road until it comes to the remains of a high bridge that was once a part of the abandoned railway. St Ciarián's Well is just beyond.

More to Experience

Loughcrew Historic Gardens

Loughcrew Historic Gardens [(0)49 854 1356] are a charming mixture of ruins and earthworks, including a roofless church and what remains of a seventeenth-century garden, complete with yew trees and a medieval motte, and delightful plantings and herbaceous borders. An opera is held in the summer. The coffee shop provides excellent food and interesting books and souvenirs. Loughcrew House is available as a B&B or self-catering accommodation. Directions are above, under the section on Loughcrew. http://www.loughcrew.com

Castlekeeran (Castlekeiran) High Crosses

Castlekeeran (Castlekeiran) High Crosses are a ten-minute walk from St Ciarán's Well. A legend recounts that St Ciarán/Kieran was told to build his monastery close to the wells by a boar, a salmon, and a stag—totem animals of the three major pagan deities of this area. The Vikings sacked the hermitage in 949 and the Anglo Normans in 1170; later, it belonged to the Knights Hospitallers. Still visible are three relatively plain high crosses, a fifth-century Ogham stone, and an early medieval grave slab. Legend says that there was a fourth high cross, but St Columba threw it into the nearby Blackwater River when St Ciarán caught him taking it to his monastery in nearby Kells. Castlekeeran is 5 km (3 mi) west of Kells, approached via R163 (Kells-Oldcastle), taking the minor road to the north (right), 2 km west of Kells. Then walk across a farmer's field and over a field stile. Signposted.

Kells

The market town of Kells is an important monastic site that includes ancient and medieval remains. Worth noting are the monastic layout of the town, the monastic enclosure with the high crosses, the round tower, St Colmcille's house, and the heavily restored Scriptural Market Cross now located at the entrance to the Heritage Center. Kells is famous for the exquisite illuminated manuscript *The Book of Kells*, probably produced in Iona in the eighth century and brought to Kells sometime in the eleventh century. The original is on display at Trinity College, Dublin, but the town has three facsimiles. http://www. kells-on-line.com/.

Clonmacnoise, Co. Offaly N 53 19 35 W 7 59 11

Perhaps it was the time it took to get there, driving down narrow country roads. Or perhaps it was the dark and grieving statue of a weary pilgrim resting on his staff, located beside the path that leads from the parking lot to the visitor center. Or perhaps it was the stony remnants of the 1400-year-old pilgrims' path still visible behind the ruins of St Ciarán's church. Whatever it was, I found Clonmacnoise a deeply moving place. Two high towers, evocative ruined medieval churches, replicas (impossible to tell unless you knew) of elaborate high crosses, numerous ancient gravestones—the past lies thick but lightly on the place. (Elyn)

Clonmacnoise Monastic Settlement

Although Clonmacnoise is technically in "the Midlands" of Ireland, it is easily reached from Roscommon and Clon-

106

fert (see pp. 294-297).
St Ciarán founded
the monastery on the
east bank of the river
Shannon sometime
between 543 and
549 CE, only to die
seven months later at
the age of thirty three
of the yellow plague.
He was the son of a
craftsman (perhaps a
carpenter), born near
the royal seat of Con-
naught, Rathcroghan,
in the early sixth cen-
tury. He studied with
St Enda on the Aran Islands and St Finian in Clonard, and
tales of his ability to work miracles soon followed him—as
did a dun-colored cow, which gave enough milk to supply
the needs of any monastery where he stayed.

O'Rourke's Tower and the North Cross

Clonmacnoise comes from Cluain Mhic Nóis, which
means "Water Meadow of the sons of Nós," perhaps so-
named because much of the green, fertile land was flooded
by the Shannon during the winter. Although today Clonmacnoise seems remote, in the Middle Ages it was at the
crossroads of important medieval routes linking Ireland
internally. Situated beside the Shannon and along the old
Pilgrims' Road—the great esker (a raised glacier sand and
gravel ridge) road—it was in a prime location. The early
settlement of wood-and-wattle and beehive huts soon
grew to include a cluster of stone churches and a cathedral,
three high crosses, numerous dwellings for lay people as
well as monks, two round towers, a corn drying kiln, an
iron foundry, and an extensive graveyard where some of the
kings of Connaught and Tara were buried.

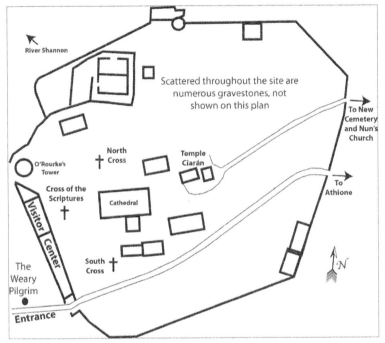

Plan of Clonmacnoise

The monastery thrived from the seventh to the twelfth centuries and was famous as a center of learning and fine metal craftsmanship. *The Annals of Tighernach* and *The Book of the Dun Cow* were written here. The latter, *Lebor na hUidre,* is the oldest surviving book in the Irish language and contains part of the earliest known form of the *Tain Bó Cuailnge, The Cattle Raid of Cooley* (see p. 291).

(see p. 291).

For more than 500 years, Clonmacnoise was a very important monastic settlement—*literally* a very powerful place. Over the centuries it was sacked, burned, pillaged, subject to plague and pestilence, hit by lightning, and

Page from Lebor na hUidre

plundered by Irish, Vikings, and Anglo-Normans, yet it continued to thrive. It was finally reduced to ruin by the English in 1552. Given the litany of disasters that occurred there, it appears that being a powerful place is not necessarily positive.

Unlike medieval pilgrims who arrived on foot or by boat, modern pilgrims arrive by car or bus. The tree-shaded path that leads from the parking lot to the OPW Visitor Center sets a meditative mood. At least it did for us, perhaps because we were there on a relatively quiet day. The imposing sculpture of Aedh, the weary pilgrim—the first recorded at Clonmacnoise, he died soon after arriving in 606—strikes a serious note. This isn't Disneyland.

Aedh, the weary pilgrim

The Visitor Center provides an informative context for the ruined monastic complex. Exhibits include a sampling of the 700 decorated grave slabs discovered in the cemetery, as well as extensive educational displays and two original high crosses (replaced in the graveyard by replicas), properly oriented and dramatically lit. The Cross of the Scriptures includes a charming cat and mouse under the northern side-arm on one side and the Hand of God with a nimbus behind it under the side-arm on the other side. The same carver or school of carvers who carved the

The cat and mouse figure on The Cross of the Scriptures

Muiredach High Cross at Monasterboice (see p. 68) may have carved this cross.

The Cross of Scriptures with the Cathedral in the background

An eleventh-century stone path leads from behind Temple Ciarán, which perhaps contains the grave of St Ciarán, through the New Cemetery. After 500 meters (1/3 mile), it reaches the ruins of the twelfth-century Nuns' Church, considered one of the best surviving examples of Hiberno-Romanesque architecture. A small Sheela-na-gig is carved high on the left side of the chancel arch, seventh figure up.

Queen Devorguilla founded the church in 1167, after she had, in effect, played the role of Helen of Troy. Although she was married to Tiernan O'Rourke, king of Breffny, Diarmuid McMurrough, king of Leinster, abducted her. The story goes that she was compliant, if not complicit. A year later she was returned to her humiliated husband. When the chance arose in 1166, Tigernán and his allies drove Diarmuid from Leinster. Diarmuid fled to France and petitioned Henry II to help him regain his throne, thus instigating the devastatingly successful Anglo-Norman invasion of Ireland.

Getting there

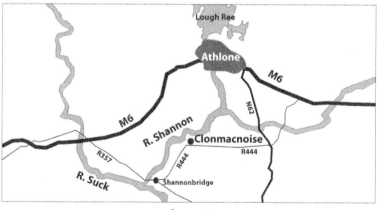

Area map

Clonmacnoise is well sign-posted; it is 21 km (13 mi) south of Athlone. Take N62, turning on R444. From Ballinasloe take R357 turning left on R444. It is on the east bank of the Shannon and it takes longer to get there than you might expect. OPW entry fee or Heritage Card.

More to Experience

St Ciarán's Holy Well

St Ciarán's Holy Well (see p 99) is about 400 m (1/4 mile) from Clonmacnoise. It is found along the road south of Clonmacnoise on the Shannon side, in a field beside a thorn tree. There are a number of carved stones around the well; the Pattern day is 9 September, and on that day the earth at St Ciarán's church in Clonmacnoise is supposed to have magical properties. Part of the annual Pattern includes visiting the well.

The Clonfinlough Stone

The Clonfinlough Stone, said to be the oldest carved stone in Ireland, is 4 km (2.5 mi) east of Clonmacnoise, signposted off R444 to Athlone. Park at the Clonfinlough church and take the path to the stone. It's a ten-minute walk, round trip. The stone is a large limestone boulder, about 2.5 m (8 ft) by 3 m (10 ft), lying in rough pasture. It is covered with deeply incised carvings, including stylized human figures, handprints, and cups and rings. It is simi-lar to decorated stones in northwestern Spain dating to the Bronze Age. It is still frequently visited. http://www.offalyhistory.com/articles/61/1/A-History-of-Offaly-Through-its-Monuments/Page1.html.

Southeast Ireland

Piper's Stones (Athgreany Stone Circle), Castleruddery Stone Circle, and Glendalough Monastic Site, Co. Wicklow

Athgreany Stone Circle (Piper's Stones) N53 04 18 W6 36 45

Getting there is part of it. Walking up the hill, wondering where "The Place of the Sun" is, and then seeing a large, misshapen thorn tree lying on its side, its roots and branches clinging tightly to scattered chunks of stone. You can't see the Athgreany circle until you get to the top of the rise, and then it appears like magic. The stones were "quiet" when we arrived, but I circled three times around and then touched them one by one. Gradually they seemed to wake from slumber. We watched in delight as energy began to rise from the stones, energy that looked like a faint haze against the grey background sky. (Elyn)

Athgreany comes from the Gaelic Achadh Greine or "Field of the Sun." The name probably reflects its use as an ancient ceremonial site connected with calendrical events. There is conflicting information and opinion about exactly which calendrical events were celebrated at this site, in part because many of the stones have shifted or been moved over the millennia. Another part of the problem—here and at other sites, including Stonehenge—is that it is hard to know exactly which stones in combination with which landscape gaps, hilltops, or distant alignments were being used to mark a recurring astronomical event.

The Athgreany Stone Circle, showing the thorn tree

One researcher, Helen O'Clery, determined that the shadow cast at sunrise and sunset by what she called the "pilot stone," found under the fallen thorn tree, marked the cross-quarter days (http://source.southdublinlibraries. ie/bitstream/10599/4971/2/HelenOCleryBiography. pdf). Other researchers emphasize the importance of the outlier stone (the Piper) to the northwest or focus on sunlight striking a recumbent stone to the right of the big upright in the circle. Still other researchers fail to find any verifiable markers for any astronomical event.

Although we can't be sure of its original astronomical purpose, we can still experience the stone circle, the outlier, and the setting. Athgreany is a powerful place, regardless of what you know, think you know, or don't know about it.

The stone circle may date from the late Bronze Age (1400-800 BCE), though its age is difficult to determine. It is approximately 23 m (75 ft) in internal diameter and contains 14 granite porphyry boulders. The grey-colored

114

stones contain large quartz crystals and, occasionally, white quartz veins. The 1841 Ordnance Survey recorded 29 stones at the site; of the 14 that remain, 5 stones are en situ, 5 fallen, and 4 displaced. Nonetheless, the Piper's Stone Circle still feels complete and coherent, as if the energies created by the circle can flow across the gaps where standing stones are missing.

The entrance is probably on the northeast, marked by two tall stones. The outlying Piper stone is 40 m (131 ft) away in the fields to the northeast. It is a natural glacial erratic, almost 2 m (6 ft) tall, but clearly an important part of the megalithic site. Like one of the fallen stones in the southeast part of the circle, it has a deeply grooved cross shape on top. Several other stones have deeply carved channels across the top. Are these the remains of mega-

> Sometimes when you arrive at a site, nothing seems to be happening. Remember BLESSING and ECOLOGY (p. 4). Introduce yourself to the "spirit" or "guardian" of the place and ask permission to enter. Establish a relationship with the site, perhaps by circling in a sunwise direction, or by making an offering, or simply by "being present." You may be surprised at what happens next; we certainly have been.

> Elyn "heard" the stones saying, "Rounded and mounded, hounded and bounded..." Perhaps the latter referred to the efforts made in recent centuries to destroy the circle and deface the stones.

lithic sacred art or an attempt to Christianize the site—or a combination? A similar deep groove is found on a stone at Harestone megalithic site, Harestone Down, England, where it may be intended as goddess symbolism (Knight, p. 38).

The standing stones alternate, more or less, between rectangular flat-topped boulders and dia-

A groove in one of the stones

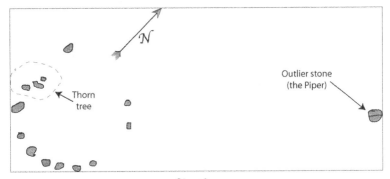

Site plan

mond-shaped. They range in height from 1.3 to 1.9 m (4.3 ft to 6 ft). Elyn "got" that the stones are masculine and feminine: rounded, recumbent ones resembled pregnant bellies; rectangular taller uprights are (not surprisingly) masculine. She felt a huge "heart opening" when she stood in the circle and imagined hand-fastings or weddings taking place there. It's possible that she was "picking up" contemporary rituals and ceremonies at the stones, but she doesn't know. A friend described hearing music and singing at the site, but again, whether she was "picking up" ancient or contemporary usage was unclear.

An impressive hawthorn tree leans over at the edge of the circle, its roots entwining with fallen stones. It is considered a faery tree and guardian of the site. People have left offerings in its branches or tucked into crevasses. (For videos and oral history, go to http://www. voicesfromthedawn.com/ and search for Athgreany.)

One legend associated with Athgreany states that faeries play the bagpipes there at midnight. Another legend asserts that the stone circle and outlier were dancers and a piper who were turned to stone for dancing on Sunday. This is clearly a Christian story, but it may perhaps echo an ancient perception that stones are energetic beings, an "enlivened" part of the landscape. There are at least five other Piper's Stones circles in Ireland, and similar legends exist in

England and France of pipers, dancers, and maidens petri-
fied for violating the Sabbath.

Getting There

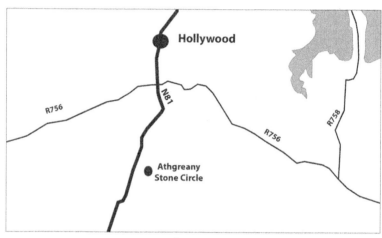

Area map

Athgreany Piper's Stones Circle is 3 km (1.8 mi) south of
Hollywood on N81, a route that was probably important in
prehistoric times because it goes to the west of the mountains. The circle is 13 km (8 mi) south of Blessington and
17.5 km (10.5 mi) north of Baltinglass. Signposted. Pull
off the road near the brown and white signpost and enter
through a large swing gate. Walk about 183 m (200 yd) to
an information plaque. With the plaque to your left, walk
up the hill.

Castleruddery Stone Circle (Druidical Circle)
N52 59 28 W6 38 12

Early Bronze Age Castleruddery Stone Circle is located on a gentle rise overlooking the river Slaney; to the south is Spinan's Hill (AKA Brusselstown Ring) with its massive Iron Age hill fort, the largest in Europe, visible from the stone circle. Some 30 m (98 ft) in diameter, Castleruddery (from Caisléan' an Ridear, "Castle of the Knight") is unusual for several reasons: its huge quartz boulders and the surrounding bank and ditch.

Two enormous recumbent quartz boulders mark the entryway in the east. They are 2.4 m (8 ft) by 1.2 m (4 ft) and 3 m (10 ft) by 1.8 m (6 ft), tapering at their outer ends. Quartz has unusual properties, including piezo-electrical qualities (e.g., it develops electrical potential on the application of mechanical stress), and is often found associated with megalithic sites in Ireland. The Irish word for quartz is *grian cloch*, which means "stone of the sun."

Another standing stone is found a little to the east of the entrance. A huge bank, somewhat similar to the one at Grange Stone Circle (see p. 166), surrounds the stone

The quartz boulders at the entrance to Castleruddery Stone Circle

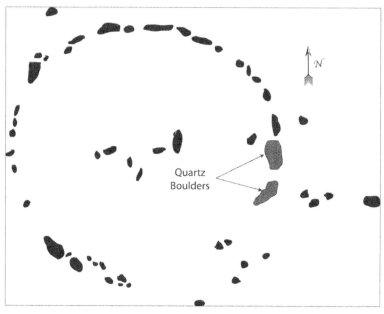

Site plan

circle. The bank is approximately 40 m (131 ft) in diameter, as much as 4.5 m (115 ft) wide, and 1 m (3 ft) high. Beyond this bank is an outer ditch, perhaps 60 m (197 ft) in diameter. Aerial photos show an even larger enclosure, 80 m (262 ft) in diameter, surrounding the circle, and a trench, 50 m (164 ft) in diameter, between the two. These ditches and banks around the circle are unusual because they combine what would appear to be a ceremonial setting with defensive enclosures.

Some 29 boulders remain in the circle, which is largely intact at the northern end but disturbed at the south. Some of the stones are upright, others recumbent. There is evidence of intentional destruction of a number of stones.

Outside the circle, under the spreading branches of a thorn tree, are a number of moss-covered boulders. One has at least seven human-made cup holes, six of them lined up across the domed top of the stone. Were they used as re-

> "Quartz has always had significance at sacred sites. It reflects light without absorbing it, very different from granite which absorbs and is changed by the sun's rays." Meehan, pp. 319-320.

ceptacles for offerings? Were they a kind of bullaun stone, used to capture water that was considered sacred, with healing properties? Or are they evidence of a quarryman's unsuccessful effort to split the boulder?

For Elyn, Castleruddery had a very different "feel" than Athgreany Piper's Stones. Athgreany felt heart-centered, balancing masculine and feminine, somehow "personal." Castleruddery felt solemn, impressive, and serious. It felt like a powerful political center (judicial perhaps? Having to do with kingship?) that had fallen into disre-

> A bullaun stone (from Irish *bullán* or "bowl") is a small boulder or large stone with one or more deep spherical depressions in it. Water collects in the "cup" and is often considered to have healing properties. Sometimes round or ovoid stones sit in the depressions; according to tradition, these stones may be turned for blessing or cursing. Bullaun stones may have originally been used for grinding, but no one knows. Nowadays they are often considered sacred. They bear a certain resemblance to Neolithic cup-marked stones.

pair. Elyn felt that the stones at Athgreany were still connected, forming a circle of energy, despite gaps between the stones. The stones at Castleruddery, however, felt like they were no longer a circle; instead, they were merely a disordered group of stones, some upright, others not.

What do you experience? See if you notice a difference in energy as you walk between the two quartz boulders. Spend time

Entrance gate

Human-made cup holes

in and outside the circle, visiting different stones, and see
what you notice.

Getting There

Castleruddery is
8.5 km (5 mi) north-
east of Baltinglass, off
N81 (Dublin-Baltin-
glass). Take the minor
road east off N81 to-
wards Glen of Imaal/
Donard for 1 km
(0.6 mi). The stone
circle is on south side
of the road, 0.5 km
(0.3 mi) beyond Cas-
tleruddery Cross.

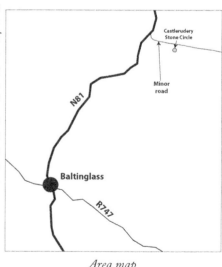

Area map

Glendalough Monastic Settlement
N53 00 38 W6 19 38

We approached Glendalough from the south, driving over the Wicklow Gap and down into a narrow valley with two lakes. A pilgrim's trail, St Kevin's Way, headed off to the right, and we considered walking to the monastic settlement but decided to keep driving. The wooded hillsides were shrouded in mist; gentle rain covered the grey stone buildings and round tower with an otherworldly veil. (Elyn)

Glendalough (Gleann Dá Locha, "The Valley of the Two Lakes"), pronounced "glendalockh," is the beautiful site of one of the most famous religious centers in early Christian Ireland. St Kevin founded the monastery in the sixth century. He chose a site that had been sacred in pre-Christian Celtic times, "where farmers traditionally drove their cattle through the water at Beltaine to keep them healthy for the rest of the year" (Meehan, p. 314).

Like Clonmacnoise (see p. 105), Glendalough monastic settlement includes several ruined churches, a round tower, a high cross, and an extensive medieval cemetery. Unlike Clonmacnoise, Glendalough is set in a secluded, glacier-carved valley with two lakes, located in the Wicklow Mountains instead of on the banks of the river Shannon. The monastery flourished for over 600 years, despite Viking raids. It only declined in importance after the English partially destroyed the monastery in 1398. Glendalough ceased functioning in 1539 with the Dissolution of the Monasteries, but pilgrims still came, especially on St Kevin's feast day on 3 June. Relatively close to Dublin, pilgrims and tourists continue to visit Glendalough, at times turn-

122

ing the tranquil setting into a buzzing hive of activity.

St Kevin is said to have lived 120 years, from 498-618 CE. Born into nobility, he left a life of privilege to live as a hermit but ended up founding a famous monastery. One legend relates that the miracle-working young Kevin fled the care of clerics and escaped to nature, where he lived in the hollow of a tree above the Upper Lake at Glendalough. Discovered at last, he

A doorway in Glendalough

regretfully returned to his religious studies, but he always longed for solitude. Another legend says that he rejected the advances of an ardent female follower by rolling in a bed of nettles—or by beating her with the nettles.

Yet another legend recounts that while he was at prayer, a blackbird laid an egg in one of his outstretched hands. He left his hand outstretched until the egg hatched, demonstrating great self-discipline and great compassion. He seems to have had a good relationship with animals and birds, but perhaps more difficulties with humans. At any rate, he was a hermit at heart (http://www.irishcultureandcustoms.com/ASaints/kevin.html).

Under St Kevin's supervision, the monastery at Glendalough became a center of learning and caring

Modern icon of St Kevin

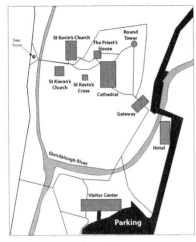

Site plan

for the sick. After he died, the settlement became an important pilgrimage site. Seven pilgrimages to Glendalough were said to be the equivalent of one to Rome. Despite the sixteenth-century suppression of the monastery, pilgrimages continued until the 1860s.

Today, Glendalough monastic settlement is entered through the double stone arch of the Gateway (the only one of its kind in Ireland), passing from secular space into sacred. Pick up a map at the excellent OPW Visitor's Center (entry fee includes guided tour), which features numerous interactive displays and a very interesting video, "Ireland of the Monasteries." The Center displays the Hollywood Stone, found near Hollywood village, a granite boulder engraved with a seven-circuit labyrinth thought to perhaps date to the early Iron Age, though it may be later and early Christian.

A minimum of two hours is required for a quick tour of Glendalough, but a full day is better, giving you time to wander on trails into the surrounding hills. Many of the buildings date from the eighth to twelfth centuries and were restored during the 1870s; few if any actual remains from St Kevin's time are visible.

The Gateway

124

There are two groups of ruins, less than 1.5 km (1 mi) apart. The largest is on the east side of the Lower Lake; the other group is by the Upper Lake. At the east end of the Upper Lake, the Wicklow Mountains National Park Visitor Center provides details of local walking routes. "St Kevin's Bed," the little, perhaps manmade, cave on a ledge above the west bank of the Upper Lake, is not accessible but remains evocative. It is a short distance east of the Church of the Rock.

The Hollywood Stone

Close to the Visitor Center is the 30 m (91 ft) high round tower. It rises up out of the atmospheric graveyard, which remains a highly evocative place. Nearby is the Cathedral, the largest ruin at Glendalough. Other buildings include the Priests' House, St Kevin's Kitchen, St Mary's, and Reefert Church.

There are some 30 bullaun stones in the area. A path leads from the cemetery across the river to the Deer Stone, a bullaun that St Kevin reputedly used to collect deer's milk for an infant whose mother had died in childbirth. Not too long ago, pilgrims would visit the stone and perform a specific set of ritual acts to receive a cure.

The Round Tower

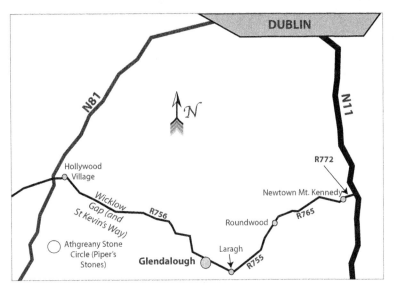

Area map

Glendalough monastic site retains a powerful "odor of sanctity." It still feels like a powerful place, despite being in ruins and over-run at times with tourists. If it is crowded, forget about visiting the ruined buildings and head to the Upper Lake. Remember, St Kevin was attracted to the natural beauty of Glendalough, and that is still there to be experienced.

Getting There

St Kevin's bus from Dublin to Glendalough runs on a schedule (http://www.glendaloughbus.com) and private tours go there. If you are driving, take N81 south from Dublin to Hollywood (between Baltinglass and Ballymore Eustace), then R756 through the Wicklow Gap. This route more or less follows St Kevin's Way. (The Piper's Stones, p. 112 are south of Hollywood on N81.) The fastest route from Dublin is to take N11 south and turn onto R772 to Newtown Mt. Kennedy. Continue on R765 to Round-wood, then R755 to Laragh and Glendalough.

If you drive to the site, try to arrive early during tourist season. Entrance fee or Heritage Card is required for the Visitor Center, but visiting the grounds is free. If you prefer to walk to Glendalough, you can follow St Kevin's Way from Hollywood (see below). Don't miss the large labyrinth cut into the grass between the parking lot and the Visitor's Center.

More to Experience

St Kevin's Way

St Kevin's Way (or St Kevin's Road), once a popular pilgrimage route, begins 30 km (18 mi) to the northwest of Glendalough, at the village of Hollywood. It passes through the scenic Wicklow Gap on its way to Glendalough. Legend says St Kevin was looking for a new place of retreat, but he and his companions found their way blocked by trees. He told them to keep walking, and the trees parted for them. According to Meehan (p. 317), "Kevin blessed [the trees] and put a curse on anyone who would cut them down. This gave the name Holy Wood or, as it is today, Hollywood. Perhaps this reflects a tradition of a sacred grove here?"

St Kevin's Way has been waymarked for walkers. Numerous inscribed stones can be found near the path, some of which may be Christianized standing stones. See http://www.visitwicklow.ie/walk/st_kevins_way.htm or http://www.heritagecouncil.ie/recreation/heritage-council-initiatives/the-pilgrim-paths/st-kevins-way/ for details.

Brigid in Kildare and Two St Brigid Holy Wells, Co. Kildare

Brigid, Goddess and Saint

Kildare (from Gaelic Cill Dara, "the Church of the Oak-wood") is a pleasant town set in the midst of rich pasture-land. The mythic goddess Brigid and the historic St Brigid blend in this area and imbue it with their powerful united presence. We encounter Brigid at many places in Ireland. Her story encapsulates the melding of Irish paganism and Christianity, neither of which can contain her.

The Celtic goddess Brigid, "the Exalted One," was a fertility goddess venerated in Ireland, Britain, and many European countries. Daughter of the Dagda (the Irish father god) and the Morrigan, and originally a sun goddess, Brigid was associated with livestock, fertility, childbirth, the dairy, poetry, learning, fire (of both the hearth and foundry), sacred wells, and healing.

The Christian St Brigid is known as "Mary of the Gael" and as the foster mother of Jesus. It was said of St Brigid that "flames of fire appeared to come from any house in which she slept" (Healy, p. 29), a vivid indication of her ongoing association with fire and the sun. St Brigid was bountiful, generous, a great dairywoman, a renowned brewer of

Modern icon with Brigid's cross

ale, associated with birth, fertility, growth, and fruitfulness, the sacred flame, a staunch defender of women's rights, and patroness of poets, blacksmiths, and scholars. It's obvious how the goddess and the saint have morphed into one. Numerous healing wells are associated with Brigid that were originally dedicated to the goddess. (For more on Brigid, see http://www.goddessgift.com/goddess-myths/celtic-goddess-brigid.htm.)

According to one tradition, Brigid was born about 450 CE at Fochard Muirtheimne, later known as Fochard Bríde (Faughert), a few miles north of Dundalk (see p. 84). A relic of her skull is in the church at nearby Kilcurry. But according to another tradition, Brigid was born at Umeras, about five miles northwest of Kildare Town. Her pagan father, Dubhthach, was a lo-

"Because Kildare is *Cill Dara*, the Church of the Oak Tree, and the oak was the sacred tree of the Druids, it is suggested that there already existed a pagan sanctuary at Kildare which was Christianized by a holy woman of the Fothartha (Dubhthach's tribe). Thus the name of the Brigid goddess and the cult of the sanctuary, including its sacred well, would have become attached to her." Healy, p. 31.

cal chieftain. Her Christian mother, Broicsech, was a bond-maid (slave) in Dubhthach's household. Brigid is said to have died around 523 or 524 and been buried in Kildare.

In 480, St Brigid built a religious house in Kildare, next to the ancient oak on Drumcree. Tradition says that the King of Leinster granted St Brigid as much land as her cloak would cover. She threw down her mantle, and it spread until it encompassed 5000 acres.

The archbishop, either responding to inner guidance or by error, consecrated Brigid a bishop rather than a nun. She presided over two communities, one for men and the other for women. The Kildare community was a center for metal

The story goes that after Brigid's death, nineteen women kept tending the fire, one being responsible for guarding it each night. On the twentieth night they would call upon Brigid: "Brigid, keep your own fire, for the night has fallen to you," and go to sleep. In the morning, the flame would still burn. If you want to participate in this ancient tradition, go to http://www.obsidianmagazine.com/DaughtersoftheFlame/keepers-of-the-flame.htm or http://www.ordbrighideach.org/raven/index.php.

work and decorative art, manuscript illumination, and architectural ornamentation. It included a school of great renown and became a center of political power.

After founding her Christian sanctuary (or Christianizing a previously pagan one)

beside the oak tree, St Brigid maintained the earlier practice of the fire temple. The twelfth-century chronicler Gerald of Wales (Giraldus Cambrensis) reported that the sacred flame was tended within a henge, from which all men were excluded (http://brigid-undertheoak.blogspot.com/2009/02/gerald-of-wales-and-perpetual-fire-at.html). The flame was extinguished at some point, perhaps in the sixteenth century when the Reformation and the suppression of the monasteries snuffed it out.

On 1 February, 1993—the date of St Brigid's feast day, Candlemas, and Imbolc—Sister Mary Teresa Cullen, the leader of the Brigidine Congregation in Kildare, rekindled the perpetual flame to open a justice and peace conference. Every Candlemas/Imbolc the flame is lit again at the fire temple on the north side of Kildare Cathedral. An annual five-day Féile Bríde precedes Brigid's feast day. Organized by the Brigidine Sis-

"Pattern" or "Patron" refers to the day of special devotion of a saint at a particular well. Usually a set of prescribed ritual acts (called "stations") is performed that day, such as picking up stones, reciting "Hail Marys" and "Our Father," and so on, along with perambulations, usually sunwise, around parts of the site. Irish holy wells often have a plaque detailing the station(s).

ters, a pilgrimage and a peace and justice conference are core components.

The Sisters keep the flame alight in their sanctuary, *Solas Bhride* (the Light of Brigid) (http://www. solasbhride.ie/), and send Brigid's perpetual flame to numerous peace and justice conferences around the world. According to *Solas Bhride* website, "The flame burns as a beacon of hope, justice and peace for our country and world."

Brigid in Kildare N53 09 35 W6 54 32

Brigid is omnipresent in Kildare. A number of sites pay homage to her, including St Brigid's Flame monument. This is a modern metal sculpture of a flaming torch, erected beside the Kildare Town Heritage Center (Market House) near St Brigid's Cathedral. The cathedral has a thirteenth-century structure but was largely reconstructed in the nineteenth century. There are some interesting gargoyles outside, and inside is the sixteenth-century tomb chest of Bishop Walter Wellesley, moved to the cathedral in 1971.

The chest has a Green Man carved on one corner and a splay-legged acrobat (sometimes mistakenly identified as a Sheela-na-Gig) in another. Behind the south transept (outside) is the Wishing Stone—a hole in the wall. Tradition claims that if you put your arm through it and touch your shoulder, your wish will be granted. The cathedral is closed October – April. To visit during that time, contact the

The Flaming Torch

Brigid reportedly wove "Brigid's crosses" as she traveled around the country making converts. The cross is derived from a four-armed pagan sun symbol or, perhaps, represents the Big Dipper turning around the Pole Star. It is traditionally woven out of reeds on St Brigid's Day. http://www.irishcentral.com/roots/How-to-make-a-Saint-Brigid-Cross---SEE-VIDEO-114998679.html, retrieved March 2011.

Heritage Center at kildaretownheritage-cen@ireland.com.

West of the cathedral is the well-preserved round tower, one of only two in Ireland where (for a fee) you can enter and climb ladders to the top (http://www.voicesfromthedawn.com/?p=583). The view is impressive. Southeast of the cathedral are the foundations of a circular structure, heavily restored, called "Brigid's Kitchen" but probably a fourteenth-century burial vault.

Just north of the cathedral is the reconstructed foundation of Brigid's fire temple (and perhaps the original sanctuary?), sunken beneath the current ground level. People still leave offerings there. Spend time in this ancient temple, where the eternal flame was kept burning for thousands of years. It's a powerful place to connect to light, the creative spark, and the transformative power of fire.

St Brigid's Cathedral

St Brigid's Fire Temple

St Brigid's Parish Church

A short walk away, St Brigid's parish church honors Brigid not only in name but also in décor. Its walls are decorated with Brigid crosses that seem to wheel and spin in the air. The bronze panels on the door have raised Brigid's crosses, and the altar, constructed of blocks of granite, repeats the image of Brigid's cross. We found this modern church to be a powerful place—not a "knock your socks off" or "get all tingly" kind of place, but rather suffused with a gentle, sweet, centering sacredness, perhaps similar to the energy that radiated from Brigid. It is a lovely place to meditate.

Two St Brigid Holy Wells

At the edge of town, two holy wells are dedicated to Brigid. One holy well, thought to have pre-Christian Brigid connections, is a wayside well located inside the parking lot at the Japanese Gardens. It is shown on the 1837 Ord-nance map and was enclosed by the OPW in the 1950s. If you are driving (or walking), head south to the Japanese Gardens. Turn into the Gardens' parking lot; go left to coach (bus) parking and all the way to the end; then drive toward the stone wall of the gardens and park. You'll see a rag tree, a low stone wall, and a gate. Walk in and you enter the semicircular alcove that protects the holy well.

The well is small but well kept, restored in 1953, and ob-viously still a place of veneration. The Irish inscription on the well translates as "St. Brigid, Mary of the Gael, pray for us." When we were there, we saw a reed Brigid's cross float-ing in the well. While we stared into the well, we saw little bubbles rising from the water. It was mesmerizing. Like St Brigid's church, this is a lovely spot for meditation, a pow-erful place to connect with Brigid, goddess and/or saint. The well water is thought to have strong healing properties, so many people bring bottles in which to collect it.

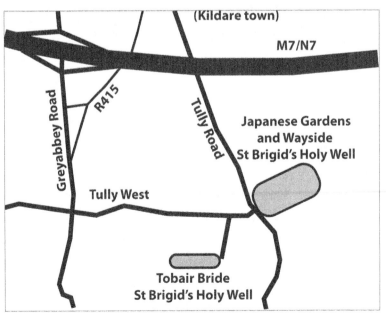

Detail map of the holy wells

The wayside St Brigid Holy Well

Although this wayside well is popular with individuals, the nearby Japanese Gardens and extensive road traffic make it difficult for holding public ritual, and pedestrians should take care crossing the roads.

For a number of years, ceremonies have been conducted at the other St Brigid holy well, also near Tully. Brallistown Commons or "the Greallachs" has long been associated with St Brigid, including the tradition that Brigid kept her cow there in the marshy ground. To reach this holy well, turn right off of Tully West before the Japanese Gardens and follow signs. Park and walk over a foot-bridge and through an arbor into a charming park-like setting, renovated by the people of Tully in 1952.

At the far end of the garden is the stone-encased holy well. A nearby tree dangles with rags and ribbons. The water from the well is channeled through the long, narrow garden, passing alongside a stone arch and a lovely bronze statue of Brigid. Frozen in motion, Brigid seems to stride beside the stream, holding a torch in one hand and a crosier in the other. Tradition states that two granite stones in the stream are the "shoes" or "cows" of Brigid. A small mound beside the stream has been a site of pilgrimage for generations.

While we were there, several families came and went, leaving garlands and other gifts at the feet of Brigid. One woman told us she comes as often as she can, even for a few minutes, to "soak in" the peace and silence. This holy well is a place of regeneration and peace, a fitting sanctuary for Brigid, both saint and goddess.

Tobair Bride, St Brigid's Holy Well and grotto

136

Getting There

Kildare is 50 km (31 mi) southwest of Dublin on the M7/N7. It is possible to spend time at the Brigidine Sisters' Center if you make advance arrangements http://www. solasbhride.ie/ (See QR code on p. 130.)

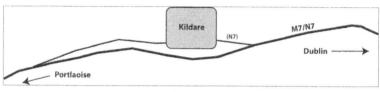

Area map

Brownshill Dolmen, Kilkenny, and Moone High Cross

Brownshill (aka Browne's Hill or Kernanstown) Dolmen, Co. Carlow
N52 50 15 W6 52 52

Chnoc an Bhrúnaigh stands in the middle of a field, surrounded by encroaching civilization. From a distance, it looks like an ungainly giant mushroom, its huge capstone barely supported by stubby stone legs. But as we draw near, we begin to sense that the dolmen has a powerful presence. Even though its capstone lists to one side, the imposing dolmen still radiates a lot of "juju." (Elyn)

Brownshill Dolmen's claim to fame is its huge capstone, estimated at between 100-150 tons, making it the heaviest of any portal tomb in Europe. The capstone is 2 m (6.5 ft) thick, 4.7 m (15.5 ft) wide, and 6 m (20 ft) long. The east-

The Brownshill Dolmen

ern end sinks into the earth; the other is supported by three upright stones, 2 m (6 ft) high, dwarfed by the size of the horizontal slab. Two other stones lie recumbent at the other end. Built some 5000-6000 years ago, it was probably covered by an earthen or stone mound. It must have resembled a cave or an entry into the Otherworld. (See http:// www.rootsweb.ancestry.com/~irlcar2/dolmen.htm.)

Brownshill Dolmen is located east of Carlow, in a field near a busy highway and a car dealership. The town has encroached relentlessly on the dolmen, destroying two nearby megaliths recorded in a survey in the late 1800s. This is not exactly a pristine rural setting, so we didn't expect to experience much. But when we approached the dolmen, we found that despite the surrounding urban hubbub, it was enveloped in stillness. It is still a powerful place.

As Meehan points out, "This is a stunning monument. It is a clear reminder that the capstone was more than just a roof. The bigger the capstone, the more potent the structure" (p. 371). The power we felt around the dolmen was probably due to the huge mass of stone, to the underground energies, and because it has never been excavated. Whatever human remains or artifacts were ritually deposited there, they still rest undisturbed.

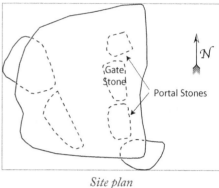

Site plan

Getting There

Drive 3 km (2 mi) east of Carlow just off R726. Park in the well-marked parking lot, then walk up the paved path that runs alongside the field.

Another view of the dolemn

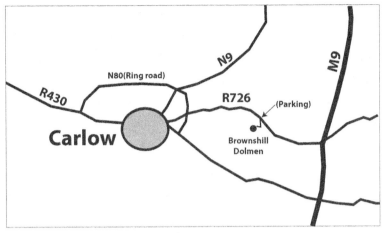

Area map

Kilkenny, Co. Kilkenny N52 39 06 W7 14 51

Kilkenny is touted as "Ireland's loveliest inland city" and is a popular tourist destination for many Irish vacationers (http://www.southeasttourism.ie). If you are in the area, it's a good place for taking a break or basing yourself for a few days. It is close to a number of interesting sites, including Jerpoint Abbey, 19 km (12 mi) to the south. Kilkenny is often very crowded, so allow plenty of time to find a place to park near the town center.

Kilkenny has a strong cultural and artistic tradition as well as carefully restored historic buildings. Don't miss the scenic medieval downtown, the Norman castle, St Canice's Cathedral, the Kilkenny Design Center (which often hosts crafts exhibits), and The Hole in the Wall bar/music venue. This restored pub was "the most popular tavern in Ireland in the 1700s," reached through an actual hole in a wall. It is down a narrow alley behind the Old Archer House. Mi-

Michael Conway, owner of The Hole in the Wall

chael Conway, the owner/bartender, will give you a quick but remarkably informative Irish history lesson. He says it takes tourists two hours to find the place, but it takes locals two years. (Search for Hole In The Wall Kilkenny on Facebook or http://www.holeinthewall.ie/.)

On a more serious note, in 1324 Dame Alice Kyteler of Kilkenny was the object of one the earliest European witch trials, probably on trumped-up charges by people who envied her "merry widow" lifestyle. She escaped punishment by fleeing to England, but one of her servants was not so lucky. A surprisingly powerful replica of her resides in the basement of her old house, which has been turned into Kyteler's Inn, a "medieval tavern" (http://www.kytelers.ie/index.asp and http://annieshearth.blogspot.com/2010/05/dame-alice-kyteler.html).

Getting There

Kilkenny is on M9, southwest of Dublin.

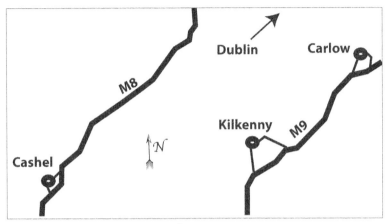

Area map

Moone High Crosses, Moone, Co. Kildare
N52 58 45 W6 49 31

The Moone High Cross is hard to find but worth the effort. The famous high cross and fragments of another are exhibited inside the ruins of a late medieval church. The high crosses were moved into the glass-topped church for preservation. Moone (from Maoin Choluim Chille, 'Gift of Colmcille") is the site of a monastery allegedly founded by St Columba in the sixth century, although there are no historic references to it before the tenth century (http://www.kildare.ie/southkildareheritagetrail/moone.htm).

142

"Probably because of the difficulty of carving in granite, the sculptors of the crosses adopted a uniquely simple, geometrical style, and—whether by accident or design—produced one of the most attractive of all high crosses." Halpin and Newman, p. 326.

The Moone High Cross probably dates from the ninth century. It is slender, with a tall, pyramidal base. It is 5 m (17 ft) high, beautifully carved with flat, naïve figures. The granite cross is carved with beasts, stylized geometrical designs, spirals, bosses, and other motifs. The base contains charming scriptural scenes, including Daniel in the Lions' Den, and Adam and Eve and the Tree of Knowledge. Fragments of another high cross are displayed at the west end of the church. It is probable that the cross was originally painted and very colorful (See http://highcrosses.org/moone/index.htm for numerous photos; see p. 68 for more on high crosses.)

The isolated setting is quite atmospheric. We pulled off the narrow country lane at the sign and walked around a walled enclosure to reach the ruined church. We had not expected to be greatly impressed by the high cross: it wasn't in its original location in the churchyard; it had been restored because it was found broken into three parts; and so on. However, it is striking. It is artistically stunning, but there is more to its attraction than mere aesthetics. Soaring to the sky within the confines of the ruined

The Moone High Cross

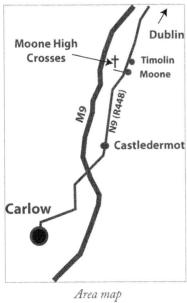

Area map

chapel, it remains a compelling testament to faith. Maybe something in the location itself enables the cross to maintain its function as an axis mundi, connecting earth to heaven. Spend time with the cross, and see what you discover.

Getting There

Drive 17 km (10.5 mi) northeast of Carlow on N9 (Dublin-Kilkenny Road). Follow signs to Moone village and take a minor road to the west. Signposted. The church and cross are hidden from direct view by a wall.

Detail of the top of the cross

Lower Shannon and Southwest Ireland

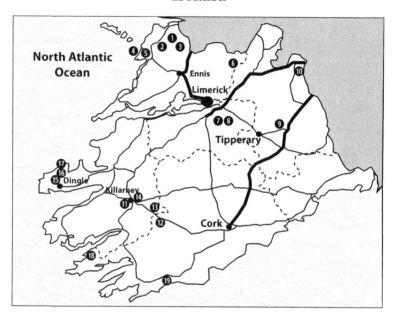

1. The Burren
2. Poulnabrone Dolmen
3. St Colman's Oratory
4. Cliffs of Moher
5. St Brigid's Well
6. Holy Island
7. Lough Gur
8. Grange Stone Circle
9. Rock of Cashel
10. Kilcooley Abbey
11. Killarney National Park
12. Ballyvourney
13. Paps of Anu/Danu
14. Seven Sisters
15. Gallarus Oratory
16. Kilmalkedar Church
17. Mount Brandon
18. Cailleach Beara
19. Drombeg Stone Circle

Lower Shannon

The Burren, Poulnabrone Dolmen, St Colman's Oratory, Cliffs of Moher, and St Brigid's Well near Liscannor, Co. Clare

The Burren is a fascinating region in northwest County Clare, encompassing approximately 250 square kilometers of karst landscape eroded by wind, rain, and glaciers. The word "burren" comes from the Gaelic *boireann*, meaning "rocky land," an appropriate name for this limestone plateau with its fissured surface of broken limestone slabs.

Sheltered valleys provide grazing for cattle but, denuded after 6000 years of human habitation, few trees except stunted hawthorn grow in the region. Numerous rare plants and flowers, a mix of arctic, Mediterranean, and al-

The Burren

pine species, thrive in the cracks in the limestone pavement that covers large areas of the region. The best months to see the numerous flowering plants and ferns are May and June. Numerous butterfly species live in the area as well.

Tourists are drawn to the Burren's seaside resorts and the annual matchmaking festival in Lisdoonvarna. But there are many other reasons to go to the Burren, including caves, impressive megaliths (four portal dolmens and over 130 wedge-shaped galleries), Iron Age ring forts, early Christian remains, and the breathtaking Cliffs of Moher.

A number of guidebooks provide driving routes, so we won't; instead, we'll describe a few of the powerful places we have experienced. It is helpful to have a detailed map of the area. We've used a three-part set published by Tíreolas, but we've heard that Tim Robinson's maps are excellent (available from Amazon). We've also heard that "Burren Hill Walks" organizes very good walking tours.

Poulnabrone Dolmen, the Burren
N53 2 50 W9 8 25

The stark stone skeleton of Poulnabrone seemed to shimmer in the air. I blinked and looked again. The distorted, wavery vision remained. What could it be, I wondered. It was a cool, overcast day, so the distortion wasn't caused by heat waves. Could it be a portal into another dimension? I walked slowly around the perimeter of the dolmen, watching the shape-shifting interference pattern. I could go no closer, since a rope fence surrounds the dolmen. Given the power of the place, perhaps it was just as well I was kept at a distance. (Elyn)

Poulnabrone Dolmen

Poulnabrone Dolmen is a portal tomb, erected in approximately 4000 BCE. Its name comes from *poll*, a hole or pit or dark place, and *brón*, which means sorrow: in other words, Poulnabrone Dolmen is the "Dark, Sorrowful Place" or the "Hole of Sorrows," a brooding name for a powerful place.

The dolmen stands isolated in the middle of a broken and fissured limestone plateau, in the center of a low mound of stones about 9 m (30 ft) across. The mound of stones was never higher, indicating that a cairn never covered the dolmen and it was always stark and dramatic. It is oriented north-northeast, tapering to the south-southwest. One side has three upright stones; the other has two upright stones, the third now lying on the ground. The flat, thin capstone measures 3.6 m (12 ft) by 2 m (7 ft) and balances on two stones on either side and an end stone. It tilts upwards from the back to the front and forms an overhanging rooftop. The portal stones in the front are 1.8 m (6 ft) high. The disarticulated bones of between 16 and 30 adults and

Mara Freeman's psychic intuition is that Poulnabrone (like certain other dolmens) is a portal to the Land of the Dead, to a sacred space where wisdom was available for the living. Mara sensed that shamans would go there, acquire "information," and bring it back to their community. http://www.chalicecentre.net; personal communication, 2007.

children were found in the chamber; they were buried sometime between 4200-2900 BCE. A later, Bronze-Age burial of a newborn was also discovered at the dolmen. In addition, a number of animal bones and artifacts were found, including a stone ax, beads, a bone pendant, flint arrowheads, coarse pottery sherds, and two quartz crystals. This is evidence that Poulnabrone was used for millennia for ritual and other ceremonial activities.

The dolmen is surrounded by a low fence, which effectively keeps visitors away. Even from a distance, however, you can sense its power. Center yourself and focus. See if you can experience the shift in energies, an "interference pattern" that becomes visible at certain angles at certain times.

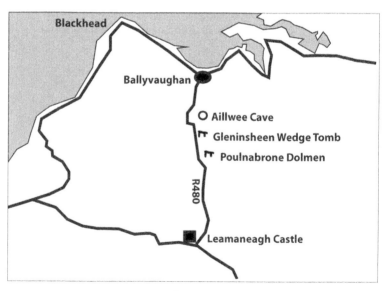

Area map

Getting there

Poulnabrone is between Leamaneagh Castle and Aillwee Cave on R480, in the direction of Ballyvaughan. It is visible on the right. One km further north is Gleninsheen Wedge Tomb. Coming from the north, it is 8 km (5 mi) south of Ballyvaughan on R480; sign-posted. Parking off-road near Clare's Rock.

St Colman's Oratory and Tobar Colman McDuach, the Burren N53 4 31 W9 0 30

We parked the car, walked past a jagged dry-stone wall, and then crossed the fractured limestone Burren, pausing to admire the tiny flowers peeking out of the fissured surface. We reached a thick barrier of hawthorn trees and found a gap. On the other side were meadowland and more thorn trees. We passed through another gap in another line of thorn trees and another, at last entering into a magical faery glen. It was dripping with green: green moss, green ferns, and green lichen-covered trees. Everything was green—except for the crystal-clear water in the holy well. The presence of Nature Spirits was intense. A hazelwood, the tree of wisdom, hangs down over the holy well, its branches dangling with ribbons. (Elyn)

If you can spend a day walking through the Burren, don't miss St Colman's Oratory, a tiny ruined chapel hidden on the Slievecarran hillside, close to the equally hidden holy well, Tobar Col-

St Colman's Oratory

man McDuach, and a small hermit's cave, 9 m (30 ft) above the oratory.

Sometime around 595 CE, St Colman McDuach retreated to the Burren to live a life of solitude and devotion. He was said to be so holy he meditated in the cave for seven years, eating nothing but berries and fruit. The path to the site is called "the Way of the Dishes" because one Easter, when St Colman

Holy cave

wanted to end his Lenten fast, angels miraculously carried the local king's dinner (and plates) over the Burren to his feet. The king and his retinue followed fast behind, eager to learn where the banquet was going. (For more details on St Colman, go to http://www.stcolman.com/ life_burren.html.)

Discovering this hidden Burren treasure is a pilgrimage to a very special place. There is a holy well, a cave, and an "enchanted" glen…. Spend time sitting beside the well, listening to the sound of water, the birds, the rustling leaves. Perhaps you'll hear something else, if you listen carefully with your "inner ears." Tune in to the

According to Nora Judge, if you leave a ribbon at a well, disconnect intentionally from outcome. As the ribbon disintegrates, "your petition is dispersed and carried by the wind—much like Tibetan prayer flags. The winds in Ireland hold great wisdom." Nora Judge, http://www.taracelebrations.org/, personal communication, 2 April, 2011.

Elyn at Tobar Colman McDuach, the holy well. Notice the ribbons.

Another view of St Colman's Oratory

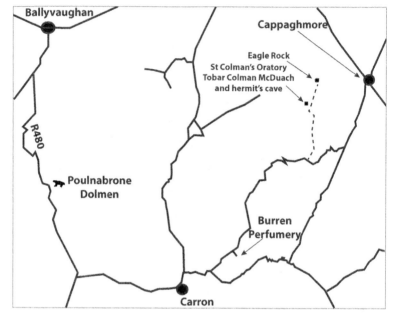

Area map

Spirit of the Place. If you feel so moved, say a prayer or ask a boon, then tie a ribbon on the hazelwood beside the well.

Getting There

Take the road that leads from Carron to Cappaghmore. Signposts to the Burren Perfumery (off to the right) indicate the way. Continue past the perfumery to a signposted turnout to Slieve Carran Nature Reserve and Eagle Rock. The path is to the left. You might consider booking a walking tour, perhaps one offered by http://www.burrenwalks.com. Also check out http://www.burrenbeo.com, a very helpful organization.

The Cliffs of Moher N52 58 17 W9 25 29

We were ready for a holiday. We'd seen so many powerful places that we were experiencing a kind of "energetic indigestion." "Let's take a break," I said, "and go to a popular tourist site like the Cliffs of Moher." We paid to park in the huge car lot and then walked up the wide path to the top of the cliffs. The undulating cliffs create a visual rhythm of layered rock, green on top, dark and light and green and dark below, worn by sea and wind and curving into the distance. Far below, waves crash against the stones, gradually transforming solid mineral into sand. It is an awesome place, where the elements join in a wild dance of wind and water, sunlight and stone. Surely ancestral people worshipped at this powerful place, this end-point of land

The Cliffs of Moher

*meeting water, of sun setting into sea. I said a silent prayer and
cast an offering into the wind. (Elyn)*

The sandstone and shale Cliffs of Moher rise 200 m
(650 ft) straight up from the Atlantic, breathtaking in their
abruptness. Birds wheel and swoop, then head for their
nests hidden on sheltered ledges. The vertically layered
cliffs undulate 8 km (5 mi) from Hag's Head to the west
to just beyond O'Brien's Tower, constructed in 1835 at the
cliffs' highest point. On a clear day, you can see the Aran
Islands and Galway Bay. The rays of the setting sun illuminate the cliffs and sea in a spectacular way, but any time of
day is a good time to visit.

We had heard complaints because the Cliffs of Moher
Visitor Center requires you to pay for access to the cliffs,

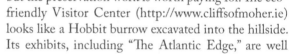

but the preservation work is worth paying for. The eco-
friendly Visitor Center (http://www.cliffsofmoher.ie)
looks like a Hobbit burrow excavated into the hillside.
Its exhibits, including "The Atlantic Edge," are well

O'Brien's Tower

> Center yourself. Bring your awareness to the four elements—earth, fire (sunlight), water, and air—and how they dance together at this meeting place of sea and land. Open all of your senses, paying attention to each in turn: the shifting colors of the cliffs, the smell of the sea, the sounds of the waves and the birds, the feeling of the wind on your skin, the taste of salt.... Nature is the true temple.

done, as are the paths that lead up to the edge of the dramatic cliffs.

It takes about 15-30 minutes to walk uphill from the Visitor Center to O'Brien's Tower. There are also longer walks, including an 8 km (5 mi) walk to Hag's Head Overlook.

Getting There

The Cliffs of Moher are 8 km (5 mi) south of Doolin and 5 km (3 mi) north of Liscannor on R478. Admission fee. Hiking trails lead along the cliffs, including a 3-hour coastal walk from Doolin to the Cliffs of Moher. Take a cruise from Liscannor's pier (http://www.cliffs-of-moher-cruises.com) for a different perspective.

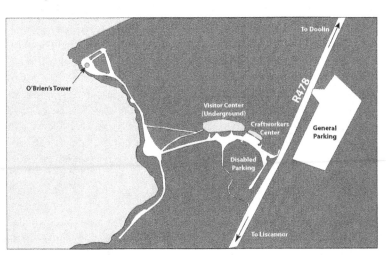

Area map

St Brigid's Well, Liscannor
N52 57 2 W9 25 11

Inland from the Cliffs of Moher on the Doolin-Liscannor road is St Brigid's Well, one of the most important holy wells in Ireland. It has been a place of worship for over 2000 years, dating back to when the site was used (as was Croagh Patrick) for major Lughnasa celebrations. Its pagan origins are still present, barely hidden beneath a veneer of Catholic devotion.

The main pilgrimage festival used to be held on Garland Sunday, the last Sunday in July, a date close to Lughnasa. It began the night before and often became quite boisterous by morning. Another festival was traditionally held at the well on 1 February, Candlemas, the feast day of St Brigid and the date of Imbolc. The vigil is now held on 15 August,

"In Irish mythology, Brigid, Brigit, or Brighit ("exalted one") was the daughter of the Dagda (and therefore one of the Tuatha Dé Danann) and wife of Bres of the Formorians. She had two sisters, also named Brighid, and is considered a classic Celtic Triple Goddess. … Brigid was the goddess of the Sacred Flame of Kildare and the patron goddess of the Druids. She was the goddess of all things perceived to be of relatively high dimensions such as high-rising flames, highlands, hill-forts and upland areas; and of activities and states conceived as psychologically elevated, such as wisdom, excellence, perfection, high intelligence, poetic eloquence, craftsmanship, healing ability, druidic knowledge and skill in warfare. She seems to have been the Celtic equivalent of the Roman Minerva and the Greek Athena, goddesses with very similar functions and apparently embodying the same concept of 'elevated state', whether physical or psychological. … After the Christianization of the Celts, Brigid was considered the foster mother of Jesus and was often called St. Brigid, daughter of the druid, Dougal the Brown." (http://en.wikipedia.org/wiki/St_Brigid%27s_Well, 28 March, 2011)

Figure of St Brigid near the well house

the Feast of the Assumption, displacing the celebration
further and further from its pagan origins. Today, one is
more likely to encounter a busload of tourists at St Brigid's
well than a sincere devotee, but it remains a powerful place.
(For more on Brigid, see p. 127.)

In the nineteenth century, Cornelius O'Brien (who also
built O'Brien's Tower at the Cliffs of Moher) constructed a
well house over the well after the miraculous waters healed
him. A serene, life-size statue of St Brigid stands near the
well house, encased in glass and surrounded by flowers.
Above the well house is an ancient cemetery in which the
Uí Bhrian, the Kings of Dál gCais, are buried. On the hill,
a large cross, statues, and a walkway form part of the stations performed at the holy well. The well was held in such
high regard that people from the Aran Islands would make
a pilgrimage to pay homage to Crom Dubh or St Brigid at
the well, beginning their vigil on Saturday, the night before,
and returning home the next day. Apparently, making "the

rounds" at the well was more important than attending Mass.

A flight of stairs leads down from the hillside to the well house, a tiny, cave-like building. Its fern-sprouting walls are covered with offerings and ex-votos, including crutches, photos, letters, testimonials, rosaries, statues, and medals. Water flows from underground into a stone basin set into the floor. Legend says that if you see a white trout swimming in the well waters, your prayer will be granted.

St Brigid's Well at Liscannor is a powerful place, filled with longing and hope—and gratitude. The presence of Brigid, healing goddess and Christian saint, is very strong.

Getting There

Drive 2 km (1 mi) north of Liscannor on R478; on the left-hand side of the road.

Mara Freeman outside St Brigid's Well

Interior of St Brigid's Well

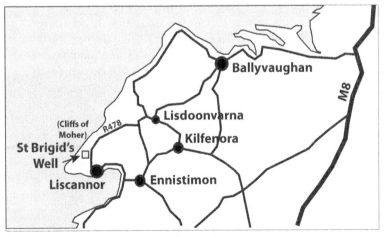

Area map

More to Experience

Some local towns

Kilfenora town is a center of "trad" Irish music; it is also famous for its high crosses, including Doorty's Cross, now placed inside the ruined twelfth-century Kilfenora Cathedral for preservation. The Burren Center interpretive exhibits are located nearby (http://www.theburrencentre.ie). Doolin is a tiny village 8 km (5 mi) north of the Cliffs of Moher. It is another center for "trad" music. Don't miss the evening music sessions at O'Connor's Pub. Boats depart from Doolin Pier to the Aran Islands and the Cliffs of Moher (http://www.doolinferries.com and http://www.cliffsofmoher.com [see p. 153]). It is a pleasant base from which to explore the Burren. A coastal hiking path leads from Doolin to the Cliffs of Moher; allow about three hours.

Ennistymon is a charming small town located in a wooded valley. It is known as "the town of old shop fronts," and waterfalls on the River Cullenagh are visible from the seven-arched bridge. Ennistymon has an "artsy" feel, lively "trad" music, an ATM, and is well located as a base for the area. Lisdoonvarna contains Ireland's only operating spa using mineral water from several wells. The Spa Wells Health Center has provided sulphur baths and other treatments since the nineteenth century. Avoid Lisdoonvarna in September, when it hosts the hugely popular international matchmaking festival.

The Aran Islands, Co. Galway (accessible from Doolin)

Across the sea, across the wind-swept waters, the ferry goes to and from the Aran Islands. The Aran Islands: famous for intricately knit Aran sweaters, their unique patterns serving as an identity card for the fishermen who wear them—if, perchance, they drown at sea. But other thoughts arise once we reach the island of Inishmore, remote and bleak. The ancient fort, Dún Aonghasa, is on the edge of a cliff, which is collapsing into the sea, and those who don't mind heights hang their heads and arms over the unprotected cliff edge. No guardrail holds them back; no "Do Not Enter" sign warns of the danger that awaits. Here on the islands, life is lived without a safety net. (Elyn)

The Aran Islands include Inis Mór (Big Island), Inis Meáin (Middle Island), and Inis Oírr (East Island), also known as Inishmore, Inishmaan, and Inisheer. Austere and isolated, they remain a center of traditional Irish culture. Most visited and the largest is Inis Mór, with its ruined churches, including Teampall Chiaráin and the Seven Churches (Na Seacht dTeampaill), and Dún Aonghasa, a breathtakingly situated Iron or Bronze Age fort. The Aran Heritage Center at Kilronan's main harbor is worth visiting. Plan to spend the day exploring Inishmore by jaunting car (pony and trap), minibus, or bicycle. It's a dramatic place, but is it a powerful place? That's for you to determine.

Getting There

The islands are reachable by ferry from Galway or from Doolin, and by commuter plane from Connemara Airport. A number of companies offer transportation.

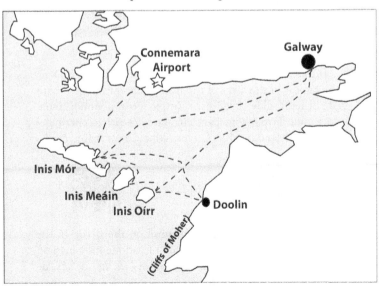

Area map

Holy Island (Mountshannon), Co. Clare, Lough Gur and Grange Stone Circle, Co. Limerick, and the Rock of Cashel and Kilcooley Abbey, Co. Tipperary

Holy Island (Inis Cealtra or Inishcaltra)
N52 55 51 W8 25 53

As we drove down the tree-lined road alongside Lough Derg, I felt a shift in energy. I glanced over at the lake and saw a small island with a tall tower: Inis Cealtra, the Holy Island. I caught my breath, taking in its beauty, glad that soon we would be walking on that sacred soil. I could feel it drawing me to it from across the waters. But then the wind kicked up and the rain set in. The boatman shook his head. He wouldn't risk the journey. We looked at his tiny boat, rocking fiercely on the choppy waves. Sadly, we agreed. So near and yet so far. Sometimes the journey can't be made; the distance can't be crossed from this shore to the other. It wasn't far, but we couldn't walk on water. (Elyn)

Inis Cealtra is a small island in the middle of Lough Derg, the largest of the lakes of the river Shannon, at the mouth of Scarriff Bay inlet (see http://www.mountshannon. com and http://homepage.eircom.net/~eastclareheritage/ Holy%20Island.html). Colum Mac Cremthainn estab-

lished the first Christian foundation on the island in the sixth century, but there had been at least one holy man on the island a century earlier. Other saints, including St Cai-

Holy Island (courtesy of East Clare Heritage)

min, soon arrived, and a monastery was built that became a center of learning. Inis Cealtra is also called the Island of Seven Churches, indicative of the continuing importance of the number seven in sacred places in Ireland.

In the sixteenth century the churches were abandoned, but in 1608 Inis Cealtra was named one of twelve "notable shrines" in Ireland by Pope Paul V. He honored it with a Plenary Indulgence on St Caimin's feast day, 24 March. The opportunity to receive this important indulgence immediately brought numerous pilgrims to the island, and until the mid 1800s it was one of the most popular pilgrimages in Ireland.

There is much to see on the island: pre-Christian bullaun stones (the water in the depressions was believed to have healing properties); a ring fort; a round tower; the Saints' Graveyard with grave slabs from the sixth to twelfth centuries; St Caimin's church, begun in the tenth century and later rebuilt; and three other churches, including one dedicated to St Brigid and one to St Mary. East of St Mary's church is a holy well. The pilgrimage round began and ended at the holy well. On the highest spot, in the middle of the island, is St Michael's Garden, an ancient enclosure within the remains of a ring fort. It includes a children's burial ground, unconsecrated by the Church, and has been considered holy land from ancient times.

Although we were unable to get to Inis Cealtra, it felt like a very powerful place. We hope you will have better luck reaching the island than we did.

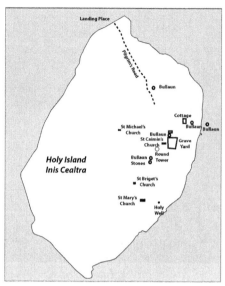

Map of Holy Island

 If you are in the area, Mountshannon's Aistear Iniscealtra Community Park is worth a visit (http://www.mountshannon.com/index.php/local-features/aistear-park/). It has a multi-layered, 3D Irish history maze that you can walk on, over, and through, as well as a delightful Chartres-style (11-circuit) labyrinth overlooking the nearby lake. The circuits or paths are mowed in the grass, and plants form the labrys shapes at the turns. In the center is a boulder with the labyrinth path engraved on the top. The setting is peaceful and soothing.

Getting There

Inis Cealtra is near the west shore of Lough Derg. Drive on R352 between Scarriff and Mountshannon. You will see the pier signposted. The ferry service is operated by East Clare Heritage: http://www.eastclareheritage.com/ (see p. 162) or http://www.discoverireland.com/za/ireland-things-to-see-and-do/listings/product/?fid=FI_15953.

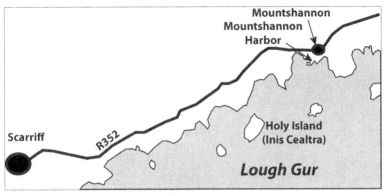

Area map

The phone number for the Heritage Center is (0)61 921351. Gerard Madden, a local historian and author of books on the area, ferries people across if the weather is good. You may need to go to the Mountshannon harbor to meet him. Telephone in advance: (0)61 921 615, mobile (0)86 874 9710, or email him at ger@eastclareheritage.com. Aistear Iniscealtra Community Park is located in the village of Mountshannon, between the harbor and the main street.

More to Experience:

Relatively near is Brian Boru's oak, a splendid tree said to be 1000 years old and one of Ireland's oldest oaks. http://twitpic.com/bc4i9 for photo. http://www.limerickleader.ie/news/local/tuamgraney_s_mighty_oak_ was_growing_at_time_of_brian_boru_1_2179074. To get to Brian Boru's oak in Raheen Wood, go to Tuamgraney. Follow the road from St Cronan's Church toward Killaloe for 2.4 km (1.5 mi); turn left into the hospital grounds. Just before the building, take the foot lane on the right. 0.8 km (0.5 mi) further you'll see the tree on the right, at the edge of Raheen woods.

Lough Gur and Grange Stone Circle
N52 30 51 W8 32 33

It is impressive: large standing stones touching side to side, surrounded by an earthen mound, sheltered by towering trees. We walked slowly around the outside in a sunwise direction before entering the circle through a gap between two monumental stones. We continued walking clockwise, gradually spinning off one by one to come to rest at the monolith that called to us. Eyes closed, my back against the cool granite surface, I imagined that I saw and heard an ancient, torch-lit procession still circling inside the stones. (Elyn)

The area around Lough Gur is important for Irish archaeology because of the quality, density, and range of sites located in a well-preserved landscape. There are over 130

View across the Grange Stone Circle

listed sites and monuments ranging in date from Neolithic to medieval times. Drainage of the lake in the 1850s (part of an unemployment relief scheme after the famine of 1847) lowered the level by 1.2 m (4 ft), revealing an archeological treasure-trove of artifacts on the exposed foreshore. A campaign of archeological excavation between 1936-1954 provided the basis of modern Irish archaeology.

Grange Stone Circle is located on the west of the lake and is part of a wider ceremonial landscape that originally included an even larger stone circle (no longer visible) immediately to the north, with a smaller surviving circle to the northeast. Grange Stone Circle is 45.7 m (150 ft) in internal diameter and consists of a continuous ring of 113 large upright stones enclosing a floor of earth, raised 60 cm (2 ft) above the original ground level. The stones are in sockets, their backs nestling into a low bank of earth and stones that is over 9 m (30 ft) wide and up to 1.5 m (3-5 ft) high. It was constructed during the Bronze Age and dates to 2000 BCE.

Drawing of how the circle might have originally appeared

The circle appears to have many astronomical alignments, some of which may be the result of modern "over-ceremonializing" the stones. The midsummer sun shines through the narrow entryway and into the center of the circle. The entrance faces northeast, roughly aligned to sunrise on the harvest festival of Lughnasa (1 August)—fitting, perhaps, since the circle is associated with Crom Dubh, the

Celtic harvest god, and the largest stone, the prominent Black Stone, is called Ronnach Croim Duibh. It is over 4 m (13 ft) high and weighs 40 tons. These associations indicate that the circle continued to be important into the Iron Age. Opposite the entrance, two tall stones perhaps point to sunset at Samhain (1 November).

"The entrance stones are matched by a pair of equally impressive slabs ... , whose tops slope down towards each other to form a v-shape. It has been calculated that these stones and the entranceway were aligned with the sunset of the Festival of Samhain. The locals won't come near this place after sunset because the belief is that the place returns to the Fey and the otherworldly beings. The entities tolerate visitors during the day, but at night it belongs to them and we're to respect that." http://www.sacredsitetour.com/sacred-sites-of-ireland/grange-stone-circle.html, retrieved 25 March, 2011.

There is also an alignment from the entry stones and the stones on the opposite side to the midsummer moon. The problem is, it is often hard, if not impossible, to know which of the so-called alignments are intentional and which are the result of people with a theory who find stones to match it.

Animal bones were found within and beneath the bank, as well as an unusually high number of broken pots from the Beaker period. It appears that the pots were ritually broken during construction and the food may have been part of the ritual.

Although Grange Stone Circle is associated with Crom Dubh, the Knockadoon region has connections with the sun goddess Áine as well—and with Diarmuid and Gráinne, and Fionn Mac Cumhaill's adventures. Since Gráinne is an alter ego or sister of Áine, the association is not surprising. Áine is said to be the daughter of Manannán mac Lir, the sea god.

Entrance into the Grange Stone Circle

Áine is said to appear at Lough Derg, which she created, in the forms of a mermaid, a maid, and a hag, images
suggestive of the Celtic triune goddess. According to one
legend, the first Earl of Desmond met Áine combing her
hair and stole her cloak, thus putting her in his power. (It
was traditional for the tribal chief to seek acceptance of the
goddess of the land at his inauguration, a custom reflected
in this legend.) Áine agreed to bear the earl a son, Géaroid
Iarla, but forbade the earl to show surprise at anything the
son did. Later he violated the prohibition, and his son had
to return to the faery realm. "It is said he lies sleeping beneath Knockadoon with his knights, waiting for the time
when they will ride forth and gain freedom for all Ireland"
(Meehan, p. 423). This legend of the sleeping knight is
reminiscent of legends of Kesh Corran and of Glastonbury.

Another story recounts that every seven years Lough Gur
disappears by magic, revealing a supernatural tree growing
from the bottom of the lake: in other words, the *axis mundi*.
In another legend, the tree is covered with a green cloth

and a woman sits under it weaving. Clearly, we are in a powerful place filled with myth and magic.

The archeological park at Knockadoon, at the northeast corner of the lake, offers an interpretive center of Neolithic life. Entrance fee. A site map available at the visitor center will help you explore the area. http://www.shannonheritage.com/Attractions/LoughGur/ For more stories and a video of midsummer sunrise at Grange Stone Circle, go to http://www.voicesfromthedawn.com, then search for Lough Gur. Audio self-guided walks can be downloaded at http://www.loughgur.com/.

Getting There

Drive 20 km (12 mi) south of Limerick on R512 towards Kilmallock.

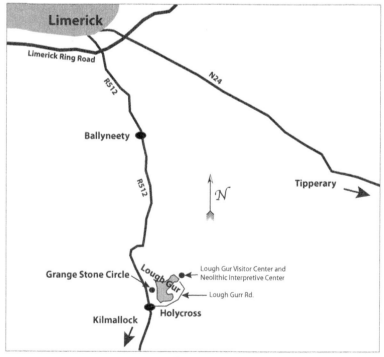

Area map

The Rock of Cashel N52 31 12 W7 53 52

We were told that the Rock of Cashel, "Ireland's Acropolis," was a must-see place to truly understand Ireland. It was the seat of the Munster kings from around 370-1101 CE, until the Kings of Munster handed Cashel over to the Church, which built a flourishing religious center on top of the rock. In 1647 Cromwell's army besieged Cashel and many residents fled for safety to the cathedral on the Rock. The army proceeded to set the cathedral on fire. All told, the army massacred 3000 inhabitants.

The Rock of Cashel is a stunning site, especially when lit up at night. It is a dark mass of limestone rising out of the Tipperary plain, with a round tower and several once-

The Rock of Cashel

172

important edifices on top. Despite the dramatic setting, the ruined cathedral and the Hall of Vicars Choral, now a museum, felt devoid of energy when we were there.

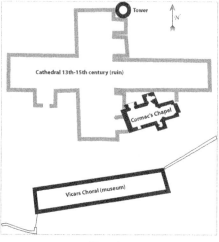

Site plan

Cormac's Chapel, however, is still a powerful place. Consecrated in 1134, it contains superb Romanesque sandstone carvings and wall paintings undergoing restoration. In the tympanum over the north door, a centaur wearing a helmet (Sagittarius?) aims his bow at a lion. We stayed in the chapel for a long time, admiring the diverse carved geometric motifs and human and animal heads—and, more importantly, enjoying the sweet, harmonizing energy that filled the space. Elyn said it brought her back into balance, and she could imagine that worshippers would have enjoyed a sense of renewal and well being. This special feeling results from a combina-

Cormac's Chapel

tion of sacred geometry, specific proportions and measurements used to build the chapel, and, we presume, the energies of the rock itself.

A grinning, jug-eared Sheela-na-gig resides on the wall in the restaurant corridor of the nearby Cashel Palace Hotel. The loquacious bartender told us the stone carving had been found in a nearby field. We learned later it was found 12 km away, but perhaps that qualifies as "nearby." He said it was a fertility symbol for good luck, but the Catholic Church had perverted it into something bad. He also told us (perhaps erroneously) that 30 to 40 such carvings had been found in the fields, facing toward the Rock of Cashel. The Cashel Palace Hotel has lovely gardens, and the Bishop's Walk leads from Main Street through the gardens up to the Rock.

Getting There

Cashel is east and a bit south of Limerick. Take N24 between Limerick and Waterford, then take N74 north to Cashel; or continue to N8 north (toward Dublin). Entry fee or Heritage Card.

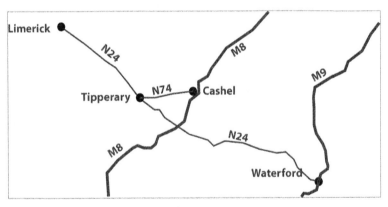

Area map

Kilcooley (Kilcooly) Abbey
N52 40 22 W7 34 9

We visited the ruins of the Cistercian Kilcooley (from Cill Cúile, "the Church of the Nook" or "the Church in the Corner of the Angle") Abbey in Co. Tipperary. We went there to see a mermaid carving, similar to the one at St Brendan's cathedral. We discovered much more than just the mermaid: we discovered another powerful place.

Founded around 1182, the abbey was burned in 1418 and again in 1444, later rebuilt, then abandoned after the dissolution of the monasteries. Today it is in remarkably good repair for a ruined abbey. The sacristy screen wall in the south transept features a number of intriguing carvings, including a naïf crucifixion scene with Mary and John,

Approaching Kilcooley Abbey

> "There is a pulse to Kilcooley Abbey, a glisten in the stone even on the most dreary day (and I've seen it in all weathers) that belies its dereliction. There is a quality to the light there, there is a shimmer in the grey, an echo that tells us that its story has not ended yet. It commands the landscape solidly yet in an understated way and it winks at you when you least expect and suddenly you want to go and embrace it." Maura Barrett, personal communication, 6 April, 2011.

with exaggerated feet; a pelican plucking at her breast (a symbol of eternity and self sacrifice, since she feeds her young with her own body and does not die); St Christopher carrying a large baby Jesus and a sprouting staff, and fording a stream while eels swim at his web-like feet; an angel swinging a metal incense burner (a thurable), facing east in honor of the rising sun/resurrection; and a mermaid holding a mirror and comb while pointing at two fish, perhaps representing souls she would lead astray. The wall may have decorated a private chapel of the Butler family. (See Maura Barrett's book, *Kilcooley Abbey*, for additional details.)

Kilcooley Abbey contains three extremely well-preserved tombs and numerous medieval grave slabs. The knight-effigy tomb of Piers Fitz James Oge Butler (d. 1526) is especially noteworthy. The abbey also features an elaborately carved prior's chair and an abbot's chair, and one of the most beautiful Gothic flame-tracery windows we have ever seen. The yew tree in

Sacristy screen wall

the cloisters seems to be keeping guard over the place. The cloisters felt peaceful, harmonious, and sacred.

Kilcooley Abbey is reached by walking down a narrow lane and across a field. A rare Irish columbarium (dovecote) stands in the field to the left and other outbuildings can be explored around the abbey. The

The Gothic east window

setting is lovely and the energy luscious. Bring a picnic and spend the afternoon. It is sufficiently off the tourist path that you may be able to enjoy the surroundings without any other visitors. Contact Maura Barrett at Slieveardagh Rural Development at (0)52 915 6165 for a private tour.

 http://www.slieveardagh.com/kilcooly_abby/index. html. Also, Liam Noonan is a "key holder" for the abbey and we are told he is an excellent guide; his contact phone is (0)56 883 4277; or his mobile, (0)86 396 9356.

Getting There

Drive 32 km (21 mi) northeast of Cashel on M8. Go north to Urlingford; then take R689 and 690 south for 5.5 km (3.5 mi); park in parish church carpark and walk 0.5 km (500 yd) to the abbey.

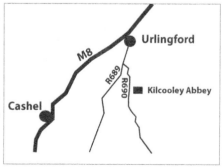

Area map

More to Experience

The Glen of Aherlow, Co. Tipperary

The Glen of Aherlow, Co. Tipperary, is a lush valley running between the Galty Mountains, Ireland's highest mountains, and the conifer-covered ridge of Slievenamuck. It is filled with hiking trails and walks, with holy wells, abbeys, and megaliths. The glen runs 26 km (16 mi), following the River Aherlow. http://www.aherlow.com. Getting there: 3.2 km (2 mi) south of Tipperary on R664.

The Southwest

Co. Kerry has stunning scenery—lakes, mountains (including the highest range in the country, the Macgillycuddy's Reeks)—and a wealth of prehistoric and early Christian remains. It has three peninsulas, Iveragh, Dingle, and Beara.

Iveragh Peninsula: Killarney National Park, Ballyvourney Monastic Site, Paps of Anu/Danu, the Seven Sisters, Co. Kerry

Killarney National Park N52 3 36 W9 31 6

Huddled in our long narrow boat, protecting ourselves from drizzle and spray under a waterproof tarp, we saw deer prancing and sheep grazing on the steep slopes of the mountains on either side of Long Range River. An eagle circled overhead. The landscape was all about contrasts: green forests, grey rocks, glistening obsidian water. There were no signs of human habitation—no roads, no buildings, no electric lines. In the odd, pervasive stillness, I realized we had entered a primeval landscape. The mountains really were *beings; the strange inky black water really* was *Niamh, the faery goddess of the lakes and waters of Killarney. I held my breath, spellbound. (Elyn)*

Located just south of Killarney on N71, Killarney National Park, first of Ireland's six national parks, can be explored by car, boat, bicycle, horse and cart, or foot. It is a lovely place to spend a few days. The park, designated a UNESCO Biosphere Reserve in 1981, includes three lakes linked by the Long Range River. It has the most extensive covering of native forest in Ireland and the only native herd of red deer. A "Gap of Dunloe/Lakes of Killarney" excur-

View from the lake

sion is an excellent way to experience the area. A ride in a "traditional" boat (narrow outboard motorboat) will put you in direct contact with the elements. (http://www.killarneynationalpark.ie/visit.html)

Be sure to visit Innisfallen in Lough Leane, with its evocative, ruined medieval abbey and numerous yew trees. We had (perhaps) a close encounter with a shape-shifting faery deer that leaped out of a field of ferns beside the narrow path that we were following around the island. Or perhaps it was a Sika deer that had swum across the river. Tour boats leave from Ross Castle on a regular basis.

The large Muckross estate begins 3 km (1.8 mi) south of Killarney off N71. Muckross Friary or Abbey is now in ruins, but it is still a powerful

"We can see how humans have expressed and interpreted the sacred spirituality of the land through churches and monuments, but the Killarney National Park is the chance for a very personal experience of connecting directly with the land." Nora Judge, personal communication, 10 April, 2011.

180

place to visit. A massive yew, surrounded by a low metal fence, shades the center of the two-story cloister. The tree may have been planted in the fifteenth century, when the Franciscan friary was established. Undisturbed, it has continued to grow inside the arcaded cloister, long outlasting the religious community. The friary is opposite Muckross Park Hotel on N71 going south from Killarney. Park and walk in.

The yews on Innisfallen

 The nineteenth-century neo-Elizabethan Muckross House and Gardens with its traditional farms is a pleasant tourist diversion (entrance fee; http://www.muckross-house.ie). It is 1 km (0.6 mi) further south.

The Muckross Peninsula, between Lough Leane and Muckross (Middle) Lake, has several nature trails and one of Europe's finest yew woods. Be sure to walk through the gardens to the Muckross Lake. Spend time meditating, perhaps on a boulder overlooking the water, and connect with the Spirits of the Place.

"Nature is the true temple," and there are many places to experience the power and sanctity of nature in Killarney National Park. One of these is the Blue Pool, a nature reserve known mostly to locals. A magical place, local limestone and other minerals color its waters. Tourists haven't discovered the site, but kingfishers and squirrels know it well. Take N71 south from Killarney for 4 km (2.5 mi), then turn left on the southern side of Muckross Park Hotel/ Molly Darcy's Pub. Entrance on left after 200 m (0.12 mi).

Getting There

Killarney Town can be reached from Cork by driving north on N22, from Kerry Airport south on N22, from Killorglin on N72, or from Kenmare on N71.

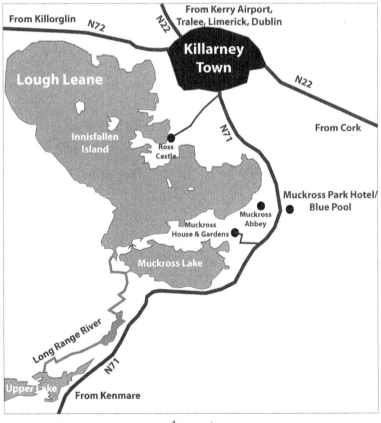

Area map

Ballyvourney Monastic Site
N51 56 40 W9 10 16

Ballyvourney Monastic Site includes a number of power-ful places and is one of the most visited pilgrimage sites in the Lee Valley. St Gobnait, who may have lived in the sixth century, is the patron saint of beekeepers. She was famous for her care of the sick, so her connection with bees may be because the healing properties of honey were well known in the sixth century.

Or perhaps the bee connection comes from a different source. Irish sites dedicated to female saints are rare, and such sites often indicate Christian expropriation of an earlier goddess tradition. St Gobnait's association with bees may hint at a pagan predecessor. "Gobnait" is the equivalent of the Hebrew name "Deborah," which means Honey Bee. Priestesses of Demeter and Artemis were

"The bee, found in Ancient Near East and Aegean cultures, was believed to be the sacred insect that bridged the natural world to the underworld. Appearing in tomb decorations, Mycenaean *tholos* tombs were even shaped as beehives. Bee motifs are also seen in Mayan cultures, an example being the Ah-Muzen-Cab, the Bee God, found in Mayan ruins, likely designating honey-producing cities (who prized honey as food of the gods)." http://en.wikipedia.org/wiki/Bee_%28mythology%29, retrieved 29 March, 2011.

called "bees." Some Irish say that the soul leaves the body as a bee or butterfly—and an unexpected bee is the sign of a departed loved one.

Legend says that St Gobnait was born in Co. Clare but fled to the Aran Islands; there an angel instructed her to

St Gobnait statue

travel to a place where she would find nine white deer. She traveled across southern Ireland, building churches. Eventually she reached Ballyvourney, encountered the nine white deer, and founded a religious community for women on land given to her by St Abbán. A white deer is sometimes associated with Jesus, but deer are very important in Celtic mythology—perhaps another hint of Gobnait's pagan antecedents. Her saint's day is 11 February, which, using the Old Style Julian calendar, was 1 February (Imbolc), the feast day for Brigid.

Ballyvourney contains a number of sacred sites to experience. There is a pensive statue of St Gobnait, erected in 1950. She is depicted standing on a beehive decorated with bees. A long strand of rosary beads hangs from around her neck. There are three holy wells. One is near a circular stone-walled foundation, about 10 m (33 ft) in diameter, excavated in 1951 and referred to as "St Gobnait's House." Since the excavations, that well has become a place of veneration.

To the east is Ballyvourney graveyard and the ruins of St Gobnait's church, Teampall Ghobnatan. On the south wall, just above the window, is a worn Sheela-na-gig carving. Rubbing the figure (perhaps on the genitals) is part of the *turas* (sacred journey) associated with the pilgrimage on 11 February, although it is also performed at other times. This is one of the few remaining Sheela-na-gigs that still plays an active part in pilgrimage ritual (http://www.irelands-sheelanagigs.org/archive/index.html)

184

St Gobnait's grave is a stone slab marked with a cross, next to a slab with three bullauns. Or perhaps her grave is the slab with the three holes; information differs. Offerings are left on both.

Sheela-na-gig above window

Some 60 m (197 ft) south of the graveyard is the second holy well. The path is marked with a large sign, "Tobar Ghobnatan Holy Well." The metal archway features a white deer. Follow the wide path through the woods and you will arrive at a very special clearing. The holy well is covered by a stone structure and reached by descending a set of steps. Cups are often left there for drawing water, but you might want to bring your own, along with an empty bottle for water. A metal rack draped with rosary offerings stands next to the well. The well is cool and dark, shaded by the overhanging linden tree, its trunk adorned with offerings of photos and rosaries.

Tobar Abbán, the third holy well, is 70 m (230 ft) to the east of Tobar Ghobnatan. It is dedicated to St Abbán and visited on 16 March.

Ballyvourney is an area filled with powerful places,

Spend time at St Gobnait's holy well, experiencing the energy of this sacred place. Fresh, clear, healing water: what a blessing! Ask permission, say a blessing or prayer, and draw water from the well. Perhaps you will anoint your forehead or the forehead of your companion with the holy water. What do you sense? Does this place, does this water seem powerful to you?

Tobar Ghobnatan

not all of which we have described. Explore the different sites in the surrounding woods, sensing the energies of Nature.

Getting There

55 km (34 mi) west of Cork on N22, between Macroom and Killarney (or 30 km southeast of Killarney). It is 15 km (10 mi) west-north-west of Macroom on the Killarney road. The church is just outside of Ballyvourney on the south side.

Signposted. Follow the road over the bridge to the Church of Ireland church.

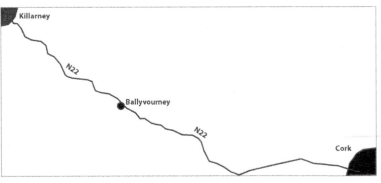

Area map

Seven Sisters Stone Circle (Lisseyviggeen or Lissivigeen Stone Circle) N52 3 29 W9 27 44

This stone circle is a powerful place, but you may not be able to experience it. The last time we went, the landowner had installed an electric fence around the field, perhaps to protect it, thus blocking off access.

If you are able to enter the field, you'll find two outlying stones, 2 m (7 ft) and 2.5 m (8 ft) tall, standing guard to the south of a bank (a low, raised ring of earth and stones) covered with trees. These two outliers form a doorway—both figuratively and energetically—to the stone circle. If you soften your eyes, you may be able to detect energy flowing between them; or you may be able to feel the energy as you

The two outlying stones

The Seven Sisters in their grove

walk between them. If you focus on each stone in turn, perhaps you can sense whether the energy moves up or down. Touch the stones and notice whether the stones have different temperatures. They did when we were there, but each time you visit a powerful place, the experience is different.

The Seven Sisters themselves are located inside the grove. Silently (or aloud) ask permission to approach and, if you are given it, enter the stone circle in a sunwise direction. Then visit each of the seven moss- and vine-covered stones in turn, sensing the different energies. Gary "sensed" that they were a family. Later we heard a legend that the outlying stones are the parents and the seven stones are the children, and that the family was turned to stone for dancing. A version of this story is also told about the Athgreany Piper's Stones (see p. 112).

Although the seven stones may not have always been seven, seven is a significant number. There are seven days in the week, seven dwarfs, seven Christian virtues, seven cardinal sins, seven heavens, seven colors in the rainbow, seven chakras—and so on.

Getting There

Take N22 east from Killarney toward Cork; after about 2.5 mi, turn left for Lissivigeen (the sign may say Upper Lissivigeen). The stone circle is accessed (or was accessible) from the green lane on the left by crossing the field.

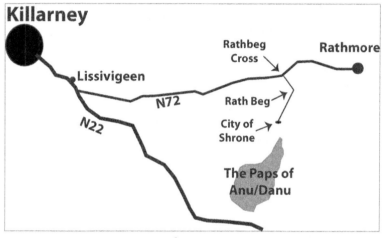

Area map

The Paps of Anu/Danu

The Paps of Anu are twin, rounded hills, the Mother's breasts rising out of the land. Their feminine energy is palpable. According to Howard Goldbaum, "Each 'breast' has at its peak a megalithic 'nipple,' a prehistoric cairn, perhaps containing burial passages. They have not been excavated" (http://www.voicesofthedawn.com, "City of Shrone" entry).

Danu (pronounced Donna) is the ancient mother goddess of the mythical Tuatha Dé Danann, who brought prosperity to Munster province until their defeat by the Milesians. Danu was venerated throughout Europe, giving her name to many rivers, including the Danube. There is

> "Earth is the ancient Mother, and the hills and mountains, the fertile soil and deep caves are her body. She is the rivers, springs, and lakes—the waters emerging from the underground to fertilize the lands." Delyth, p. 46.

an intriguing association between Anu/Danu and Ste Anne; in Brittany (and elsewhere) places sacred to Ste Anne were often previously sacred to Danu (see *Powerful Places in Brittany*).

We're told that the nearby City of Shrone (Cathair Crobh Dearg), located in the shadow of the Paps, is a very powerful place, a focus of pilgrimage and veneration since Neolithic times, complete with a holy well, cross-inscribed slabs, and an Ogham stone. See http://www.voicesofthedawn.com (QR code on p. 188) and search for City of Shrone to listen to an interview with Dan Cronin, author of *In the Shadow of the Paps*. Also see http://www.goddessalive. co.uk/issue3/issue3.html for an interesting discussion of the Paps.

The Paps can be climbed. See http://climbingire-landsmountains.blogspot.com/2009/10/paps-east.html or http://mountainviews.ie/mv/index.php?mtnindex=125.

Getting There

Drive 17 km (10 mi) southeast of Killarney. The Paps are best viewed from Rathmore on N72 toward Mallow. To get to the City of Shrone, head from Killarney toward Rathmore on N72. A road west of Rathmore leads to the site. (See map on p. 188)

More to Experience

Ring of Kerry

The Iveragh Peninsula is an area of much natural beauty—mountains, bays, and beaches—along with ancient monuments and charming villages. The Ring of Kerry is a popular driving tour, 203 km (126 mi) on N70 that follows the coastline of the Iveragh Peninsula between Killorglin and Kenmare (http://www.ringofkerry-tourism.com/). Killorglin is famous for its Puck Fair in mid August, in which a Billy goat is crowned. The festival was probably originally a Lughnasa celebration (see http://www.puckfair.ie/. The ring road takes you by numerous noteworthy locations, including stone forts, Ogham stones, stone alignments, and lovely beaches.

Skellig Islands

The difficult-to-reach Skellig Islands, site of a medieval monastic settlement established in the sixth century, are 16 km (10 mi) offshore from Slea Head. This UNESCO World Heritage Site can be reached by boat, weather (and courage) permitting, from Portmagee Harbor on Valentia Island, which can be reached by a land bridge from Portmagee. Skellig Michael defines "White Martyrdom," the early Irish Christian practice of retreating to an isolated location

for prayer and solitude. Between ten to twenty monks lived a Spartan existence on this isolated rock—but not so isolated that Vikings didn't raid it on occasion.

Skellig Michael rises abruptly and inhospitably 218 m (600 ft) above the sea. To visit the ruined beehive huts and other remains

The stairway on Skellig Michael

of the ancient monastic settlement, you must climb the 1000-year-old stairway (without rails) that leads from the tiny pier to the top of the barren rock. In the last few years, several tourists have been killed and others injured by falling from the dangerous staircase. If you go, be very careful.

The Skellig Experience visitor's center is located on Valentia Island (http://www.skelligexperience.com) directly opposite the village of Portmagee. It is much easier to get to the center than to the Skelligs. Cross the bridge from Portmagee and the entrance is located on the left hand side of the road (http://www.skelligexperience.com/location.html).

Dingle Peninsula: Gallarus Oratory, Kilmalkedar Church, and Mount Brandon

The Dingle Peninsula in the extreme west of Ireland is rich in heritage. It remains one of the strongest *Gaeltacht* (Gaelic-speaking) areas in Ireland, known as Corca Dhuibhne (from "the followers of Davinia," a Celtic goddess). It is visually stunning, with rough and varied terrain. An L-shaped ridge of mountains on the north is topped with holy Mount Brandon; at 951 m (3121 ft), it is the second-highest mountain in Ireland. The Dingle Peninsula is reached from Tralee.

The peninsula contains a number of ancient monuments, many preserved by the State although others are in private hands, so you may need to pay the landowner a small fee for access. Sites include Iron Age fortifications, beehive huts, early Christian monuments, and Ogham stones. Guidebooks and websites (http://www.dingle-peninsula.ie) describe the peninsula in detail, so we will focus on Gallarus Oratory, Kilmalkedar Church, and Mt Brandon.

Gallarus Oratory (Séipéilín Ghallarais, "The Church of the Place of the Foreigners") N52 10 25 W10 21 13

Plain and unadorned, Gallarus Oratory resembles an up-turned boat. A deep-set, round-headed window lets in light from the east. Austere, simple, and compelling, it provides an archetypal image for the religiosity of early Irish Christians—or at least for their places of worship. (Elyn)

Early Irish churches were usually constructed of timber and, as a result, none survive. Gallarus Oratory, however, was constructed of dry gritstone between the sixth and ninth centuries and still remains watertight and intact. The oratory is approximately 8 m (26 ft) long, 5 m (16 ft) wide, and 5 m (16 ft) high. Because the stones were laid at a slight

Gallarus Oratory

angle, sloping downward on the outside, water runs off the walls. The corbelled roof is formed by the gradual rise of the side walls from the base upward. Dry-stone construction and corbelling have been in use in Ireland since Neolithic times—including at Newgrange—so this church partakes of an ancient tradition. What may be the remains of an ancient stone altar are located beside the church. Outdoors worship was an important part of early Celtic Christianity.

A small private Visitor Center, open June, July, and August, is a short distance from Gallarus Oratory. It provides a video and other information, as well as selling unnecessary tickets to get to the Oratory. The OPW access road is just around the corner and admission is free.

Nearby to the south is an old pilgrimage way (Cosán na Naomh) and modern walking trail that goes up the southwest face of Mount Brandon to an oratory and shrine at the summit, dedicated to St Brendan (see below).

Getting There

The Oratory is 6 km (3.7 mi) northwest of Dingle off R559, between Murreagh and Ballyferriter.

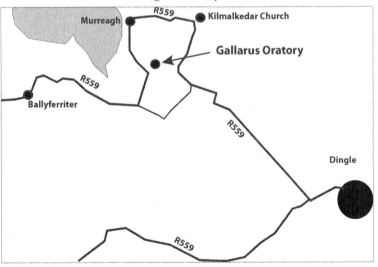

Area map

Kilmalkedar Church N52 11 12 W10 20 14

Kilmalkedar Church (Cill Maolchéadair) is one of the most important ecclesiastical sites on the Dingle Peninsula, built over a pagan center of worship. The name comes from *kil* = cell = church; *maol* = male tonsure; and *ceadair* = cedar of Lebanon, the wood of the true cross. In other words, it is the "Church of the Tonsured Male of the True Cross." It was named for Maolceadair, a saint who died around 640 CE.

The Romanesque church was built in the twelfth century; it remained the parish church for the area until the mid-sixteenth century or possibly later. Although it is partly in ruins, it retains much of interest, including the tympanum and various carvings. In the graveyard outside the church are an early sundial, a large stone cross, and an Ogham stone.

Kilmalkedar Church

Kilmalkedar Church is situated in the foothills of Mount Brandon. A post at the front entry to the church shows a pilgrim, outlined in yellow, with a stocking hat and a curved staff. This indicates that the church is on the pilgrimage route to Mt Brandon. It was the main assembly area for pilgrims before tackling the final stage to the top of the mountain (see below).

Getting There

Drive 8 km (5 mi) northwest of Dingle; signposted on R559 west of Dingle, about 1.6 km (1 mi) past the turn for Gallarus Oratory. (See map on p. 193.)

Mount Brandon

Mt Brandon is a holy mountain associated with St Brendan the Navigator (see p. 295). The mountain is an ancient pagan site, once called Sliabh Daghda or the "Mountain of the Daghda," the father god of the Tuatha Dé Danann. St Brendan of Clonfert is reported to have prayed for three days on top of the mountain, which was later named after him. When at last he fell asleep, he dreamed that an angel

Mount Brandon

came to him and promised to guide him to a beautiful island: Paradise. He set off immediately on his fabled transatlantic journey, sailing from Brandon Creek at the west foot of the mountain.

The annual pilgrimage up the mountain probably replaced an early Lughnasa harvest assembly that took place on the mountain on "Crom Dubh's Sunday," the first Sunday in August (see http://en.wikipedia.org/wiki/Crom_Dubh). Popular in medieval times, the pilgrimage had almost died out in the nineteenth century; the Bishop of Kerry reinstated it in 1868. Pilgrimage to the summit also used to take place on St Brendan's feast day, 16 May. Nowadays, a pilgrimage takes place on St Brendan's Festival Day, the last Sunday in June. Crom Dubh's Sunday—and Lughnasa—have once again become times of great festivity on the Dingle Peninsula, although not on top of Mt Brandon. Check out http://www.dingle-peninsula.ie/calendar.html for details.

Today the old pilgrimage way (Cosán na Naomh) up Mt Brandon has been transformed into a waymarked hiking trail (http://www.discoverireland.com/us/ireland-things-to-see-and-do/listings/product/?fid=FI_70393). The 18 km (11 mi) trail starts at Ventry Strand and passes by the Gallarus Oratory, the Chancellor's House, and Kilmalkedar Church, among other sites. Traditionally, the pilgrimage way ended at the top of the mountain but now the trail finishes at the base at Baile Breac Grotto, apparently because climbing the mountain can be hazardous. For evocative and informative geological descriptions of the mountain, read Chet Raymo's *Climbing Brandon*. (http://www.heritagecouncil.ie/recreation/heritage-council-initiatives/the-pilgrim-paths/cosan-na-naomh/ and http://homepage.eircom.net/~botharpub/activities/mountain.html.)

Getting There

Mt Brandon can be seen from much of the Dingle Peninsula, particularly along R559. Trail maps for the annual
pilgrimage are available from the Heritage Council.

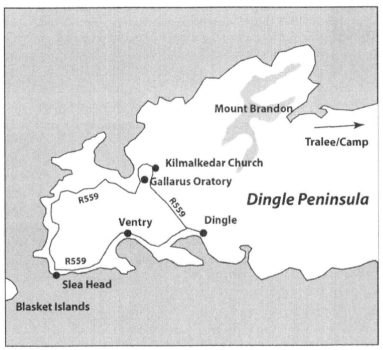

Area map

More to Experience

Dingle Way

The 180 km (110 mi) long Dingle Way hiking trail,
which begins and ends in Tralee, heads west to Camp and

then circles the rest of the peninsula. It takes about 8-9 days to walk. (http://www.dingleway.net).

Blasket Islands

Take a boat trip to the Blasket Islands, 3 km (2 mi) off the Dingle Peninsula. The islands were abandoned in 1953 (http://www.blasketisland.com); the rich and varied literature of the Blasket Islands captures life on this isolated location.

Slea Head

Slea Head is located on the south-facing slopes of Mount Eagle and contains numerous beehive huts and ring forts.

Dingle Town

Dingle town is a center of "trad" music and a pleasant base from which to explore the peninsula. It is home port to one of Ireland's largest fishing fleets and has become a popular tourist resort. Its harbor is home to Fungie, a sociable bottlenose dolphin. You may be able to swim with him, if you make advance arrangements.

Beara Peninsula: Rock Shrine of the Cailleach Beara and Uragh Stone Circle, Gleninchaquin Valley

The Beara Peninsula is named after a local tribe, not a bear. It is located between Kenmare (a good base for both the Beara Peninsula and the Ring of Kerry) to the north and Bantry to the south. Bleak moorland, high mountains, spectacular scenery, and wonderful hikes characterize the peninsula. The Ring of Beara is a 137 km (85 mi) long driving tour, beginning at Kenmare. The Beara Way is a 200 km (124 mi) waymarked path that takes approximately 9-11 days to walk (http://www.bearatourism. com). Both are fine ways to experience this isolated land, once a haven for smugglers. You may want to begin your journey by visiting the tourist information center in Glengarriff.

Cailleach Beara (The Hag of Beara) Stone
N51 42 57 W9 57 47

We could see the Hag of Beara silhouetted on the horizon—a large, lumpy metamorphic rock on the side of a hill, looking out over the water. Perhaps four feet high, the Hag of Beara has been a pilgrimage shrine for centuries. Ancient mother, maker of the hills, islands, waters, mountains—fertile, untameable, bestower of sovereignty—she has left this bit of herself for us to contemplate. I sat on the hillside beside the Hag and realized that I was resting on her body. Eons of time flew by. Life and death took on a new perspective. (Elyn)

The Hag of Beara is said to be the Cailleach Beara turned to stone, waiting here for her consort, Manannán mac Lir, god of the sea. She resides on a ridge overlooking Coulagh

The Hag of Beara silhouetted against Coulagh Bay

Bay at the western end of the Beara Peninsula. We also encounter the Cailleach at Loughcrew (see p. 86) and near Carrowmore (see p. 260). She is present at (and in) many locations in Ireland and the British Isles.

Here, she is a specific goddess who lives in a particular place and is known as the "shaper of the lands." She is also mother of the goddess Áine, whom we encountered at Lough Gur (p. 166). The information plaque at the site describes her as Goddess of Sovereignty.

The Hag of Beara is located near an ancient ruined church, Kilcatherine, which was built over an early Christian monastic settlement "estab-

Despite the usually grim presentation of the Cailleach Beara, a different view is expressed in the following description, collected early last century: "She never brought mud from this puddle to the other puddle/ She never ate food but when she became hungry./ She never went to sleep till she grew sleepy./ She never threw out the dirty water till she brought in clean water." http://www.brigitsforge.co.uk/pilgrimage_to_visit_the_hag_of_beara.htm

> "Rocks and stones are the ancient bones of our natural landscape. For the early people, power adheres to the rocky places. ... Mountains and hills connect the earth to the heavens, they are the body of the ancient Earth Goddess." Delyth, p. 46.

lished by the 'nun' or 'saint' named Caitigern, the cat goddess..." (Roberts, p. 46). A carving resembling a cat's head (or possibly a snake's head) is found over the doorway. Powerful feminine energy is strong in the area.

At other megalithic sites, we have heard of pipers and dancers, parents and children turned to stone for frolicking on the Sabbath. Here, however, the mythic context is different. A powerful goddess—"shaper of the lands"—has been transformed into rock. Rather than being a punishment, this transformation acknowledges a powerful truth about the relationship between creation and the created.

The Hag of Beara is a geological oddity. The lump of metamorphic rock is attached to the land and is natural. According to Jack Roberts, there are no other such extrusions in the landscape, and no other such geological structures in

Meditating near the Hag of Beara

202

the entire southwest region. The Hag is indeed a "shaper of the lands"!

Spend time experiencing the energy that emanates from this ancient, windblasted rock. It is unlike anything else in the area. It is an anomaly that calls attention to itself. Meditate, perhaps make an offering. See whether She will bestow a response upon you.

"All over the Gaelic world in Ireland and Scotland, down to the present age, traditions of the Cailleach, the supernatural female elder, are to be found attached to natural features of the physical landscape—mountains, lakes, rivers, tumuli, caves whose shape she has molded and whose location she has fixed—and feature also in the abundant stories of supernatural encounter between humans and the native otherworld.... In many ways the most prominent of these *cailleacha* is the Cailleach Bhéarra or Supernatural Female Elder ('Hag') of Beara, one of the great peninsulas of the southwest Irish coast." Ó Crualaoich, p. 28-29.

Getting There

The Cailleach Beara is located between Ardgroom and Eyeries but it is on the coastal road. It (or "she") is signposted on the coast road, east of Kilcatherine Point, near Kilcatherine Old Church. Find the turn to Loch Fada, keep on the coast road for another mile and the Hag is on

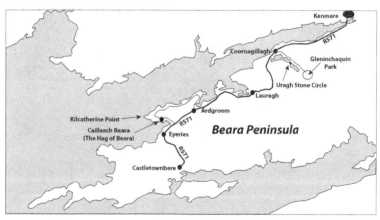

Area map

your left at the top of a steep hill. You may have to cross 20 m of boggy ground to the track, so wear wellies.

Uragh Stone Circle, Gleninchaquin Valley

The small circle (2.4 m or 8 ft in diameter) is composed of five squat stones and a 3 m (10 ft) tall alignment stone. It is in a stunning setting, on a terrace overlooking Lake Gleninchaquin and Inchaquin waterfall, surrounded by glaciated hills with views down the valley and across to Macgillycuddy's Reeks. When we visited Uragh Stone Circle, a trio of musicians was playing Celtic instruments, and the wind plucked the harp strings. It was, indeed, magical.

Getting There

Go southwest from Kenmare toward Lauragh on the Beara Peninsula. Opposite the Peacock Camping Site, you will see a sign directing you to Gleninchaquin. Follow this road for about 6.4 km (4 mi) until you come to a junction. The circle is off to your right. If you keep driving, you'll come to Gleninchaquin Park (fee), with well laid out walking trails. See map on previous page. Also check out http://www.isleofalbion.co.uk/sites/122/uragh.php

Some Sites in Co. Cork

Ardgroom Outer Stone Circle

Ardgroom Outer Stone Circle, Co. Cork, is east of Ardgroom, signposted from R571 inland. Follow the land to the farm gates; you'll see it on the right, overlooking Ardgroom Harbor. Originally it had 11 stones and an outlier. There is an unusual conical hill nearby.

Ballycrovane Ogham Stone

Ballycrovane Ogham Stone, Co. Cork, is the tallest in Ireland and probably an ancient megalith that was later inscribed upon. It is quite impressive, located on a knoll with views over the coast. North of Eyeries: take the coast road north from Eyeries, or leave R571 south of Ardgroom towards Kilcatherine Point and the Cailleach Beara. It is signposted as you continue east to Ballycrovane Harbor.

Drombeg Stone Circle

The Drombeg Stone Circle, also known as "The Druid's Altar," is in a lovely location: a stone terrace that looks to sea. It is a very popular site, so arrive early to avoid the stream of visitors. Dromberg Stone Circle has 17 stones; the most westerly one is recumbent and has cup marks. It is 9 m (30 ft) in diameter. The axial stone in the southwest appears to be in line with the midwinter solstice sunset. Within sight, only 40 m (130 ft) away, are the remains of two stone huts and a *fulacht fiadh*, possibly a communal cooking place, although archeologists have not found any food remains in the vicinity. The site was probably in use up until the fifth century CE. The "kitchen" features a hearth for heating stones, a well, and a trough. Hot stones could have been placed in the water-filled trough, and then meat may have been added and cooked. People lived here, close to the stone circle. Were they guardians of the site? Seasonal visitors? We have no way of knowing.

Coming from the west, the stone circle is signposted off N71 east of Skibbereen, 2.4 km (1.5 mi) east of the village of Glandore (along the southern coast of Co. Cork). Coming from the east, from Clonakilty take the N71 west to Rosscarberry; just after the causeway take a left turn onto the R597, then after about 4 km take a left turn, sign-post-

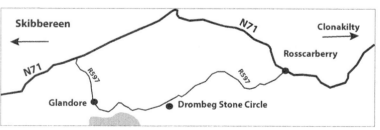

Area map

ed for Drombeg Circle. There is a carpark on your right about 400 m down this road. The circle is a short walk along a track from this carpark.

Gougane Barra (Guágan Barra)

Gougane Barra was the site of the sixth-century hermitage of St Finbarr, founder and first bishop of Cork. It is an ancient pilgrimage site—and we are told it is still a very powerful place, tranquil and serene. The ruins on the island, linked to the mainland by a causeway, date from around 1700, and were erected by another, more modern hermit. The tiny chapel on the island dates from the late nineteenth century and was perhaps influenced by Cormac's Chapel in Cashel (see p. 171). Guágan Barra Forest Park is a scenic driving route, with numerous walking trails. Most of the trees were planted beginning in 1938. http://www.cork-guide.ie/gouganebarra/gouganebarra.html

Getting there

Guágan Barra Forest Park is located 5 km west of Ballingeary on R584 to Bantry, at the Pass of Keimaneigh.

The North, Northwest, and West of Ireland

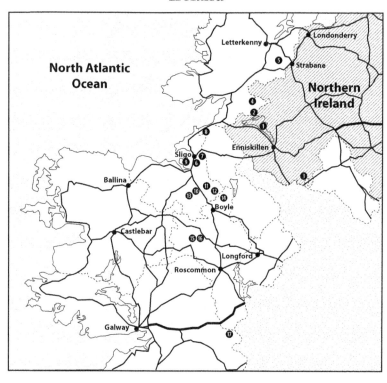

1.	Lough Erne	10.	Carrowkeel
2.	Boa Island	11.	Heapstown Cairn
3.	Crom Estate	12.	Labby Rock
4.	Station Island	13.	Kesh Corann
5.	Beltany Stone Circle	14.	Keadue Holy Well
6.	Tobernalt Holy Well	15.	Rathcroghan Complex
7.	Deerpark Court Cairn	16.	Oweynagat Cave
8.	Creevykeel Court Tomb	17.	Clonfert Cathedral
9.	Knocknarea/Medb's Cairn		

The North of Ireland

In this chapter we describe four powerful places in the north of Ireland that are easily reached from the Boyne Valley or Co. Sligo. Crom Estate and Boa Island are in Co. Fermanagh in Northern Ireland. Station Island (St Patrick's Purgatory) and Beltany Circle are in Co. Donegal in the Republic of Ireland.

Note that the currency in Northern Ireland is British pounds, not Euros.

Other places to experience in the north include the impressive, though heavily reconstructed, Grianán Aileach (Ailigh) Ring Fort, Co. Donegal, near Derry, one of only five Irish locations marked on Ptolemy's second-century-CE map of the world; the beautiful Kilclooney portal dolmen, Co. Donegal (http://www.voicesfromthedawn.com/?p=33); Derryveagh mountains, Co. Donegal; the stunning Slieve League cliffs, the highest in Europe, close to Glencolumcille, southwest Co. Donegal, with its 15 penitential stations and impressive isolated setting (http://www.voices-fromthedawn.com; search for Glen Colum Cille); the Rock of Doon, near Lough Gartan, central Co. Donegal, the ancient inaugural platform of kings, surrounded by rowan trees; nearby Doon Well, an ancient pagan healing well that still has a living well keeper and vigils on New Year's Eve and Mayday; The Burren, at the Co. Cavan/Co. Fermanagh border—not the Burren in Co. Clare—complete with woodland faery walks, dolmens, and stone circles; Beaghmore stone circles, alignments, and cairn, Co. Tyrone. In the east of Northern Ireland, Legananny dolmen, Co. Down, is worth visiting (http://www.voicesfromthedawn.com/?p=86).

Lough Erne, Co. Fermanagh (Northern Ireland)

Lough Erne is actually two connected lakes, created by a broadening of the river Erne. The river flows in a north-westerly direction, first flowing north, then curving west into the Atlantic. The southern of the two lakes is further up the river and is named Upper Lough Erne. It is a warren of twisting channels and islands. The northern lake is Lower Lough Erne, a broad expense of water and islands, popular for fishing and cruising.

The region has been inhabited for thousands of years. Early settlers from Britain and Scandinavia traveled up the Erne in small boats and lived near the banks of the rivers and lakes. Neolithic relics have been found, along with Bronze Age artifacts from 2000 BCE, including spear heads, axes heads, swords, and daggers. Iron Age fragments of gold torcs have been discovered in the area. Ancient Celtic stoneworks dot the countryside, and the ruins of early Christian monasteries are visible on the islands. The area around Lough Erne was and still is an important oak woodlands and wetland wildlife refuge.

Crom Estate N54 10 11 W7 27 01

As we approached the two 1000-year-old yew trees, I saw what looked like a tangled mass of dark green, spreading across the meadow like a huge overgrown bush. Up close, the interwoven trees came into focus. We walked "inside" and stood beneath the sheltering branches. The atmosphere shifted, the air felt more refined. The space within the canopy of the yews is a powerful place, a holy place, a place of stillness and timelessness. Nature is indeed the first temple. (Elyn)

Crom (pronounced "crumb") Estate is just over the border from the Republic of Ireland, on the southeastern shore of Upper Lough Erne. The area is rich in history and prehistory, with evidence extending back 6000 years. The island opposite the Crom Estate National Trust Visitor Center is Inishfendra. Its 400-year-old oak forest is home to the largest colony of nesting herons in Ireland. Nearby Galloon Island was the site of a monastery founded in the sixth century CE by St Tierney. Between Galloon and Wattle Bridge is "The Druids Temple," a megalithic burial ground closed to the public.

The name "Crom" may refer to Crom Cruach (Cromm Crúaich), a pre-Christian Irish fertility and/or solar deity purportedly associated with human sacrifice. His cult image was located in nearby Co. Cavan, and a standing stone identified with him is found in Drumcoo townland, Co. Fermanagh. *Crom* means crooked, bent, or stooped. It is possible that Crom comes from the Phoenician word for "shrubbery of trees"—but that seems a little farfetched.

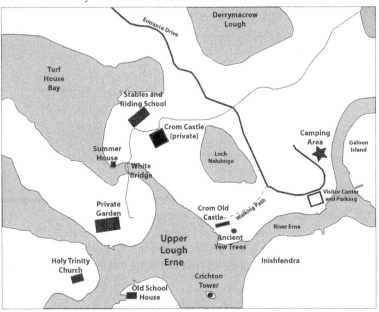

Site plan

Ruins of Crom Old Castle

(If you're interested in pursuing this largely discredited Phoenician connection, check out *Phœnician Ireland*, by Joaquín Lorenzo Villanueva, published 1833/37, available on Google Books.)

Until 1607 the land belonged to the O'Neills and Maguires, who fought against the English Crown and left Ireland after the defeat at Kinsale—a forced migration known as the Flight of the Earls. Legend says that one of the O'Neills came to the yew trees on the estate to bid goodbye to his beloved before he fled to Spain in 1607.

The land was confiscated and granted under the terms of the Plantation of Ulster to Michael Balfour, a Scottish laird. He built Old Crom Castle in 1609-10 but soon sold it. The Old Castle survived several sieges but accidentally burnt down in 1764. The New Castle was designed by Edward Blore, an important architect, and completed in 1838.

The National Trust representative told us that the owners had planned to construct the new castle near the ruins of the old, but the workmen's tools kept disappearing. Finally they decided the area was a "faery ring" and moved the new castle to its current site. William Gilpin beautifully landscaped the grounds, and the area was popular for garden parties and games. The Farmyard, now the Visitor Center, was created in 1835-38 as a model farm. Other developments continued, perhaps as famine relief projects.

Today Crom Estate comprises almost 2000 acres of woodland, wetlands, farmland, and parkland. It is one of Northern Ireland's most important conservation areas, home to the largest surviving oak woodland in Northern Ireland. It provides habitat for a number of rare and endangered species, including plants such as orchids and frogbits, and insects such as hairy dragonflies and butterflies.

One could spend several days at Crom Estate, walking nature trails, boating on the river, exploring the walled garden, visiting reconstructed buildings, perhaps staying in one of the holiday cottages. But our visit was more focused. We came with one purpose only: to see the 1000-year-old mated yew trees, reputed to be the oldest in Ireland.

Yew trees were sacred to the Celts, associated with healing, magic, communicating with the ancestors, death, and rebirth. The entire tree (berries, leaves, and wood) is poisonous, but modern researchers have discovered that taxol, which comes from the bark of the yew tree, can be used to fight cancer. Sometimes, the tree appears to bleed, emitting a blood-red sap. In hot weather the tree gives off a vapor, which shamans may have inhaled to initiate Otherworld journeys. Its wood was also used to make longbows that were both strong and flexible. Carving Ogham script spells on yew was powerful magic. http://www.ancient-yew.org/mi.php/trees-in-mythology/79 and http://www.whitedragon.org.uk/articles/yew.htm.

To visit the yew trees at Crom Estate, follow the path behind the Visitor

Approaching the ancient yews

Center and the holiday cottages. A sign on the left points to "Old Castle"; follow the gravel/shale tree-lined trail. You may note an energy shift when you pass through the wooden gate on the left, as if you had crossed an invisible boundary. The trail becomes a grassy path and crosses a large meadow. At the far end you will see the ruins of the Old Castle, complete with towers and a wall added in the nineteenth century to make the vista more romantic. Keep walking toward the ruins.

Note the oaks that form a large circle around the meadow. This is what is known as the "faery ring." The oaks were planted 400 and 200 years ago. Although the trees are comparatively recent, we wondered whether there was an earlier nemeton at the site. After all, the archeological evidence proves the area was inhabited for thousands of years, and folklore associates the area with otherworldly forces. The New Castle (not open for visitors, although one can rent

Elyn, inside the ancient yews

its West Wing) is visible to the right, peeking through the trees.

Continue walking to the ruins. You will see a sign on the left. Turn through the gap, look left, and you'll see a large mass of dark green foliage. This is the two, nearly 1000-year-old, entwined male and female yew trees. The female yew is to the east of the taller male yew. Upper Lough Erne is to your right as you walk to the trees.

Approach the yew trees politely, just as you would a stone circle or a respected elder. Remember ECOLOGY and BLESSING (p. 5). You might choose to walk around the yew trees several times in a spiraling clockwise direction. As you draw closer, you might sense concentric rings of energy, the "aura" of the trees. Ask permission to enter and, if it is granted, walk toward the sacred space created by these two ancient beings. Follow the path between them and into their sheltering embrace. Low-lying branches sink to the ground, weaving over and under each other. Higher up, tree limbs cross and criss-cross, forming an elaborate pattern that may remind you of a Celtic interweave motif.

Standing under the protective canopy, breathe slowly and center yourself. See what you feel, what you hear, what you notice. You are in the presence of two very old beings, one male, one female, who have intertwined over the centuries.

Inside the sacred enclosure formed by these ancient trees, Elyn felt so good she was practically purring, and Gary found the energy uplifting and powerful. We both felt our crown chakras open. We think the sweet, harmonious energy results from the balanced polarity of the masculine and feminine trees, mated for nearly 1000 years.

Standing in the center, words come to Elyn: "Curving, intertwining sanctuary of age and green, spiraling trunks and branches, moss green, red flesh showing through peeling bark. Sweet, so sweet, nature's sacred enclosure, masculine, feminine, embracing each other."

Gary dowsed a crossing of fire and water lines in the center between the trees, an underground earth-energy pattern often found beneath the altar in Christian churches. Try to find the crossing and stand on it. Shift your position a few feet in either direction and see if you notice a difference. Does one place feel better to you than another?

Getting There

Crom Estate is 5 km (3 mi) west of Newtownbutler on the eastern shore of Upper Lough Erne. It is open from mid March through September. The National Trust Visitor Center includes an interesting museum and a pleasant tea-room and shop. Entry fee or National Trust membership. http://www.nationaltrust.org.uk/main/w-cromestate. If you plan to visit a number of National Trust sites in Northern Ireland and England, you might want to purchase an annual pass.

Although the New Castle is not open to the public, the West Wing is now available as a luxury holiday rental (http://www.cromcastle.com/).

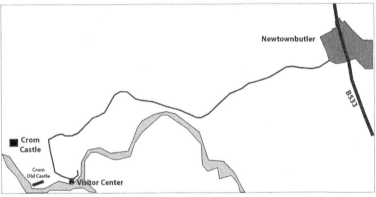

Area map

Caldragh Cemetery, Boa Island
N54 30 29 W7 52 09

Moss-covered stones and broken boulders thrust up from ill-kept grass; a two-faced stone figure stares in opposite directions. The statue stands guard, sheltered under a recently erected green awning. A smaller stone figure sits just outside the shelter, apparently not worthy of protection. Why are these pagan-looking figures in a Christian graveyard? A fence encloses the burial ground, keeping something in—or something out—I'm not sure what or which. It is a moody, evocative place, with shifting energy shimmering around the edges. (Elyn)

The first thing to realize is that things aren't what they appear to be. Although Boa Island is an island, you can drive directly onto it from the shore. Its name comes not from the constricting snake but from Badhbh, a Celtic war goddess. The stone Janus figure in Caldragh Cemetery has nothing to do with the Roman god Janus—and might be feminine. The Lusty Man Idol next to it isn't lusty: it's named after Lustymore Island, where it was discovered. And the Christian graveyard might, in fact, be something else: the remnants of a megalithic site. At least that's how it felt to us.

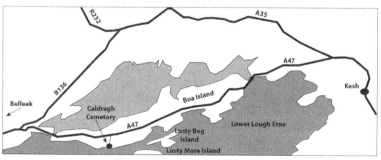

Boa Island

Boa Island (Inis Badhbha in Irish, meaning Badhbha's Island) is located near the north shore of Lower Lough Erne. Narrow and 8 km (5 mi) long, it is the largest island in Lough Erne and is connected by causeways to the mainland. The Irish Celts called battlefields "the land of Badb," and the *Annals of Four Masters* reports many battles in the Lough Erne area in the 600s. An ancient, denuded cairn is found on the southern tip of the island at Inishkeeragh Bridge.

The island's current claim to fame is Caldragh Cemetery with its two Scheduled Historic Monuments, the Boa Island Janus statue and the Lusty Man Idol. The grey, white-lichen-spotted Janus figure is two sided, hence its name, referring to the two-faced Roman god Janus. It does not represent Janus, however, so it would be more accurate to refer to it as a bilateral figure. It is 73 cm (29 in) high, 45 cm (18 in) wide on its two broader surfaces, and 30 cm (12 in) wide on its two narrow surfaces.

The statue is generally thought to represent a bearded pagan god or god-hero, but it might represent a goddess. Given its location on Badhbha's Island, named after a Celtic goddess of war, it is certainly possible that the statue is feminine. One writer (http://www.megalithicireland.com/Boa%20Island.htm) has suggested that the east side is masculine and includes a pointed penis, and the west side, with its protruding tongue, is feminine. Whatever else it may be, the Janus statue is obviously a kind of Rorschach test.

The Boa Island Janus Figure

The details of the carving are hard to decipher, but most notable are the two large flat heads, pointed-oval in shape, with staring, almond-shaped eyes and half open mouths. They appear to have entwined hair, visible as cross-hatching on the narrow sides. The heads are not identical although they are similar. A depression between the tops of the heads is often filled with mementos and offerings left by visitors. Each torso has two limbs, usually assumed to be arms, which cross in front of a double incised line, which may be a belt. The Janus statue is placed on a cement pedestal. Lying on the ground next to the figure is its lower section, recently found half-buried beside the statue. This part of the statue has two hands with elongated fingers.

The Janus figure might date to the Iron Age or, possibly, be as recent as the ninth century. It bears some similarity to the sculpted ninth- to tenth-century figures found at White Island, 5 km (3 mi) away by boat to the southeast (see p. 221). As far as is known, it has always been located at this unlikely spot: an early Christian cemetery in use from 400-800 CE. But what is it doing here? What does it mean?

The grey, white-lichen-spotted Lusty Man Idol was brought to the cemetery in 1939 from an early Christian cemetery on nearby Lustymore Island. It is smaller (70 cm/27.5 in high), one-sided, but equally enigmatic, and it has a similar pointy chin. Apparently cut off at the waist, it sits on a low stone pedestal. It has one eye fully carved and the other blank, perhaps blind.

The Lusty Man Idol

Celtic legends describe a number of war goddesses who are blind in the left eye, and Ireland has a long tradition of deities/heroines/images with one eye closed looking inward at inner wisdom and the other open looking outward at the world. Perhaps, like the Janus figure, the Lusty Man Idol is not masculine but is feminine. Or perhaps it's a Sheela-na-gig, its arms and hands directed towards its missing genitals. Or, if the Lusty Man Idol was carved in the Christian era, the "blind" or "closed" eye might be a reference to Matthew 5:29, "If your right eye causes you sin, pluck it out...." Or the apparent blindness might simply be the result of damage.

The Lusty Man Idol is more worn than the Janus figure and is thought to be older. Both of these figures may be Iron Age Celtic images, but if so, they are unique. They may be early Christian images, created at a time when pagan and Christian imagery were mixed together. But what are they doing in a Christian cemetery?

It is easy to get so involved in puzzling over these figures that one forgets to "be present" to them and to experience the power of the place. Contemplate the figures and notice what you feel. Perhaps you'll feel nothing other than curiosity.

Pay attention to your surroundings. Enclosed by hazel trees and a low fence, surrounded by water, the ancient cemetery is a jumble of broken, moss-covered stones poking out of the grass. We noticed one new tombstone, white and bright in comparison to the others.

A number of the large stones in the graveyard did not appear to be tombstones; several had interesting cup-like markings. Gary dowsed that this was an ancient

Matthew 6:22-23 (King James Version). "6:22 The light of the body is the eye: if therefore thine eye be single, thy whole body shall be full of light. 6:23 But if thine eye be evil, thy whole body shall be full of darkness. If therefore the light that is in thee be darkness, how great is that darkness!"

Mystery at the edge of the cemetery

pre-Christian ceremonial site. If he is correct, perhaps some of these stones are the remains of a 2300 BCE court tomb, combining ceremony and burial. If so, this site has been a place for the dead for millennia, eventually morphing into an early Christian burial site that was still in use as recently as 2007.

Elyn noticed something hazy hanging in the air just beyond the fence toward the lake, to the right of a big tree. Was it a guardian? A portal into another dimension? She stood between two large boulders, one with a cup hole, the other without. Was she standing in a "thin place," where it is easy to cross from one reality to another? With a shiver, she moved away. She wondered whether the statues were intended to draw attention away from what was really going on—or whether they were erected there because of the spooky energies. A friend later described a similar experience at the site. Caldragh Cemetery is a strange, evocative place, dreamlike in setting and in interpretation.

Getting There

Boa Island is 33 km (20 mi) northwest of Enniskillen on A47 (Kesh-Belleek) road. It is 10 km (6 mi) west of Kesh at the northern end of the Lower Lough Erne. The cemetery is signposted off A47 about 1.6 km (1 mi) west of Lusty Beg Island. Drive slowly so as not to

Sign to the cemetery

miss the sign to Caldragh Cemetery; turn, drive down a narrow lane, and park. The graveyard is through the wooden gate to the left of a building.

More to Experience

White Island

The ruined Romanesque church on White Island is famous for the eight peculiar carvings, including a possible Sheela-na-gig, set into its north wall. These ninth-to tenth-century carvings are interesting decorations but nothing more. The ruined church didn't seem like a powerful place, but after we walked rapidly three times around the exterior walkway, we could see energy rising like heat waves from the top of the stone walls. A huge thorn tree near the dock is worth visiting, and the island itself has a lovely feeling.

Getting there: Ferries leave the Castle Archdale Marina in summer for the island. The brief (15 minute) journey is quite scenic. Fee for ferry.

Lower Lough Erne

A tour of Lower Lough Erne is a pleasant option, beginning in Enniskillen with its famous castle; then moving on to Devenish Island with its important medieval monastery, originally founded in the sixth century by St Molaise, and impressive round tower; then Castle Archdale Country Park and a visit to White Island; then Boa Island; then Castle Caldwell Forest Park; and ending in Belleek, famous for its pottery.

Cairns and Alignments

Numerous cairns and alignments dot the area. This ritual landscape is said to form a sort of amphitheater opening southwestwards onto Lough Erne and Boa Island (Halpin and Newman, p. 169). Drumskinny, Co. Fermanagh, has a stone circle that originally had 39 stones, an alignment, and a cairn. Despite being restored, the place still feels very active. It is located 11.5 km (7 mi) south of Castlederg, Co. Tyrone, off B72 (Kesh-Castlederg). Another complex at Montiaghroe townland, 1.5 km to the south, includes four stone circles and various standing stones and alignments. Detailed directions are needed to see all of them (http://www.megalithic.co.uk/article.php?sid=354).

Station Island and Beltany Stone Circle, Co. Donegal (Republic of Ireland)

Station Island/St Patrick's Purgatory, Lough Derg N54 36 29 W7 52 17

I have no plans to go to Purgatory when I die, but the opportunity to visit St Patrick's Purgatory while I live was too good to pass up. A boatman waited to take us across the choppy, peat-dark waters of Lough Derg to the tiny island. I admit I was relieved that the boatman bore no resemblance to Charon, the mythic Greek ferryman who conveys the souls of the departed across the River Styx. But appearances can be deceiving. You never can be sure. Soon we reached St Patrick's Purgatory, which barely rises above the rippling surface of the lake. The island is completely covered with religious buildings. Inexplicably, tears filled my eyes: I had arrived. But where? (Elyn)

St Patrick's Purgatory, AKA Purgatorium Sancti Patricii, AKA Lough Derg, AKA Station Island, is not a place you go to by accident. It's at the end of a dead-end road, no pun intended. Only about two acres in area, the name "Station

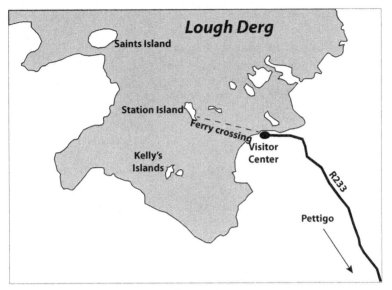

Area map

Island" comes from the Latin *statio*, a word associated with penitential "post of duty"—for example, the Stations of the Cross followed during Lent. At Lough Derg, "station" refers to the specific set rituals (prayers, circumambulations, etc.) performed at the six stone "penitential beds" (the reconstructed remains of medieval monastic cells or beehive oratories) dedicated to different saints. The term also refers to the pilgrimage itself, as in "going on station."

Some say the name of the lake, "Lough Derg," comes from the Irish *deirc* and refers to "the lake of the cave." Others say that the name of the lake (*dearg* or red) comes from the blood of the great serpent or demon mother that St Patrick slew in the waters. One legend reports that Corra, a warrior aspect of the Celtic triple goddess, called Patrick to the lake, turned into a water serpent, and swallowed him. "It took two days and nights for him to cut himself free, killing her in the process" (Meehan, p. 104). Hence, Patrick experienced a kind of death and rebirth in the lake, along with destroying a female representative of the ancient religion.

Why call the island St Patrick's Purgatory? One story relates that Jesus showed St Patrick a cave on the island where he saw the torments of the Otherworld. Another, that Patrick fasted for 40 days on the island and was given a vision of purgatory. As a result, the place became known as St Patrick's Purgatory and people

"Others say it was Fionn mac Cumhaill's son, Conan, or even Fionn himself who killed the serpent. Whatever his name, the hero is swallowed by the Great Swallower, Corra or Caoranach, and returns to the womb or underworld from where he is reborn" (Meehan, p. 105).

believed they could be purged of their sins there. The story (if not the island itself) may have inspired Dante's famous Divine Comedy. Other legends declare that St Patrick and the Druids had their final confrontation inside the island's cave. No proof exists that St Patrick ever visited the island in the fifth century, but there is a strong tradition that St Dabheoc, a local abbot, established or presided over a monastery on the island during the lifetime of St Patrick.

Whatever its origins, St Patrick's Purgatory has been famous since at least the twelfth century as a center of pilgrimage. One story relates that in 1152, Devorguilla, wife of Tiernan O'Rourke of Breffny, ran away with Dermot Mac Murrough while her husband was on pilgrimage to Lough Derg. The aftermath of their one-year elopement was

1666 drawing of Station Island

Approaching Station Island

the devastating Anglo-Norman invasion of Ireland (see pp. 18-19).

Lough Derg gained international fame with the story of Knight Owein, recorded in the mid twelfth century by Brother H. of Saltery, England. Knight Owein reportedly entered St Patrick's Purgatory to do penance for his many grievous sins. He had been warned that many had entered the cave but never returned. Inside the cave he wandered at length, experiencing torments and visions of horrific punishment. Eventually he crossed a bridge from hell to paradise and re-emerged purged of sin twenty-four hours later.

The story became widely popular. It was written at a time when Christian theology was placing increasing importance on purgatory as a place of on-going purification in the "next" world. Rather than being understood metaphorically, it was taken as describing a physical location. St Patrick, after all, had entered purgatory, and so had Knight Owein—and so could other pilgrims journeying to St

Patrick's Purgatory in Lough Derg.

The cave or pit may have originally served as a traditional Irish sweathouse where people would come to inhale medicinal smoke, much like a modern sauna. If so, the *purgatorium* in the name of

the island would have originally referred to purging and cleansing. This would suggest that the cave was a sacred place for healing long before it became a physical location for Christian Purgatory.

In the twelfth century, nearby Saints Island was taken over by Augustinian canons, who made it the mandatory reception center for the increasingly popular pilgrimage to the cave on Station Island. No one could enter the latter

Penitential Beds with the bell tower and St Mary's Church in the background

The Basilica

without passing through the former. There has been some suggestion that the original cave to Purgatory was located on Saints Island but that seems unlikely; rather, a second cave (perhaps for "overflow") was apparently opened on Saints Island but closed in 1497 by papal decree.

In 1632 the pilgrimage was suppressed by the Privy Council for Ireland, and the Anglican Bishop of Clogher supervised the leveling of the buildings on the island, including destroying the original cave. Further destruction took place in 1680, and fines were imposed in 1704 for going on pilgrimage to Lough Derg. Despite all odds and lengthy prohibition, the pilgrimage continued.

Contemporary barefoot pilgrims engage in a three-day pilgrimage in which they fast, keep vigil, repeat the Pattern, and celebrate sacramental rites. As many as 30,000 pilgrims, many of them young, come to the island between June and mid-August to undergo these ascetic practices. In the twelfth century, the pilgrimage ritual included up to fifteen days of prayer and

Statue of the Virgin and the Bell Tower

fasting, so although the modern pilgrimage is intense, it is less strenuous than it once was.

> Notes on a pilgrimage to Station Island: "Crossing the waters of death and rebirth. Despair. Exultation." Elyn

Many local Roman Catholic churches organize at least one trip a year to Lough Derg. The pilgrimage begins with parishioners fasting at home, then traveling together by bus with friends and the parish priest. En route, pilgrims repeat the rosary, "Hail Marys," and other prayers, so they are in a heightened religious state of mind even before they get on the boat to be ferried across the waters to Station Island.

The pilgrimage season is in summer, but the island is used throughout much of the year. As we wandered around the island in late September, we met several friendly staff members and an ebullient group of young people on a week-long spiritual-development retreat. Lough Derg is available for group retreats, conferences, and corporate events.

With so much history behind it, so many centuries of purgatorial associations, so much fierce determination to continue the pilgrimage despite religious oppression, we expected Station Island to be a very powerful place. Expectations can be dangerous. We don't know what others will experience, but we were largely unmoved when we paid a brief visit there out of season. It's true, Elyn felt teary-eyed when we arrived, but that had more to do with being ferried across the wind-swept water to a tiny bit of land and then being warmly welcomed with tea and cookies.

The setting is impressive: a tiny island, barely holding itself above the waters of the lake, covered with religious buildings and the evocative remains of medieval cells or huts. The fourteen stained-glass windows depicting the Stations of the Cross in the modern (1931) octagonal basilica are stunning. The Church of Mary is intimate and sweet. The outdoor labyrinth with a separate entrance and exit is confusing. The sound of water lapping against the edges of the buildings is disturbing.

Perhaps we expected to encounter demons, or a gaping entrance to purgatory, instead of a well-organized Catholic religious establishment. Although we didn't find the island a powerful place, pilgrims have been drawn to Lough Derg for centuries to willingly undergo great personal deprivation and intense spiritual practices. We would imagine that their experiences on the island make it an increasingly powerful place. Just because we didn't experience this power doesn't mean it isn't there.

Getting There

Station Island, close to Lough Derg's southern shore, is about 6.5 km (4 mi) north of the village of Pettigo in Co. Donegal via R233. Station Island is reached by boat from the jetty. To participate in the three-day pilgrimage between 1 June and 13 August, no advance booking is necessary. One can attend a much-less arduous one-day retreat in May, late August, and September; advance booking is required. It is sometimes possible to visit the island off-season without attending a retreat, but arrangements must be made in advance. Fees. Contact info@lough-derg.org or go to http://www.loughderg.org.

A reconstructed medieval Irish pilgrim path follows a 10 km (6 mi) circular path from the Station Island Visitor Center on the shore to near Saints Island. The booklet "Medieval Irish Pilgrim Paths No, 3, Lough Derg" describes the route and is available from http://www.heritage-council.ie/recreation/publications/.

Entrance to the Visitor Center

Beltany Stone Circle N54 50 59 W7 36 16

How you arrive at a powerful place matters. For example: you drive half an hour to a parking lot, hop out, walk through a gate, and you are at your destination. But are you really there? Or, you drive half an hour to a parking lot, hop out, and walk ten minutes up a tree-lined path, woods on either side. You see a clearing in the distance and what looks like boulders scattered on the ground. You take a deep breath and prepare yourself. You draw closer and reach the flat top of the hill. Suddenly the jumbled bits and pieces of stone are silhouetted against the horizon. They coalesce into a circle. Cardinal directions fall into place. You are there. You are really *there. (Elyn)*

The Beltany Stone Circle (from *Baal Tine* or Baal's Fire) in Co. Donegal is one of the best-preserved circles in Ireland—but it might not be a circle. It might be the remains of a cairn that was once surrounded by kerbstones. The view in all directions is impressive, and the sheep wandering among the stones create a very picturesque scene. The fence-line to the left as you walk up to the circle runs generally north/south.

The circle currently consists of 64 stones of many shapes

Tom FourWinds describes the circle as fitting "snuggly on the top of the hill like a big stone crown" http:// www.megalithomania.net/ show/site/1171/beltany_ tops_stone_circle.htm, retrieved Feb. 19, 2011.

and sizes, varying in height from 30 cm (12 in) to over 2 m (6 ft). At one time there were at least 80 stones. The circle is 137 m (450 ft) in circumference and about 44 m (144 ft) in diameter. It is usually dated around 2000 BCE, but some researchers think it is more recent (1400-800 BCE) and that it is the remains of a large cairn. A

The Beltany Stone Circle

carved stone head from 400 BCE - 400 CE was found at the site, which seems to indicate it continued to be an important site for many centuries. For a 3D view, go to http://www.lookaroundireland.com/donegal/beltony.php.

Within the circle of stones, an earth platform is raised about 70 cm (2 ft) to 1 m (3 ft) above the surrounding land. This platform is filled with various hummocks and depres-

sions, possibly the remains of a tumulus and certainly the remains of disruptive amateur excavations in the early twentieth century. It is possible that some of the stones from the tumulus (if such it was) were scattered around the inner circumference of the stone circle/kerbstones. White quartz rocks are strewn on the ground.

The stone head

232

There may be several astronomical alignments. A nearly 2 m (6 ft) high outlier is 20 m to the southeast, and an upright, triangular stone carved with cup marks is in the east-northeast. The cup-marked stone and the largest stone in the southwest quadrant of the circle align with Tullyrap, a hill 8 km (5 mi) away, where the sun rises on 1 May. Mayday is the cross-quarter festival of Bealtaine, which marks the beginning of summer and for which the circle appears to be named.

However, if this megalithic monument was originally a tumulus surrounded by kerbstones, what do we make of the apparent Bealtaine alignment? There would have been a lot of earth blocking the view between those two stones, making it unlikely the alignment was intentional. Perhaps the tumulus originally opened in that direction? Or perhaps the alignment stones were moved into position at a later date? Tradition states this was a stone circle used at Bealtaine, so perhaps there never was a tumulus. Much remains a mystery.

Gary and a friend dowsed the circle and found a strong energy line running more or less northwest to southeast. Elyn found a powerful vortex near the center of the circle. She kept feeling turned around directionally and felt disoriented.

Remember to ask permission before entering a stone circle, even if the circle seems broken and disturbed.

Beltany Stone Circle from an outlying stone

Spend time getting to know the stones and their setting. Enjoy the expansive views. Experience the outlier, the orientation of the circle toward Bealtaine (1 May). Walk around the outside, walk around the inside, noticing the different shapes and carvings on some of the stones. Is this a circle with a badly excavated center or the remains of a huge tumulus? Do you get a sense of the ancient Fire Festival that might have been held here? Don't hurry. Let the stones reveal themselves to you. See if you can hear the stories they have to tell.

Getting There

The entrance gate

From Letterkenny, drive 13 km (8 mi) southeast to Raphoe. Beltany Stone Circle is 3 km (2 mi) south of Raphoe (originally "Rath Bhoth," the name for an Iron

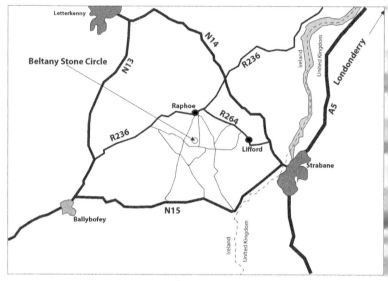

Area map

Age fort). In Raphoe town square, take the road that runs beside the Mason's Hall, painted blue at one time, south toward Castlefinn (signposted). Follow the signposts for 2.5 km (1.5 mi) and park at the Department of Agriculture Food and Fuel Development Potato Center. Follow the wide gravel path to the right through the trees for about 400 m (1/4 mi). The gentle uphill walk will take about 5-10 minutes. At the clearing at the top of Tops Hill is more signage.

Northwest

"Yeats Country," Tobernalt Holy Well, Deerpark (Magheraghanrush) Court Cairn, and Creevykeel Court Tomb, Co. Sligo

Part of WB Yeats' evocative poem "The Stolen Child" is set at Glencar Waterfall. I wanted to experience what inspired him—perhaps, even, be spirited away by the faeries he describes: "Come away, O human child!/ To the waters and the wild/ With a faery, hand in hand,/ For the world's more full of weeping than you can understand." Eagerly, I hurried up the well-kept path that leads to the tumbling waterfall. The cascading waters beckoned, splashing and dancing down the hillside, dropping far into the pool below. I imagined Yeats being lulled into fantasy by the sound of water, the rustle of ferns. But perhaps his poetic image was no fantasy—perhaps his was a truer vision of the waterfall than I could summon up, distracted by the numerous visitors strolling up and down the trail. (Elyn)

"Yeats Country"

Co. Sligo is a haunting county, filled with evocative locations and impressive scenery. It is one of five counties in the ancient province of Connacht and is situated on the northwest coast of Ireland, opening onto the Atlantic Ocean. It shares a border with Donegal to the north, Mayo to the west, Leitrim to the east, and Roscommon to the southeast. There is an airport 8 km (5 mi) west of Sligo Town (http://www.sligoairport.com) and train service from Dublin to Sligo. You can rent a car at the airport in Sligo or rent a car elsewhere in Ireland and drive to Sligo (see http://www.sligoheritage. com/ for general information).

Co. Sligo has numerous important prehistoric sites, including Medb's Cairn on top of Knocknarea and the megalithic cemeteries at Carrowmore and Carrowkeel. It also has

Medb's Cairn on Knocknarea

a more contemporary attraction: the Nobel-prize-winning William Butler Yeats (1865-1939), Ireland's best-known poet, spent long summer holidays in the county. He called Sligo "the Land of Heart's Desire." For many, Co. Sligo is known as "Yeats Country," although music fans know it as "Coleman County," in recognition of the fiddler Michael Coleman, who played an important role in the revival of traditional ("trad") Irish music.

Why devote most of a chapter of *Powerful Places in Ireland* to "Yeats Country"? WB Yeats was not only a poet and dramatist; he was also a leading member of the Irish Literary Revival movement and the Abbey Theatre, founded for the performance of Irish and Celtic drama. He was fascinated by the folktales he heard during his summer holidays in Co. Sligo. Myths and legends strongly influenced his writing, and he collected Irish folklore and published it, making it known (and respectable) to a larger audience. He was also a practicing esotericist—a hermeticist, a member

WB Yeats

of the Golden Dawn, and a student of Hinduism, Theosophy, spiritualism, and the occult. In 1896 he co-founded the esoteric Order of Celtic Mysteries. Thus, his mythic-laden descriptions of places and land, of mystical encounters with other Beings, should be considered as more substantive than simply "poetic license" or literary devices.

Yeats was born into an Anglo-Irish Protestant family at a time when the Anglo-Irish Ascendency was in decline. He went on to become a spokesperson for Irish nationalism and cultural independence. Although he was born in Co. Dublin, his family soon moved to England. As a youth, he spent long summers with relatives at Elsinore Lodge on Rosses Point, Co. Sligo. In later years, he drew extensively upon the landscape and folklore of the region in his writing. He wrote that "In a sense, Sligo has always been my home," and he wanted to buried there, in the shadow of Benbulben. He died in France, but nine years later his body was brought back to Co. Sligo and buried in Drumcliff churchyard.

A Journey around "Yeats Country"

We propose a clockwise driving tour of Yeats Country as a way to experience the power of Yeats' mystical vision and the power of the land that nurtured that vision. This pilgrimage of sorts begins in Sligo, a pleasant town with a thriving arts scene and numerous references to Yeats, including the Yeats Memorial Building (see http://www.sligotown.net/walkingtour.shtml for an excellent map).

An appropriate way to begin your journey in Sligo (#1) is to visit Michael Quirke's quaint shop on Wine Street. Once a butcher, Michael now devotes himself full time to carving naïf wood figures based on Celtic myths and legends while regaling visitors with Irish stories and poetry.

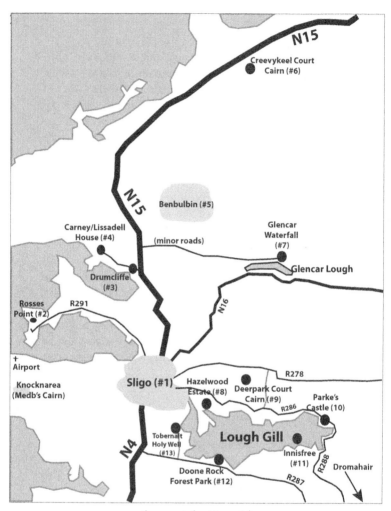

Area map (not to scale)

On second thought, if you begin at Michael's, you might not journey any further that day.

When you do manage to get away, drive northwest on N15, then R291, about 8 km (5 mi) to Rosses Point (#2), a sandy peninsula projecting into Drumcliff Bay. Yeats and his brother Jack (a well-known painter) spent many sum-

Michael Quirke

mers with their cousins at Elsinore Lodge at Rosses Point. The pirate captain Black Jack, who supposedly still haunts the ruined building, built the lodge. Wonderful sunsets are often visible from the carpark at the end of the point (see http://rossespoint-shanty.com).

Drive further on N15 to Drumcliff (#3) (AKA Drumcliffe; from Droim Chliabh, meaning "Ridge of the Baskets") to see the evocative, tree-shaded church cemetery with Yeats' grave, the ninth-century (or eleventh-century, depending on your source) high cross, and the lovely swan-shaped door handles of the early nineteenth-century Church of Ireland chapel. Yeats' great-grandfather was rector there from

1811-1846. The high cross has an interesting depiction of Adam and Eve with a tree and serpent carved on the east side; there are also interlaces, exotic animals, and mythical beasts. Across the road are the ruins of a round tower. St Colmcille founded a monastery in 575 CE at the site near the Drumcliff River.

In "Under Ben Bulben" Yeats wrote,

Yeats' grave

"Under bare Ben Bulben's head
In Drumcliff churchyard Yeats is laid.
An ancestor was rector there
Long years ago, a church stands near,
By the road an ancient cross.
No marble, no conventional phrase;
On limestone quarried near the spot
By his command these words are cut:
Cast a cold eye
On life, on death.
Horseman, pass by."

Yeats' grave is in the cemetery to the side of the chapel. The simple headstone is inscribed with the enigmatic epitaph from the poem: "Cast a cold eye/ On life, on death./ Horseman, pass by."

Spend time in the graveyard, under Benbulben's mountainous shadow, and sense the energies of the land. Pay attention to Benbulben's intense, somewhat wild presence. You might want to climb it later in your journey.

A pleasant café and craft shop are next to the church, if you want to take a break.

Next, follow signposts north of Drumcliff that point west to Carney and Lissadell House (#4), where the Gore-Booth sisters, Eva and Constance, lived and where Yeats spent time as a guest. Constance, later Countess Markievicz, devoted herself to the Nationalist cause and took part in the 1916 Easter Rising. Nicknamed "the People's Countess," she was condemned to death. Later reprieved, she was the first woman elected to the House of Commons in Westminster. She never took her seat in London; instead, she chose to represent her constituency in helping to form the first *Dáil Éireann* (lower house of the Irish Parliament) in Dublin. The Neoclassical mansion was built in 1830 and is gradually being restored; it is no longer open to the public (http://www.lissadellhouse.com).

Continue on to Benbulben (#5) (AKA Ben Bulben), part of the Dartry mountain range. Created by glaciers, Benbulben is 526 m (1730 ft) high, with a dramatic, west-facing escarpment. The massive, flat-topped limestone hill is central to many Irish legends and poems.

Benbulben plays an important role in the story of how St Colmcille (St Columba) was banished from Ireland. According to *The Annals of the Four Masters,* St Colmcille copied a Psalter (a book containing the Book of Psalms) belonging to Finian of Moville, who had been his teacher. When Finian requested the copy be returned, Colmcille adamantly refused. The High King of Ireland, Diarmuid Mac Cerbhaill, of the southern Uí Neills, was consulted, and he handed down the following decision: "To every cow its calf and to every book its copy."

Nonetheless, Colmcille, a member of the northern Uí Neills of Connacht, refused to return the copied Psalter. In 561 the armies of the High King and the southern Uí Neills met the warriors of Connacht and the northern Uí Neills in pitched battle on the slopes of Benbulben. The battle became known as the Battle of the Books at Culdreimhne. It is said that Diarmuid's Druids worked magic, but an angel aided Colmcille to win the battle, in which 3000 were slain. Perhaps this is a veiled description of Christianity conquering the native Celtic religion.

The story would have ended there, but Colmcille was stricken with remorse for all the deaths he had provoked. He traveled to Inishmurray (see below) and confessed to St Molaise. St Molaise banished Colmcille to travel "out of sight of Ireland" and convert more people than had died in the battle. Colmcille sailed to Iona, Scotland, and began his successful missionary career. (See p. 30 in *Powerful Places in Scotland* for more on Iona.)

Another Benbulben story tells of the demise of Diarmuid, who had eloped with Gráinne. The jilted Fionn mac

Cumhaill eventually sent Diarmuid to his death by magically luring him onto the side of Benbulben at night. As prophesized, Diarmuid was attacked by a wild boar. Water from a nearby holy well would have healed Diarmuid, but three times Fionn delayed in bringing it until it was too late.

Trails lead to the top of Benbulben, but beware of treacherous stones. Don't even think of climbing the dangerous north side, rocky and whipped by the Atlantic storms and winds. The south-facing side slopes more gently and is easier.

From Benbulben, take a megalithic detour to Creevykeel Court Cairn (#6) (see p. 252) or drive south to Drumcliff and east on minor roads about 8 km (5 mi) to the north shore of Glencar Lough and the 15 m (50 ft) high waterfall. Glencar is Gleann an Chairthe in Irish, "the Glen of the Standing or Monumental Stone."

The *Pursuit of Gráinne and Diarmuid* is a tale from the Fenian Cycle of Irish mythology. Going back at least to the tenth century, the story tells of the love between the princess Gráinne and Diarmuid Ua Duibhne, a warrior loyal to his chief, Fionn mac Cumhaill. Unfortunately, Gráinne fell in love with Diarmuid at her betrothal feast at Tara to the great, but elderly, Fionn. Diarmuid and Gráinne eloped and fled across Ireland. Eventually peace of sorts was made with Fionn, and they settled at Kesh Corran (see p. 274). Later Fionn achieved his long-delayed vengeance on the slopes of Benbulben.

Yeats wrote in "Towards Break of Day,"

> "There is a waterfall
> Upon Ben Bulben side
> That all my childhood counted dear;
> Were I to travel far and wide
> I could not find a thing so dear."

Along with a place called Further Rosses, described by Yeats as "a very noted fairy locality," Glencar Waterfall (#7) features in "The Stolen Child." (NB: The "we" in the following poem refers to faeries.)

"Where the wandering water gushes
From the hills above Glen-Car,
In pools among the rushes
That scarce could bathe a star,
We seek for slumbering trout
And whispering in their ears
Give them unquiet dreams;
Leaning softly out
From ferns that drop their tears
Over the young streams. ...."

Glencar waterfall

You can reach Glencar waterfall via a short footpath at the eastern edge of the northern shore of Glencar Lake. The tumbling waterfall cascades down from the rocky mountainside into a pool. Climb up the staircase that runs alongside the waterfall and you enter into a magical bower, dripping with ferns and greenery. It's a perfect place from which to contemplate the pool, even if the area is no longer as wild as when Yeats visited the waterfall. If you can be there without tourists, it is a powerful place.

Continue south to Lough Gill, a lovely lake dotted with islands and fringed by woodlands. If you approach the northern shore from the west, via R286, just east of the junction with N16 Enniskillen road is a signpost to the waterside Hazelwood Estate (#8). Yeats memorialized the location in "The Song of the Wandering Aengus":

> "I went out to the hazel wood
> Because a fire was in my head,
> And cut and peeled a hazel wand,
> And hooked a berry to a thread."

If you feel like walking and the weather is good, take the lane that leads down to Half Moon Bay. Or, follow the Hazelwood Estate's signposted 3 km (2 mi) Hazelwood Nature Trail—if it is still accessible.

From there, you can either continue on R286 along the northern side of the lake to the eastern edge, leaving Co. Sligo briefly and entering Co. Leitrim, or you can make a detour to Deerpark Court Cairn (#9) by picking up R278 and taking it to the east (see p. 248). If you continue on R286, soon you'll reach Parke's Castle (#10), the plantation mansion erected by Captain Robert Parke in the 1620s and restored by OPW in the late twentieth century. Parke's Castle is a fortified manor house, complete with a stone hut that served as a sweathouse or Irish sauna. An exhibition and audiovisual display describe the prehistoric and historic sites in the area. (Entry fee or Heritage Card.)

If your journey to Lough Gill takes place between Easter and October, try to take a boat ride to the Isle of Innisfree (#11). In "The Lake Isle of Innisfree" Yeats writes:

> "I will arise and go now, and go to Innisfree,
> And a small cabin build there,
> of clay and wattles made:
> Nine bean-rows will I have there,
> a hive for the honeybee,
> And live alone in a bee-loud glade."

The Wild Rose Water Bus (http://www.sligotown.net/wildrose.shtml and http://www.roseofinnisfree.com/) departs from outside Parke's Castle and provides an entertaining excursion, complete with commentary, poetry reading, and a cup of tea or a pint of Guinness.

Drive around to the south side of Lough Gill, stopping at Doone Rock Forest Park (#12) for extensive views over Lough Gill to Benbulben. Once this was a favorite spot for dancing and romancing, and Yeats would have heard the blind fiddler playing there on Sundays. He provided Yeats with inspiration for the following lines: "When I play on my fiddle in Dooney,/ Folk dance like a wave of the sea."

Tobernalt Holy Well N54 14 38 W8 26 46

Either drive directly back to N4 and Sligo Town or make a slight detour near Aughamore off R287. Turn right at the first intersection onto Holy Well Road (Wards Hill Road) and drive a short distance to the parking lot for Tobernalt Holy Well (#13). This is a very popular site, but if you are lucky you will get there either before the tour buses arrive or after they depart.

According to tradition, Tobernalt Holy Well was an important assembly place in Celtic times. The Irish name was probably Tobar na nAlt, meaning "Curative Well for Body Pain" or perhaps "Well of the Cliff." It was Christianized by St Patrick in the fifth century and has strong associations with the saint, although the well isn't named after him. St Patrick reportedly left the marks of his fingers impressed into one of the altar stones of the Mass Rock, which may originally have been a wishing stone used in Celtic rituals.

"The pagan Celtic tradition of individuals unburdening ills and leaving petitions at Tobernalt by tying rags and strips torn from clothing on bushes near the well has endured through the Christian centuries, and its practice is currently alive and evident around the holy well." Eamonn Boylan, p. 10.

246

During the Penal Times (approx. 1700-1829), when public Catholic rites were forbidden, Tobernalt was a safe, secluded haven for the celebration of Mass. The faithful would journey at night to Tobernalt and wait anxiously for the priest to step up to the Mass Rock and begin the service, celebrating Mass at the same site as the legendary St Patrick purportedly had, more than a millennium before. Lookouts would have been posted to give early warning of approaching English yeomanry.

Tobernalt Holy Well Shrine

Today Tobernalt is a beautifully landscaped shrine replete with Catholic themes, including a Penal cross, a candle-filled main altar, a replica Lourdes Grotto, a Mass Rock, a Shrine of St Anne, the Way of the Cross, fifteen Mysteries of the Rosary plaques commemorating high and low points in the life of Mary and Jesus, crucifixion figures—oh, and, by the way, the holy well.

A sign on the low wall around the holy well warns people not to leave offerings and not to drink the water. Despite these and other rather off-putting announcements, the wooded

The holy well

garden and statue-covered hillside radiate powerful healing energy. We felt as if we had entered a sacred grove, complete with the gently flowing stream that issues from the holy well. While we strolled along the path, an older woman and her daughter approached the altar, lit candles, and prayed fervently.

> "Garland Sunday celebrations evolved from the pagan festival of Lughnasa - the feast of harvest thanksgiving. Garland Sunday is therefore a fusion of Christian and Celtic traditions. Garland Sunday may still serve as an occasion for thanksgiving but now with a Christian dimension." http://www.holy-wellsligo.com/, retrieved 6 March, 2011.

Devotion to Mary is a strong component at Tobernalt. She is invoked when pilgrims draw water from the well; she is honored by the recitation of the Rosary; and the plaques of the Mysteries of the Rosary and St Anne's shrine draw attention to Our Lady. The feminine Spirit of the Place is alive and active, regardless of what you call Her.

Although people come to Tobernalt through the year, the main event is Garland Sunday, which takes place on the last Sunday in July, linking it to the earlier pagan celebration.

Spend time at the well, sensing into the energies of the place. It has been drawing the faithful for millennia. What do you feel? How would you describe it?

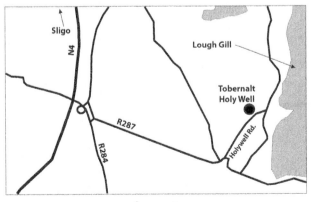

Area map

Deerpark (Magheraghanrush) Court Cairn
N54 16 45 W8 22 50

Deerpark (Magheraghanrush) Court Cairn is located near the north shore of Lough Gill, close to Sligo Town.

Starting from Elliskellen, we drove southwest and into the narrow valley leading to Deerpark Forest and Magheraghanrush Court Cairn. The energy suddenly felt very creepy. The three of us (Gary, our friend Michael, and me) felt a powerful blast of negative energy. It made our skins crawl and seemed to warn, "Keep Out! Only Authorized Persons Allowed." I "got" that the negative energy created a protective gateway for the site. However, we ignored the warning and kept driving. Fortunately, the energy shifted to neutral when we reached the parking lot at Deerpark Forest. (Elyn)

The center court of Deerpark Court Cairn

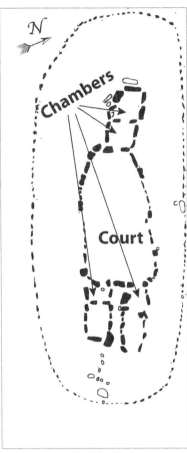

Park in the car park and walk down a path on the left to an information sign. Follow the trail on the right marked "Stone Circle." It leads to an impressive court cairn as well as a difficult-to-find cashel, a souterrain, and a wedge tomb. The walk is lovely (a 3.5 km loop), the hillsides covered with invasive rhododendron and pine forest plantation. It takes about 20 minutes to walk (mostly up, some down) to the high point, the site of the 5000-year-old Magheraghanrush Court Cairn, which sits on top of a limestone ridge overlooking Lough Gill. To the west, you may be able to see Medb's Cairn on Knocknarea.

Plan of Deerpark Court Cairn

Magheraghanrush Court Cairn (from Machaire Chon Rois, "The Plain of the Hound of Ros") is one of the best preserved in Ireland. The cairn is 30 m (100 ft) long and 18 m (60) ft wide. Unburned human and animal bones were found during excavations. Archeologists believe that the large court of a court cairn (a construction that is unique to Ireland) was designed to facilitate group ceremonies, making it primarily a temple, as well as a tomb.

Gary and Michael "dowsed" that there were three protective gateways, that the site was older than Medb's cairn, and that the place was sacred before the court cairn was built

One person may find a certain energy stimulating while another person finds it disturbing. In addition, the energies we experience at a particular site change with the seasons, the moon phases, and geological activity. They are also impacted by a number of other factors, including one's receptivity and whether someone has recently conduced a ceremony there.

upon it. The cairn has a large oval central court, about 15 m (50 ft) long, entered from the south via an entry passage. On either end are galleries that were once covered with stone cairns. There are two parallel galleries on the east, divided into chambers, one with a broken lintel stone, and one gallery divided into two chambers on the west. From above, the court cairn resembles a person with a crowned head, an oval body, and two legs. (http://www.themodernantiquarian.com/site/1044/magheraghanrush.html includes an excellent, if small, aerial photo of the site.)

Gary and Michael dowsed the site, which is oriented northwest to southeast. The court cairn is slightly bent between the northwest end and the ceremonial space. Gary dowsed a slightly bent "fire line" going through the cairn, matching the slight bend in the construction. We wondered whether the builders dowsed the energy line before they built the tomb and built the tomb to follow the line. Or whether somehow, over time, the underground energy line "bent" itself to follow the construction. (We've heard about an earth-energy line in a garden that shifted to follow a wavy line of stone pavers, and about underground water lines that seem to congregate around labyrinths after they are built.)

The cairn appears to be a place of great natural energy, perhaps manipulated for human purposes. Our experience of the energies as we drove to the site is an important reminder that not all earth energies, or "human-enhanced" natural energies, are positive or welcoming.

Although we felt very strong, aversive energy driving to Deerpark from the northeast, we felt nothing unusual when we drove away in the direction of Sligo. Perhaps we would have felt the same "Do Not Enter" energy if we were approaching the Deerpark from Sligo, but we didn't check out that possibility.

We've been told that the area north of Lough Gill is very active geologically, with underground streams and caves. Perhaps we felt this activity as emotional dis-ease and dis-comfort. Or perhaps there was a human-created compo-nent as well.

Getting There

From the northeast, head southwest from Enniskellen on A4 then take N16 to Manorhamilton to R286 toward Park Castle. Turn on R78 toward "Giant's Grave" and "Deer Park." From Sligo, take R286 toward Dromahair. Turn left onto R278/Calry road. After about 5 km (3 mi), you reach Deerpark.

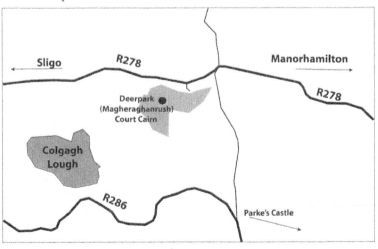

Area map

Creevykeel Court Cairn N54 26 17 W8 25 59

Creevykeel Court Cairn is reached by continuing on N15 north from Sligo town. You could go there after visiting Benbulben on your "Yeats Country" journey. Creevykeel is a heavily reconstructed Late Neolithic court tomb. Dated between 3500-3000 BCE, it originally was covered by a cairn. It is trapezoidal (wedge-shaped) and between 35 m (115 ft) and 48 m (157 ft) long, depending on the reconstruction. The entrance is in the southeast. The cairn contains a large oval court area, about 15 m (50 ft) by 9 m (30 ft), accessed through a 4.5 m (15 ft) long passageway. Opposite the passage, at the other end of the court, is a gallery containing two burial chambers. You enter the gallery by passing between two massive stones joined by a lintel. Three chambers open off the sides of the cairn behind the

Creevykeel Court Cairn

gallery; it is thought these are later additions. Excavations in 1935 revealed cremains, bowls, knives, scrapers, a stone bead, pottery shards, and the clay balls usually associated with passage tombs of a later date. In early Christian times, iron was smelted in the central court.

The megalith builders oriented Creevykeel toward the Dartry Mountains, not towards Donegal. To the left of the carpark is a path leading to a small holy well, referred to locally as "Brisheen." When we visited the cairn, a nearby rag tree was festooned with offerings, and we saw "smoke-like" energy rising from the walls at the back of the burial chambers. It remains a powerful place. (See http://www.carrowkeel.com/sites/misc/ creeveykeel.html for detailed information. http://www. megalithics.com/ireland/creevykl/crvymain.htm has a number of photos.)

Getting There

Creevykeel is located just off the N15 Sligo-Bundoran Road going north. Drive past Cliffony and slow down so as not to miss the site. A short distance (1.5 km) after the town you'll come to the carpark on the right. The court cairn is behind the carpark wall.

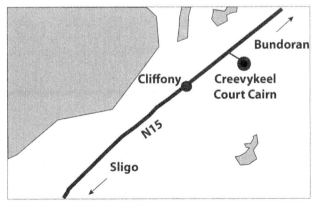

Area map

Mullaghmore, located 4 km (2.5 mi) north of Creevy-keel, is a charming village with a great beach, wonderful views of Benbulben, and excellent seafood.

More to Experience

Inishmurray N54 25 59 W8 39 41

Inishmurray (Inis Muireadaigh, "Muireadach's Island") is a deserted holy island and wildlife sanctuary 6.5 km (4 mi) out in Donegal Bay. A visit to this mystical place would probably require a full day; it's a 1 hr 40 min boat ride each way. For a description of a journey to the island, go to http://www.megalithomania.com/show/date/20/06/2010.h

On our various trips to Ireland, Gary and I have not been able to visit Inishmurray, but we are describing the island because, judging by all the legends about it, it is a very powerful place. It includes the remains of an old monastic settlement; the Church of Fire, which may have had a perpetual fire maintained on a stone hearth on the floor; a large standing stone with odd-shaped holes, visited by women praying for conception and by pregnant women praying for safe delivery; several open-air altars, including one known as *Clocha Breaca* (Speckled Stones) because of the 50 or so rounded stones on top thought to have been used as cursing stones—and much more.

According to Martin Byrne, "Inishmur-

"It is a remarkable place, with a purity of atmosphere that seems to make time stand still. ... Yet it has a rich spiritual past with links connecting it to Devenish Island and Iona in Scotland [via St Colmcille and St Molaise]....It is thought by Michael Poynder to be on a major ley line that crosses Ireland from Newgrange in Meath." Gary Meehan, p. 664.

ray is home to some of the best preserved early Christian antiquities from medieval Ireland, having one of the largest collections of engraved cross-slabs, pillar stones and altars" (http://www.carrowkeel.com/sites/inishmurray/murray.html). http://inishmurray.com is an excellent collection of information, photos, and stories about the island, including first-person accounts from people who lived there.

Caher Island, Co. Mayo, is similar in several ways to Innishmurray. It is the site of an early Christian monastery and contains the remains of a chapel in an enclosure, a number of carved slabs, a holy well—and Cursing Stones. The island is very difficult and dangerous to access, which makes the 15 August pilgrimage arduous. See http://homepage.eircom.net/~kilgeever/caher.htm and http://www.mayolibrary.ie/en/LocalStudies/IrishTouristAssociationSurvey/ClareIsland/CaherIsland/

Getting There

Inishmurray is accessible by boat in good weather from Rosses Point or from Mullaghmore pier, a little north of Creevykeel. To get there, contact Joe McGowan weeks in advance to book a spot on his boat. Contact him at (0)71 916 6267 or at joe_mcgowan@sligoheritage.com. Other resources for excursions to Inishmurray are on http://www.sligoheritage.com/island-tours.htm. For a 360 degree view, http://inishmurray.com/?page_id=246.

More resources

Martin Byrne is available as a guide for sites in Co. Sligo. He really knows his stuff—both the archeological and the mythic. Check out his websites, http://www.carrowkeel.com and http://www.carrowmore.com.

256

Knocknarea and Medb's Cairn, Carrowmore Megalithic Cemetery, and the Faery Glen, Co. Sligo

Knocknarea and Medb's Cairn
N54 15 28 W8 34 31

You can see Knocknarea (Gaelic Cnoc na Riabh or Cnoc na Rí, AKA "Hill of the Kings," "Hill of the Moon," or "Hill of the Executioners") from almost anywhere in Co. Sligo. It's a 327 m (1073 ft) high, flat-topped limestone mountain with what looks like a large grey nipple on top. That "nipple" is known as Queen Medb's Cairn. Also known as Miosgán Meadhbha, "Medb's Heap," or "Maeve's Lump of Butter," the cairn is 60 m (197 ft) wide by 10 m (33 ft) high. This enormous human-made pile of rocks—some 40,000 tons of loose stones—is one of the largest cairns in Ireland outside of the Boyne Valley. It is part of the prehistoric ritual landscape constructed on the Cúil Irra Peninsula.

Medb's Cairn has never been excavated, but many believe that it is a 5000-year-old passage tomb. Quartz lies scattered around, which may have originally formed part of the façade. An irregular earthen bank surrounds the cairn. On the northern side, six gneiss kerbstones are visible. Two "marker" stones occur on the north and south. There are seven satellite "tombs" and several other constructions scattered around the summit, including hut enclosures dated around 3000 BCE. These

According to Martin Byrne, "It has been said that by placing the cairn where they did, the ancients transformed the mountain into a monument." http://www.carrowkeel.com/sites/coolrea/knocknarea.html, retrieved 10 March, 2011.

Knocknarea and Medb's Cairn seen from Tomb #7 at Carrowmore

remains suggest that the site was an important ritual gathering place for millennia.

Although Medb's Cairn is probably 5000 years old, legend claims that it is the burial place of first-century CE Queen Medb (AKA Maeve, Maebh, or Meadhbha), the mythic warrior queen of Connacht. She is one of the main protagonists in the *Táin Bó Cuailnge*, "The Cattle Raid of Cooley" (see p. 291 for the story). Queen Medb is said to be buried upright, sword in hand, facing in the direction of Ulster and waiting for the best opportunity to attack her foes. Medb is also thought to be buried at Rathcroghan (see p. 283). But before she was a legendary and perhaps mythic queen, Medb was the Goddess of Sovereignty. Her association with the cairn on Knocknarea may harken back to a time when mystic marriage with Medb conferred the right of kingship.

Knocknarea and Medb's Cairn looms large, not only in the landscape but also in the "folk soul" of the area. Legends

258

tell of the Knocknarea dragon and the Sidhe. In "The Hosting of the Sidhe," WB Yeats wrote,

"The host is riding from Knocknarea/ And over the grave of Clooth-na-Bare;/ Caoilte tossing his burning hair,/ And Niamh calling Away, come away:/Empty your heart of its mortal dream. …"

"Although the cairn is associated with Maebh, it was never meant to be her tomb. According to a much older tradition she is the goddess of this place and very much alive in the fertility of the land, the red of the sunset, and the rising moon." Gary Meehan, p. 671.

 Martin Byrne (http://www.carrowkeel.com) has noticed lunar associations at Knocknarea, including the 18.6 Lunar Standstill. During the last one, in 2006, the moon viewed from Medb's cairn "rose over the Carrowkeel sites in the Bricklieve Mountains. If the inner passage in Maebh's cairn was open, maybe the moon, at its most southerly point, would shine inside it" (quoted by Meehan, p. 671).

Two people approaching the summit of Knocknarea with Medb's Cairn ahead

Long gone but not forgotten, Queen (or Goddess) Medb and her cairn are an imposing presence. The view from the top of Knocknarea is worth the climb. To the north is Co. Donegal; to the northeast, Benbulben; to the west, Co. Mayo. Miles of ocean beyond Sligo Bay are visible to the northwest and, to the east and south, one can see the sacred landscape of Co. Sligo. Please note: signs discourage climbing to the top of the cairn. Its loose stone covering makes it slippery and dangerous, and walking on the surface dislodges stones, leading to degradation of the cairn.

Getting There

Knocknarea is located at the western edge of the Cúil Irra peninsula. To reach Knocknarea from Sligo, drive 10 km (6 mi) west on R292 (Strandhill Road), then bear left and park after another 1.6 km (1 mi) in the carpark at the base of the mountain, on the southeastern slope of the hill. From there, it's a 4 km (1.75 mi) walk up a steep but picturesque trail to the summit. The first part of the trail is rough stone; after passing through a fence, the trail becomes grassy and quite steep, until leveling off again a few minutes before reaching the summit. Allow about 1 1/2 or 2 hours to walk there and back. Take special care if it has been raining because the grass becomes quite slippery.

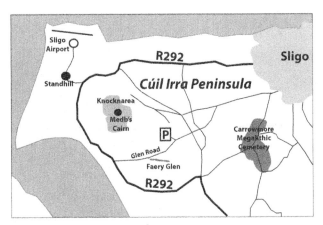

Area map

Carrowmore Megalithic Cemetery
N54 14 53 W8 30 48

Carrowmore Megalithic Cemetery is on the Cúil Irra Peninsula, 4 km (2.5 mi) southwest of Sligo. Medb's Cairn is easily visible 4 km (2.5 mi) to the northwest. Carrowmore (from Gaelic Ceathrú Mor, "Great Quarter") is in the midst of a rich, intervisible sacred landscape, much of it with feminine associations.

Numerous passage tombs are scattered over a low-lying limestone ridge that forms a shallow bowl in the midst of the surrounding mountains. Although Carrowmore is only about 3.8 km square (1.5 miles square), it is the largest of the four Neolithic cemeteries in Ireland in terms of the number of individual tombs. According to George Petrie's 1837 survey, Carrowmore originally had as many

One of the tombs in Carrowmore Megalithic Cemetery

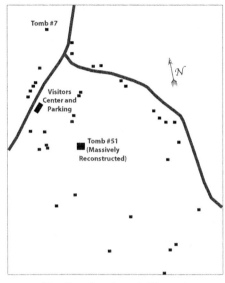

Tomb #7

Visitors Center and Parking

Tomb #51 (Massively Reconstructed)

Site plan showing visible tombs

as 60 passage graves, dolmens, and stone circles. Some 30 of the original 40+ passage tombs survive; many have been destroyed in the last 200 years.

For the most part, the chambers are small and multi-sided, open at one end. Many were constructed with five upright stones, two on each side and one at the back, with a conical- or wedge-shaped roof stone. Some have a passage leading out to the boulder curb that typically surrounds the chamber. This passage would have allowed for repeated access the tomb. Sometimes there is another circle of small stones inside the circle of boulders. It appears that some of the megaliths are paired, which may represent important dualities such as male/female, left/right, etc.—or might simply be a result of one tomb "replacing" the other over time.

Disturbed cremated human remains were found inside the satellite tombs, often with a limestone slab beneath them. Archeologists speculate that the cremains were deposited in layers, separated by limestone. The remains were cremated using oak and hazelwood. Millennia later, the Celts still considered these to be sacred trees. It is likely that the dead were exhumed and reburied in complex funeral rites. It is difficult to determine the number of individuals in any given chamber, and the depositions may have been token body parts rather than entire corpses.

It is difficult to date the site, in part because mortuary practices included bringing artifacts from other places (and times) and depositing them at Carrowmore. Just because something found inside a megalith can be dated (e.g., bone pins) doesn't mean that the tomb is that age. For example, after a gap in time, some of the sites were re-used in 600 BCE and again in 300 BCE. Coins from many places, including Trieste, Rome, and Paris, have been found at Newgrange, and a Roman figurine, bone dice, and other Iron Age items were found at Carrowmore. Were they left as offerings by descendents? By tourists? By pilgrims? We can only wonder.

OPW guide Padraig (pronounced "Porick") Meehan says that Carrowmore is "like the Egyptian Valley of the Kings. The megalith builders altered the landscape. They moved very heavy stones. And they went into inaccessible places, for example Cailleach a Bhera in the nearby Ballygawley Mountains. Even getting there is difficult—and they brought stones up there." (Conversation, September 2010)

The oldest of the megaliths at Carrowmore probably date from 4300-3500 BCE, making the site at least 1000 years older than Newgrange. The Swedish archeologist Goran Burenholt has made the controversial claim that one of the megalithic structures is as old as 5400 BCE, but that date is seriously disputed. Cremains, mushroom-headed pins of antler and bone, a rock crystal pendant, a decorated bone fragment, the ubiquitous small bone or chalk balls, pottery, and worked flint and chert have been excavated from inside various structures. Some of these materials are on display at the National Museum - Archaeology in Dublin.

"Carrowmore megaliths were sometimes re-used and re-shaped by the people of Bronze Age and Iron Age times. They remained focal points on the landscape for long after they were built. The role of megaliths as monuments and foci of ceremony and celebration, as well as markers on the landscape is emphasized by archaeologists such as Richard Bradley." http://en.wikipedia.org/wiki/Carrowmore, retrieved 14 March, 2011.

Interior of Listoghil cairn (#51)

Carrowmore's megalithic constructions are arranged in an oval, and they seem to look inward toward the empty center—empty except for one off-center monument, called Listoghil (#51). The sites are numbered, and it is possible that #7 and #13 formed an entranceway into the center, which probably served as a ceremonial grounds. Listoghil passage cairn is slightly to the north of the center of the complex. Listoghil is both the largest structure and the only one definitely covered originally by a cairn of small stones. Its size and location indicate its importance.

Listoghil cairn has been creatively (and controversially) reconstructed and can be entered. It is about 35 m (115 ft) in diameter and is kerbed with boulders. The interior dolmen and the surrounding kerbstones are original, but the large external cairn is not. It was reconstructed using the 6:1 ratio of height to diameter that, according to Padraig, our guide, seems to have been used consistently by the megalith builders—including in Medb's Cairn (60 m by 10 m). A low circular platform surrounded the cairn itself, outside the kerbstones. This can be seen on the west side.

The interior central chamber is oriented east-southeast. Like Newgrange, Listoghil is oriented towards the winter solstice sunrise, although the controversial reconstruction blocks this astronomical event.

Excavators found the remains of five adults and two children buried, instead of cremated, inside the dolmen. The interior chamber has barely visible carvings on an interior upright and

"Cailleach a Bhera is a part of the four cairn-topped hills that form the Ballygawley Mountains, 6 km from Carrowmore. They dominate the landscape on the opposite side to Knocknarea, to the southeast. The most southerly of these hills, a lovely rounded breast-shaped hill, is called the Cailleach a Bhera. The megalith on top of it is called the Cailleach a Bhera's House. By their location, this complex of monuments interplays visually with Carrowkeel, Cairns Hill, Carrowmore, and Knocknarea. Legend says that the witch or hag flying from Cailleach a Bhera's hill to Knocknarea dropped the stones from her apron to form Carrowmore. The same story is of course told at Loughcrew, also associated with the Cailleach. She is ubiquitous. She is associated with Beinn a Cailli in Broadford, Skye, and at scores of sites in Scotland and Ireland." Padraig Meehan, written communication, 25 February, 2011.

near the capstone. According to Martin Byrne's website, http://www.carrowmore.com (see QR code on p. 266), the large limestone capstone came from the Faery Glen on the side of nearby Knocknarea mountain (see p. 266).

As we walked over the gently rolling terrain, Padraig oriented us toward the horizon, describing a paired set of hills as "paps" (breasts) and another as a reclining woman. The hills on the horizon are the Ballygawley Mountains, tied in name and myth to the Cailleach a Bhera, the ancient hag of winter. We have encountered her already (see pp. 89, 199).

Begin your visit at the OPW Visitor Center to see the exhibits, pick up a map, and perhaps schedule a tour. After your guided tour, take time to wander over the fields,

experiencing the individual sites as well as getting a feel
for the overall grandeur of the place. Walk north along the
byroad to the west of the OPW Visitor Center to the "Y"
junction; then walk down the road to the right (see map on
p. 261). As you explore the dolmens large and small, dolmens ringed with boulders, and stone circles—try to imagine Carrowmore as an active ceremonial site. It must have
been very important to be the focus of so many burials over
such a long time. Perhaps you will experience Carrowmore
as a very powerful place—or perhaps it will seem like nothing more than a collection of ruined megaliths.

Getting There

From the south, Carrowmore is 5 km (3 mi) from
Sligo/Dublin road off N4, at N4 - R292 junction. From
Sligo town center, follow R292 4 km (2.5 mi) toward
Strandhill (See map on p. 258). The OPW Visitor Center,
located in a small cottage, is close to R292 and 2 km
east of Ransboro Crossroads. The center is open Easter
to October. Entry fee or Heritage Card (http://www.
heritageireland.ie/en/North-West/CarrowmoreMega-

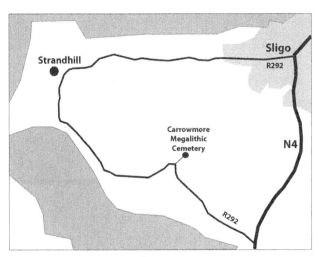

Area map

lithicCemetery/). There is an informative exhibit inside; tours can be arranged.

Padraig Meehan is an excellent, sympathetic OPW guide. He assured us that all the OPW guides are knowledgeable. Another excellent guide is Martin Byrne. See his website, http://www.carrowmore.com.

Faery Glen N54 14 55 W8 33 51

Finding the Faery Glen wasn't easy, but finally we saw a rusty open gate, nearly obscured by bushes and overhanging branches. We walked through it and into a verdant wonderland, a remarkable ivy- and fern-filled chasm, a cleft in the earth caused by a fractured limestone fissure. It wouldn't have surprised me to see dinosaurs—or faeries—or the Goddess of the Land—appearing from behind one of the many trees. The further we walked into the verdant chasm, the more peaceful and sacred it felt—and the smaller and more ephemeral I felt.

Although finding the glen was difficult, leaving it was harder. When we started back, we made a wrong turn around a fallen tree and ended up heading not back to the road but further in, in another direction. It is easy to get confused in such an otherworldly place. (Elyn)

The Faery Glen (locally known as "The Glen") is situated on the south-facing

Entrance to the Faery Glen

Limestone cliffs in the Faery Glen

slope of Knocknarea. It runs in a straight line east to west for almost a kilometer (0.6 mi). According to the Geological Survey of Ireland, the glen is probably the product of a fault line that resulted from the withdrawal of the supporting glacier ice sheet 10,000-12,000 years ago. The southern side of the limestone hill broke along a rock fracture and slid along the slippery mudstone surface beneath, forming a hairline fracture in Mother Earth.

Walk through the gate and follow the narrow path. The cliff walls on the left drip with water seeping through the limestone, depositing limy deposits called tufa. What look like stone icicles dangle from the cliff. On the right of the path, a low stone wall separates you from a deep ravine.

At first the gorge is about 6 m (20 ft) wide, but as you walk further, perhaps ¼ km (300 yd) into the limestone rift, a cliff wall rises up on the right-hand side of the path. The vegetation-covered precipices rise until they tower 18 m (60 ft) on either side, and the glen opens up to be 15-20 m (50-65 ft) wide. Profuse strands of ivy hang down from the limestone cliffs and from overhanging branches, and thickets of ferns and nettles carpet the ground. The trail continues until the glen narrows once again, but the most powerful place is the wider section, with soaring trees and copious vegetation. Sycamore, beech, Scots pine, oak, hazel,

Inside the Faery Glen

holly, and honeysuckle thrive in the moist micro-environment, along with a variety of fauna.

Take time to center yourself. Ask permission to be in this sacred place. Be aware that you are standing in the middle of a natural cleft in Mother Earth, a hairline split in the surprisingly thin skin of the planet. Be present to the vibrant energies of the land, the Spirit of the Place. There's a reason this place is popularly known as The Faery Glen. The geological activity of the fault is undoubtedly responsible for some of the power of the place, but is there more?

Getting There

The Glen is 7 km (4 mi) from Sligo and is reached by following the route to Knocknarea. From Primrose Grange, continue for 1.5 km (1 mi) on Glen Road. You'll see a sign pointing to the road up to the Knocknarea Mountain Carpark. "Instead of turning up to the Knocknarea Mountain Car Park, keep going straight for half a mile or more, until you start going down a fairly steep bit of road overlooking the sea (or the sandbanks if the tide is out), look carefully for a small well on the right-hand side of the road, when you find it, stop and park your car off the road as much as you can" (http://www.sligotown.net/theglen.shtml, retrieved 8 March, 2011). The car pull-off is marked with a sign, "Don't leave trash." The well is actually a white trough on the right and, on the left, the gate is hidden within a clump of bushes. It's almost impossible to see the gate coming from that direction until you are past it. You can park nearby in a wide spot or further up the road. (See map on p. 259.)

Wear wellies (rubber boots) because the terrain tends to be wet. Primrose Grange Court Tomb is located nearby.

Carrowkeel Megalithic Cemetery, Co. Sligo

Carrowkeel Megalithic Cemetery
N54 3 7 W8 22 27

We drove slowly up the narrow, twisting road leading to Carrowkeel Megalithic Cemetery, nearly high-centering the car. As we approached our destination, the energy shifted around us and we knew we were entering into a powerful sacred land-scape. It felt like passing through a veil. We left the car at a wide spot in the road and walked up the hillside, heading toward the tumbled-down cairns that dot the ridge. I climbed into one of the rubble-covered mounds, squeezing backwards into the nar-row passageway that sloped down into the earth. The passage expanded into a central chamber, and I felt like I had entered the womb of the Mother. Some immeasurable amount of time later, I crawled back out, "reborn" and energized. (Elyn)

View east to Lough Arrow from Carrowkeel Megalithic Cemetery

Cairn G with its lightbox

Carrowkeel, Brú na Bóinne, Loughcrew, and Carrowmore represent the four largest concentrations of megalithic sites in Ireland. Carrowkeel Megalithic Cemetery is a group of fourteen cairns constructed on five bleak limestone ridges of the Bricklieve Mountains (Breac Shliabh or "Speckled Mountains"), near scenic Lough Arrow. The ridges stretch out like fingers, running northwest to southeast. The Carrowkeel cairns have been dated from 3800-3300 BCE, making them older than Loughcrew or the Boyne Valley monuments.

Carrowkeel is an impressive site, not only because of the stunning 360° view over the surrounding country (including Knocknarea to the northwest) but especially because of the number of cairns scattered over the ridges. They seem to nestle into the side of the ridges like artificial caves, their dark entryways alluring and disturbing, beckoning from beneath rounded piles of stone rubble.

On a platform on the northern slope of the most eastern ridge (Mullagh Farna), overlooking Lough Arrow, are the remains of about 150 round huts, thought to be a Neolithic village inhabited between 3000-2000 BCE. The circular stone foundations, all that remain of the numerous huts, measure from 9 m (29 ft) to 13 m (43 ft) in diameter. During the time the Neolithic village was inhabited, the native forests of elm, oak, and hazel had already begun to diminish, due to clearance for cattle grazing, wheat and barley farming, and due to disease.

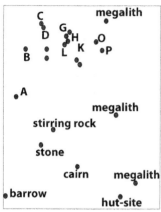

Sites that are visible in Carrowkeel Megalithic Cemetery

It is likely that the Neolithic villagers buried their dead in the nearby cairns, constructed long before they had settled in the region. More recently, the cairns were used during Christian times for the burial of unbaptised children. Carrowkeel is a powerful place, not restricted to any religion.

The cairns were brutally excavated in 1911 with the use of handpicks and sledges (local legend says dynamite, but that's an urban legend). Among the artifacts discovered were bone pins, cremains, a boar's tusk, stone beads, round balls, pendants, and pottery. Each cairn was assigned a letter to identify it, and those letters are still used today. The cairns range in size from 7.5 m (25 ft) to 30 m (100 ft) in diameter; some are 6 m (20 ft) high. They have a number of shapes, including what appears to be a combination court and passage tomb. Some of the rubble-topped cairns are surrounded with boulder kerbs; some have one or more internal cist-like boxes. Several of them contain side chambers and corbelled roofs.

The cairns were much more than tombs. Several of them have important alignments to astronomical events. Cairn G has a lightbox over the doorway similar to (though cruder than) the one at Newgrange. Instead of receiving the light from the winter solstice sunrise, however, it receives sunset light around the time of the summer solstice and the light of the setting moon at the winter solstice. Carrowkeel is still the site of an annual pilgrimage on summer solstice; every year, people climb the hills, hoping to see the sunset light shining through Cairn G's roofbox.

Cairn G, the cairn with the lightbox, "lets in the light of the setting moon for a month either side of the winter solstice. According to Martin Byrne, the cairn opens towards the most northerly point of the setting moon. The moon reaches this point every 18.6 years." Quoted by Meehan, p. 678.

This is a sacred landscape, surrounded on all sides by other sacred landscapes, several of which are intervisible. According to Martin Byrne (http://www.carrowkeel.com/sites/carrowkeel/cairnk.html) "Croagh Patrick is clearly visible on a good day, about 75 km (47 mi) away to the west southwest, and on two days of the year, Samhain and Imbolc, the sun when viewed from Cairn K, drops behind the Reek." In addition, you can see

Our guide, John Willmott, led us to an isolated limestone conglomerate called the Rocking Stone, which he says has been used for ceremonies for millennia. How does he know this? Because of the reverence for the place found in stories people tell, and because people still go there to play music and camp around it.

Knocknarea, Seelywee, and Knocknashee (in Co. Leitrim), although not Loughcrew.

Several of the cairns (including Cairn B, Cairn G with the lightbox, Cairn K, and Cairn O) can be entered. Cairn K is the most intact. It is 21 m (69) ft in diameter, with a 7 m (23 ft) long passageway into its 4 m (13 ft) high central chamber. In general, the entrance to each cairn is halfway up the cairn and slightly higher than the floor level of the chamber: in other words, the passageway slopes downward, as if one is entering an underground cave. The best way to enter the cairns is by crawling in backwards (feet first, facing outward), climbing over or behind the sillstone that blocks the entrance, then sliding carefully down the sloping passageway into the central chamber.

Center yourself and meditate inside several different cairns, experiencing the different energies. Perhaps you will feel the urge to chant or sing; if so, notice the resonance of the chamber. Perhaps you will feel energized in one chamber and depleted in another. John Willmott described one cairn as a "callbox to the Other World." Even partly buried in rubble, the cairns remain powerful places.

Getting There

Carrowkeel is about 28 km (17) miles south of Sligo off N4 from Collooney. Turn west at the village of Castlebaldwin into the Bricklieve Mountains, following the signs for Carrowkeel Passage Tombs. Turn left at the sign for the Sathya Sai Donkey Sanctuary (dedicated in 1991 by Sathya Sai Baba), and then first right, and park there. A 30 minute walk brings you to the cemetery.

It is very helpful to go to Carrowkeel with a guide such as John Willmott (http://www.celticways.com), Michael Fox

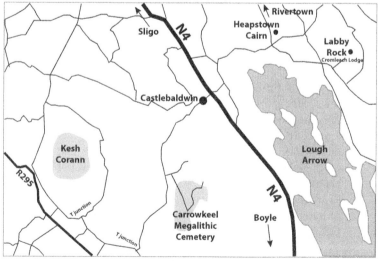

Area map

(http://www.BoyneValleyTours.com), or Martin Byrne (http://www.carrowkeel.com), who will provide you with detailed information about the cairns and the legends surrounding them. Be sure to bring a flashlight to explore the interiors of the cairns.

More to Experience

Heapstown Cairn

Heapstown is a massive cairn, never excavated, but probably containing a passage and chamber, similar to the cairns at Carrowkeel. According to legend, the cairn covers the site of a powerful healing well, the Tobar Sláine, the "Well of Health." During the legendary Second Battle of Moytura, Dian Cécht, a Tuatha Dé Danann healer, brought the dead and wounded to the well to revive them. Their opponents, the giant Formorians, the more ancient inhabitants of Ireland, decommissioned the well by capturing it and throwing stones into it, forming the great cairn. Some people report finding the cairn a very creepy place; others find it intriguing.

Getting There

Drive 5 km (3 mi) southeast of Riverstown and just north of Heapstown crossroads and the Bo & Arrow Pub. Park by the green and white gateway and follow the yellow arrows for the historical trail, "Slí Stairúil." (See map on p. 274.)

Labby Rock

Labby Rock

Labby Rock (Carrickglass Portal Dolmen) is hidden in the forest on the north edge of the ridge of Moytura. It is not on the high point; instead, it nestles in a grassy hollow, next to a low stone wall. The dolmen is remarkable for the size of its vegetation-sprouting capstone, which weighs 70 tons and is more than 2 m (6.5 ft) thick, supported on what look like stumpy legs.

Legend says that Labby Rock was one of the beds (*leaba* is Irish for bed) of the lovers Diarmuid and Gráinne as they fled across the country from the Hill of Tara (see story p. 241). Other legends claim it is the burial place of Nuada of the Silver Arm, King of the Tuatha Dé Danann, who was killed by Balor of the Evil Eye, leader of the Formorians, during the second battle of Moytura. Local folklore asserts that if a couple spends the night inside, they will benefit from the bed's "magical fertility."

The forest walk up to Labby Rock is enchanting. If you continue walking, you'll also see a ring fort and spectacular views over Lough Arrow.

Getting There

To get there from the Heapstown crossroads, follow signs to Cromleach Lodge, park in the parking lot, and walk up the driveway, following signs to the forest path up the hill. From Sligo, take N4 toward Dublin; at Castlebaldwin take the first turn left and follow signs to Cromleach Lodge. (See map on p. 274.)

Kesh Corann

Kesh Corann (AKA Keshcorann or *Céis Corran*, meaning "Hog of Corran") is an important and under-rated site, rich in legend and powerful in energy. It is visible from Carrowkeel. There are seventeen limestone caves on the side of the hill, 150 m (492 ft) up the cliffs; fourteen are in the main group and three more are about 300 m further to the south and slightly higher up the hill. The hill itself is 365 m (1200 ft) high. At the top is an unexcavated cairn 5 m (16.5 ft) high and 30 m (100 ft) in diameter.

Limestone caves on Kesh Corann

Kesh Corann is also known as Sidhe ar Crúachain, an entrance to the Otherworld and a place from which the fierce war goddess the Morrigan emerges. Another legend claims that the mountain was formed out of the dead body of the enchanted sow Cailcheir, who was lured into sleep by the harper Corann and then slaughtered by waiting warriors.

Kesh Corann is said to have been the birthplace of Cormac mac Cairt, who was stolen soon after birth and raised by wolves in the caves above. The caves also feature in legends of Fionn mac Cumhaill and his band. The star-crossed lovers Diarmuid and Gráinne are said to have made their home there for many years before returning to Benbulben, where Diarmuid was lured to his death (see p. 242).

Folklore says that the caves of Kesh Corann are connected to the Cave of the Cats in Co. Roscommon (see p. 287). It is also said that Cormac and his soldiers are asleep in the Kesh Corann caves and will awaken again when needed by Ireland. John Willmott tells intriguing stories about this site, which he links with Brigid (the Morrigan was said to be her mother) and with Glastonbury. Kesh Corann, like Glastonbury, was once surrounded by water, and Glastonbury is also reported to be where a hero (Arthur) and his sleeping warriors await awakening.

An annual family-oriented pilgrimage takes place on Garland Sunday, the last Sunday of July (a date significantly close to Lughnasa), and includes a trek up to the large cairn at the top of the mountain.

Getting There

To reach Kesh Corann from Sligo, take N4, turn right at Castlebaldwin towards Bricklieve and make a right turn at two T junctions. A new gravel road goes uphill to the east of this road; follow it to a water scheme pump house. There is room to park there if the gate is open. This will lead you to the cairn. Detailed directions are available at http://mountainviews.ie/mv/index.php?mtnindex=887. The caves can be more easily reached from nearby the village of Keash on the other side of the mountain. There is a path visible from behind an abandoned stone building, with parking for one or two cars. Take care: the path can be slippery and dangerous.

Keadue Holy Well

Keadue Holy Well, located on the north shore of Lough Meelagh, at the foot of the Arigna Mountains, is dedi-

Keadue Holy Well

280

"St Lassair's grave is on the hill above the well. Over the centuries emigrants from Ireland brought St. Lassair's clay with them to the U.S.A., Canada, Australia, etc. to bring blessings on them in their new life in a strange land." (http://www.kilronan-parish.ie/KilronanParishSite/KeadueChurchetc.htm, retrieved 11 March, 2011).

cated to St Lasair (or Lassair). It is across the road from the ruined twelfth-century Kilronan church, originally founded by St Lasair and her father, St Ronan, in the sixth century, and from the grave of the famous blind harper Turlough O'Carolan (1670-1738). Both the well water and nearby soil are supposed to have powerful healing qualities. The flagstone beside the well was at one time St Ronan's altar, and the hollowed stone was his water font.

On top of the stone altar is a rounded stone; John Willmott says that you turn it clockwise to bless and counter-clockwise to curse. A stone slab opposite the well is supposed to cure backache, as is crawling under the stone altar. Although this practice is discouraged today, we noticed a green mat under the altar. "St Lassair's clay," gathered at the

The stone altar with the "blessing and cursing" stone

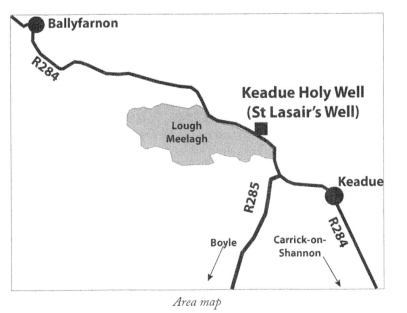

Area map

base of the nearby hill where she was buried, is purported to have healing qualities. Stations (traditional pilgrimage devotions) are performed every year on the first Sunday of September.

When we visited the well-kept holy well, it seemed energetically "empty" despite the rag tree and sweet-tasting water. Perhaps we didn't approach it with enough attention. If you go there, see what you experience.

There are a many other powerful places near Keadue, including the Knockranny Court Tomb and the Lough Meelagh *crannog* (an artificial island made of timber and rock, used for defense and habitation from the early Christian period to the seventeenth century). There are so many megaliths in Ireland that Knockranny is rarely mentioned in guidebooks, yet it is an evocative site, the kind of powerful place you are glad to have stumbled upon. For more information, go to http://www.harp.net/Keadue/Keadue.

htm or http://www.kilronanparish.ie/Kilronan-ParishSite/ArchaeologicalHistory.htm.

Getting There

Keadue is in Co. Roscommon, 12 km (7.5 mi) northeast of Boyle and east of Lough Arrow. The well is located between the road and Lough Meelagh on the south side of R284, between Ballyfarnon and Keadue. Access is via a "kissing gate." O'Carolan Harp Competitions take  place in Keadue village in August. For some interesting local history, go to http://www.kilronanparish.ie/KilronanParishSite/HistoryNotes.htm.

More Resources

John Willmott (http://www.celticways.com) is a very interesting guide and storyteller, based near Carrowkeel. His partner Claire is a wonderful singer and harpist. You can arrange to spend time at Carrowcrory cottage, walk the labyrinth, and, if you are in luck, have a private concert. Fees vary.

 Michael Fox's expertise (http://www.boynevalley-tours.com/) includes Carrowkeel and the area around Keadue.

Martin Byrne(http://www.carrowmore.com) is an excellent guide for the region.

West Ireland

Rathcroghan/Cruachan Complex and Oweynagat Cave (Cave of the Cats), Co. Roscommon

Even photos of the Cave of the Cats gave me the willies. I wasn't going to enter it, not if you paid me. I was sure of that. The others could go in if they wanted, but not me. We sloshed through the wet grass to the entrance, a dark inverted triangle almost hidden by a thorn bush. A gash, a hole in Mother Earth. "No way," I said, shaking my head. Michael, flashlight in hand, offered to go in first, and I watched him slither into the tight-fitting slit. I must face my fears, I thought. So, taking a deep breath, I wiggled in after him. The entrance opened into a tiny chamber.

While he explored the sloping inner passage that led to the cave itself, I stayed in the chamber, breathing deep and slow. A voice crooned in my ear, trying to lure me further into the cave. I knew that if I followed that voice, I'd never come back—not as I am, at any rate. Firmly, I shook my head and ignored the Morrigan's insistent call. I stayed where I was, sitting in the almost-dark, listening to my breath, listening to the whispers swirling like mist around me. (Elyn)

Rathcroghan/Cruachan N53 48 6 W8 18 13

Co. Roscommon has a reputation for being boring, but for "those who have eyes to see and ears to hear," it is anything but. Rathcroghan is an enigmatic landscape shrouded in myth and legend, the burial place of long-forgotten heroes and kings. There are over 200 sites within the area, including ancient earthworks, tumuli, ceremonial avenues, ring forts, caves, and standing stones. The Rathcroghan complex is one of the important mythological regions of Ireland, ranking with the Hill of Tara, and—like Tara—it is most helpful to explore the area with a guide who can unite mythology with history and archaeology.

Cruachan, as Rathcroghan was called in ancient times, has been a sacred site since the Neolithic, roughly 6000 years ago. Millennia later it became known as Rathcroghan and was one of four major royal sites, including Tara, in ancient Ireland. It was an important royal burial ground and the place of assemblies and royal inauguration rituals of the kings of Crúachain and, purportedly, Queen Medb. It continued to be important in medieval times. As recently as 1641, Charles O'Conor Don of Ballintubber was inaugurated as king within the complex.

The mythic warrior queen/earth goddess Medb is said to have had her palace at Rathcroghan and to have lived there with her husband Ailill, King of Connacht. She is reportedly buried at nearby Misgaun Medb or "Medb's Heap"—*not* at Medb's Cairn on Knocknarea.

Unlike Carrowmore, which faces inwards, Rathcroghan seems to face outwards, relating to powerful places on the periphery. From the main mound at Rathcroghan, known as "Medb's Palace," you can see Croagh Patrick to the west, looking like a pyramid; if the trees behind Rathbeag weren't blocking the view, you could also see Medb's Cairn on Knocknarea and the cairn on top of Kesh

"In this early manifestation, Medb was not a historical person but a goddess whose name is related to words in Irish and other languages signifying drunkenness (like the English word 'mead'); her name means 'she who intoxicates.' While the character of Medb in the *Táin* is a complex and mainly medieval creation, the earlier Medb was a goddess of sovereignty. To gain possession of Medb of Crúachain was to gain possession of the kingship, a fact that explains the unusual number of her husbands." "Rathcroghan," Waddell, Heritage Guide No. 44.

Mike Croghan describing features in the Rathcroghan landscape using photos in the Visitor Center

Corann. To the trained eye, they become visible as you drive west down N5. An old pilgrims' route led from Rathcroghan to Croagh Patrick. To the northeast you can see Sliabh an Iarainn, where legend says that the Tuatha Dé Danann arrived in Ireland, descending in a mist. Beyond that point you can see into Ulster.

Other sites include Rathnadarve (Ráth na d'Tarbh, the "Fort of the Bulls,") said to be the location of the final bloody battle between the White Horned Bull of Connacht and the Brown Bull of Cooley/Ulster (see p. 291); Oweynagat Cave, entrance to the Otherworld; Relignaree, burial place of kings and perhaps site of Queen Medb's palace; the Mucklaghs, two huge linear earthworks forming part of a ceremonial procession way, named for the rooting of a magical boar; Cashel Manannan (Cashelmanannáin), location of a Druid school and perhaps the start of a ritual route continued by the Mucklaghs; Dáithi's Stone, burial place of a Connacht king reported to have died on a cattle raid in the Alps (perhaps a mistranslation of "Sliabh n-Ealpa," but "the Alps" makes a better story) in 429 CE—and many more, including Rathra, near Castlerea (http://www.druidschool.com/site/1030100/page/3138060 http://www.themodernantiquarian.com/site/13581/rathra/html). We have been told Rathra's central hollow is best entered from the west.

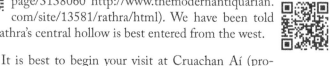

It is best to begin your visit at Cruachan Aí (pronounced "Crew-han-ee") Visitor Center (http://www.cruachanai.com), which has informative high-tech exhibits describing the area. A detailed map, available at the Visitor Center, is a necessity; a good guide is even better.

Getting there

Cruachan Aí Visitor Center at Tulsk includes excellent exhibits, a pleasant coffee shop, and a craft and bookshop (http://www.cruachanai.com or www.Facebook.com/Rathcroghan). Cruachan Aí is located where the N5 Dublin to Westport Rd intersects N61 Roscommon to Boyle Rd, a short distance north of Roscommon town. (See map on p. 287.) Tours can be arranged through the center or contact Mike Croghan at mikejcroghan@yahoo.co.uk or http://www.rathcroghantours.com. (Mike Croghan is quite knowledgeable and "attuned" to the sites. He is also a member of the last Croghan family to inhabit the area.)

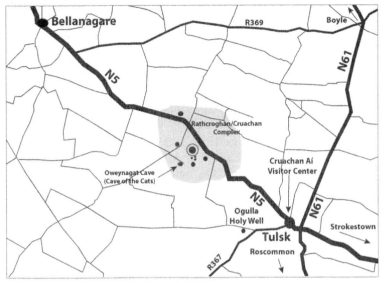

Area map

Oweynagat Cave (Uaimb na gCait or "Cave of the Cats") N53 47 50 W8 18 35

Oweynagat (pronounced "Oween-ne-gat" or "UUvna-GOTCH") or Cave of the Cats is a spooky place, filled with powerful energies both of the earth and of the Otherworld. The cat is an animal totem often associated with ancient goddess worship.

The cave has been used as a ritual site for millennia, and it continues to be visited by spiritually oriented groups. It is thought that the veil between this world and the Otherworld is thinnest at Oweynagat during Samhain. Frightening creatures are reported to issue forth from the interior, including female werewolves, malevolent birds and pigs, and a triple-headed monster. The tenth-century tale "Bricriu's Feast" (Fled Bricrenn) recounts how three war-

288

A local legend relates that long ago, a woman grabbed onto the tail of an unruly calf that ran down into the cave. They reappeared two days later in Co. Sligo. This echoes the legend that the Kesh Corann caves (p. 277) are connected to the Cave of the Cats.

riors, including Cúchulainn, were tested in the cave by terrifying cats. This story suggests that the cave may have been used for warrior rites of passage.

Several years ago we (Elyn and Gary) tried to find the Cave of the Cats without success. Or, more accurately, we did find it, but we didn't believe that the narrow triangular slit, half hidden by thorn bushes, was the entrance. This time, Mike Croghan led us to the same small opening. After hearing our story, he told us, "Many would look for the Cave of the Cats; few would find it; and fewer still would enter."

"Cats were of great significance to the Celtic people. … In one of the Irish Otherworld voyages, a little cat is encountered as a guardian of treasure; in maintaining its watch, it turns into a flaming form, and leaping its way through a potential thief, turns him to ashes." Delyth, p. 70.

The original entrance to the cave was in the field on the other side of the country lane, but this entrance was closed up and hidden once the Christians came. A souterrain was added at a 90° angle, and that is the entry that is now used. To find your way inside you will need a flashlight—or better, a candle with a sleeve to keep it from dripping, which will illuminate more of the surroundings.

To enter the Cave of the Cats, you slide or back into the triangular-shaped opening until you reach a small chamber where you can sit down. From the inside, you can see Ogham script on the lintel over the entry. The stone was probably brought to the cave from Carnfree; it translates partially as "…Fraech, …son of Medb," and refers to a leg-

Elyn slithering into the Cave of the Cats

endary Connacht warrior—more evidence that perhaps the cave was used for warrior initiations.

A downward-sloping interior passage to the left (as seen from outside looking in) leads to the limestone cave. You have to crawl through it for 10 m (33 ft), but then the passage gets taller and opens into a limestone cavity approximately 5 m (16 ft) high and an arm-span wide. The cave, formed by hydro-erosion, ends about 50 m (164 ft) from the entrance.

Elyn made it into the antechamber, which was far enough for her to experience the intense power of the place. After she crawled back out of the cave, she felt disoriented, oddly serene, and very disconnected from time. Our guide, Mike, told us that this feeling of being "outside of time" is not unusual after leaving the cave. He added, "As they say, seven years in the land of the Sidhe is one year in our land." Well, maybe that explains it!

A small opening in the ground to the left of the Cave of the Cats also has a lot of energy. Perhaps it connects to the cave. Elyn experienced the energy as moving in and out, as if the cave were inhaling and exhaling, drawing you into it. It is a very powerful place.

Mike took us to other sites in the area, pointing out the significance of a barrow here, a standing stone there. As we slogged through damp meadow grass, he reminded us that "Walking across the fields, you are walking in the footsteps of people who have used these fields for millennia. They've always been used as fields for grazing, since the Neolithic." Because the "Celtic Tiger" economic development passed this region by, many of the archeological sites haven't been excavated and imaginatively reconstructed. As a result, the integrity of the landscape at Rathcroghan is still intact.

Morrigan/Morrigu/Modron/Morgan (the "Phantom Queen") is one of the greatest "dark" archetypal Mother Goddesses of the Irish/English/Welsh tradition. She is a goddess of death, destruction, war, prophecy, sovereignty, fertility, and passionate love. She is a shape-shifter and often appears as a raven, though sometimes as an eel, a wolf, or a red heifer. She sometimes is linked to a triad of war goddesses. The Morrigan appears in Irish myth as an ugly woman offering herself to a hero or king; if she is rejected, her vengeance is dreadful; if she is accepted, she brings success in battle. She is also often said to be the mother of Brigid. (See http://inanna.virtualave.net/morrigan.html)

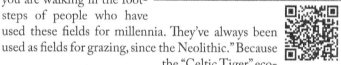

According to Mike Croghan, some people go into the Cave of the Cats and say, "It was quite lovely, I had a great time, I had a cup of tea with the Morrigan." He wonders whom they really met, "because the Morrigan would tear you apart and build you back up again for sure! Celtic spirituality is not fluffy bunnies!" He went on to say that the Morrigan is building in strength with the times. The more people work with her, the more strength she gains in the consciousness of the people. (Personal communication, Sept. 2010)

Getting there

A good map may help you find the cave, but better is a good guide. (See map on p. 287.)

The *Táin Bó Cúailnge (The Cattle Raid of Cooley)* epic is set around 500 BCE and recounts events that take place mostly in the mountains of the Cooley Peninsula, Co. Ulster. Medb, Warrior Queen of Connacht, envies her husband Ailill's extremely fertile White Bull. It had belonged to her originally but refused to "follow the rump of a woman" and wandered into Ailill's herd. She determines to capture the equally fertile Brown Bull of Cooley. She and Ailill gather their warriors at Croghan (Cruachan) and begin a war against the north of Ireland, particularly around Ulster. Medb gathered the warriors of Connacht, Munster, Leinster, and some exiled warriors of Ulster. They camped on the plains of Cruachan before setting off on the raid. Magic and myth mix in the epic, and the hero Cúchulainn is left to confront Medb's armies by himself. The two bulls end up battling each other at Rathcroghan, and eventually the Brown Bull tears the White Bull to shreds, strewing its bloody parts along the landscape as it heads back to Cooley to die from exhaustion. In *The Cattle Raid of Cooley*, the land and the legend weave together—and weave each other. For a good summary, go to http://en.wikipedia.org/wiki/T%C3%A1in_B%C3%B3_C%C3%BAailnge. Thomas Kinsella's *The Táin* (Oxford University Press, 1969) is often said to be the best translation of the story.

More to Experience

Ogulla Healing Well

Judging by the numerous Christian statues, rags, and various offerings (baby clothes, bras), this healing well is thought to be a powerful place. An eight-sided, glass-walled building dominates the site, moved there from Knock Shrine in 1980. A few years ago, the local priest had the rag-covered tree cut back, but it is growing back and people have found substitutes. Rainwater runs into the ground from Rathcroghan and resurfaces at Ogulla in two places, forming the holy well. The water then runs past the Cruachan Aí Visitor Center and a few miles further downstream enters a lake. Gary dowsed the area and found an energy line behind the building, parallel to the fence. But the octagonal building itself felt devoid of energy.

Legend says that this well is where St Patrick met Eithne and Fidelma, two daughters of Laoghaire, the High King of Ireland, although he probably met them at another location, the well of Cliabach on Rathcroghan, where they were attending the great Druid school of Cashelmanannáin. They were puzzled by Patrick's religion, which had only one god, which they couldn't see, unlike their own gods, which they could see in nature. Patrick said if they were baptized, they could see his god. They were baptized and promptly died—presumably getting a first-hand glimpse of the Christian god. The moral of the story might be, be careful what you wish for. (See map on p. 287.)

Roscommon town

Located at the crossroads of N61 and N63, Roscommon is a pleasant market town in the middle of Co. Roscommon. Worth visiting are Gleeson's, a topnotch restaurant and inn located in a restored nineteenth-century house (http://www.gleesonstownhouse.com), a bakery specializing in gluten-free products, a county mu-

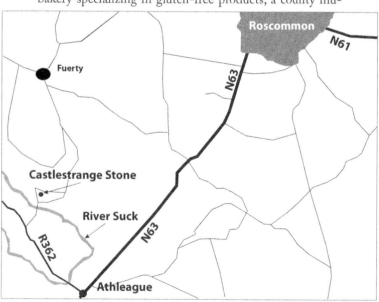

Area map

seum [(0)90 662 5613; open June to September] with the braided-hair Rahara Sheela-na-gig carving (described in http://www.beyond-the-pale.org.uk/sheela2.htm), a covered market, a ruined Dominican Friary, and the nearby ruins of an enormous Norman castle. Roscommon is a good place to take a break or to use as a base for exploring the area.

Athleague/Castlestrange Stone

The nearly 1 m (3 ft) high egg-shaped granite boulder rests in a place of honor at the edge of a field. Trees shade the stone, its curvaceous, incised spiral patterns dancing in light and shadow. Part of one side toward the top is rougher and nearly pattern-free. Did worshippers rub up against it in ancient times or scrape off a bit of patterned stone to take home? Their purpose lost, the intricate carvings remain evocative. We "got" by dowsing that the stone was used in fertility rites, but there is no way to know for sure. Silent, the stone waits for someone who can read its story.

Gary looking at the Castlestrange Stone

The Castlestrange stone is one of three La Téne-style carved stones in Ireland, dating to around 250 BCE. It was relocated to its present site, a pleasant setting with a picnic table nearby, at least a century ago.

The Castlestrange stone is located 7 km (4 mi) southwest of Roscommon town, between Athleague and Fuerty. It is signposted. There is a plaque in front of the cottage by the gate. Park there or drive up the lane to the stone on the right and another explanatory plaque. (See map on p. 292.)

An Táin cycling route

The 587 km (365 mi) long An Táin cycling route follows the route of the legendary Táin Bó Cuailgne, or The Cattle Raid of Cooley. It begins at Rathcroghan and continues to the Cooley Peninsula in north Co. Louth. A plaque next to the Roscommon church shows the route. http://www.longford.ie/longford_content.aspx?id=264&linkidentifier=id&itemid=264.

Clonfert Cathedral, St Brendan's Tree, Eddie Stones' Emmanuel House of Providence, and Our Lady of Clonfert Church, Co. Galway

After numerous detours (our own intrepid voyage of discovery), we had almost reached Clonfert Cathedral, first established by Saint Brendan the Navigator in the sixth century. We parked the car down the road and were walking toward the church when another detour loomed—a sign on a fence indicated "St Brendan's Tree and The Nun's Path." We walked through the gate and entered a sacred grove. In the center was a towering chestnut tree festooned with rags and offerings. Photos, rosaries, clothing, and caps were strewn around the base of the trunk or attached to the rough bark. The Nun's Path beckoned, but we focused on our goal and began walking back to the cathedral. A car drove by slowly, and the driver called out, "Don't miss visiting Eddie Stones." "What's that? I asked. "He's a faith

healer, a holy man. His church is just right up the road." More
detours followed on our way to an unexpected blessing. (Elyn)

We were drawn to Clonfert ("Field of Miracles" or
"Meadow of the Burial Grounds") because the cathedral
has a very unusual west façade. We found much more than
we expected, including a mermaid, a sacred grove, an ancient yew tree walk, and a Catholic faith healer.

Clonfert Cathedral N53 12 09 W8 03 44

The Church of Ireland Clonfert Cathedral is a small
building, a twelfth-century church built on or near a monastery founded in 563 (or 557) by St Brendan the Navigator.
He is supposed to be buried in the churchyard under a stone
marked with what look like bird tracks. The monastery also
included a convent for women, initially under the super-
vision of St Brendan's sister, St Briga. After St Brendan's death, the monastic community grew to over 3000 students from all over Europe. It was a religious center of great importance. The settlement was raided and burnt many times but always regenerated. It is located near the River Shannon, which made it easily accessible both to travelers and pillagers.

St Brendan the Navigator (484-577 CE) was a great scholar and founder of numerous monasteries. He is most widely known, however, for his fabled seven-year journey in search of the Blessed Isles, AKA Paradise. During this ocean voyage, he may have traveled to Iceland and possibly as far as North America. The tale was first recorded in the 900s and became quite popular. The explorer Tim Severin successfully undertook a similar journey in an oxhide *currach*, sailing from Ireland to Newfoundland. See http://en.wikipedia.org/wiki/Tim_Severin.

Clonfert Cathedral

The small size of the church and the plainness of the external walls contrast with the profusely carved west doorway and gable. The doorway is considered a masterpiece of Hiberno (Irish) Romanesque decoration. It consists of seven orders (carved semi-circular arches) adorned with various motifs, including geometrical images, human and animal heads, and foliage. Similar motifs have been identified in twelfth-century Scandinavian and western French sculpture. Above the doorway is an enormous gable. At the bottom, seven human heads peek out from blind arcades; above them, ten human heads form a triangular geometrical shape called a Tetractys. This impressive gable with its Pythagorean numerology made us wonder what else might be hidden in the ornamentation of the church.

Inside the church, intriguing fifteenth-century carvings decorate the chancel arch, including several angels, a repetitive shape that looks like a stingray with a twisted tail (a dragon?), and a mermaid holding a comb and a mirror. Over the centuries, she has been polished shiny and smooth by human hands rubbing her body—

The façade of Clonfert Cathedral

"According to Pythagoras, the numerical intelligence of the Universe was represented by the Tetractys - a triangular arrangement of ten dots, with one on top, two on the second row, three on the third and four on the fourth. Ten was considered the perfect number. The Tetractys represented the four elements - earth, air, fire, and water. It was also used to represent the ratios that form the basic intervals of the Pythagorean musical scales." http://tetractys.blogspot.com/, retrieved 24 March, 2011.

which seems a bit odd since in Christian tradition the mermaid is often used as a symbol of vanity.

According to Gary Meehan (p. 392), "Mermaids remain one of the most enigmatic figures in medieval carving. They were very beautiful and could sing with a sweetness that could not be resisted, but to follow one meant almost certain death. They symbolized something beautiful and terrible at the same time." The indigenous goddess Áine also appeared in the form of a mermaid. The comb and mirror are symbols found on sixth-to-ninth century Pictish stones in Scotland, where they may have been the attributes of a goddess. (See http://www.carlanayland.org/essays/picts_comb_mirror.htm.)

As you wander around the church, you will discover other unusual carvings, including many heads. The abundance of heads—including in the gable of the entrance—reminded us of the Celtic cult of the head, and we wondered how much of that earlier tradition had remained active as late at the twelfth century.

The mermaid figure in Confert Cathedral

St Brendan's Tree

St Brendan's Tree

Down the road from the cathedral is a fence with an open gate. A hand-painted sign announces "St Brendan's Tree and the Nun's Path." Walk through the gate and enter into a sacred grove. In the center stands an impressive chestnut tree, several hundred years old. It is festooned with offerings of all sorts, ranging from dolls to rags, photos to children's clothing—with a few medals left as offerings as well. St Brendan's Tree is obviously a place of great devotion to many. A man who lives nearby, however, spoke of St Brendan's Tree with disgust, asserting to us that there was nothing holy there. He said Travelers (an ethnic Irish nomadic group) had started leaving offerings, and everyone else followed along. He thought the offerings were a trash heap that should be cleaned up. He told us the "real" St Brendan oak tree fell over in 1903. Despite our informant's distaste for the site, we were struck by the power of the place.

Offerings at St Brendan's Tree

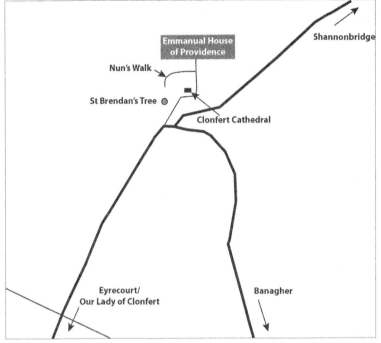

Area map

Emmanual House of Providence

Continue walking through the grove and you will come to the 1000-year-old Nun's Walk, a lovely avenue lined with towering yew trees. If you continue to the end and turn left, you will reach Emmanual House of Providence, a Catholic center for prayer and evangelization, built on the site (or very near the site) of St Brendan's monastery (http://www.emmanuelhouse.ie/). The Bishop of Clonfert appointed Eddie Stones, a highly respected lay healer, as custodian of the center. Eddie conducts healing sessions at the conclusion of Mass. There are several sanctuaries on the grounds, including the beautiful Emmanuel Oratory.

We (Elyn and Gary) arrived after the Sunday Mass and healing service; almost everyone had left. However, we were given the unexpected opportunity to tour the retreat center with the local priest and to receive a blessing from Mr. Stones. Our traveling companion was astounded at our good fortune. He said people wait in line for hours to receive a blessing, and yet we, ignorant of Eddie Stones' reputation, wandered into the center and were blessed! This synchronicity is another indication of the power of the area around Clonfert Cathedral.

Our Lady of Clonfert Church

A few kilometers (1 mi) to the south is Our Lady of Clonfert, a tidy, white-plastered church. Its fourteenth-century wooden Madonna and Child statue is renowned for performing miracles. In May (the "month of Mary") the church is packed with devotees.

According to legend, "During the time of religious suppression, someone removed the Madonna for safe keeping from one of the nearby monastic settlements of 'Medieval Clonfert,' and placed the statue in a tree. It was only in the last [19th] century that a woodcutter, while chopping trees in the area, cut through the trunk containing the statue and blood flowed freely from the trunk. He had severed the Madonna's arm! The statue was carefully removed and placed in nearby Meelick Church, on the banks of the river Shannon; however, a local tale has it, the statue kept turning back in the direction of Clonfert and for that reason, she was returned to where she wished to be . . . Clonfert." (As told in a 1938-39 collection cited in http://www.

Our Lady of Clonfert Church

emmanuelhouse.ie/index.php/our-lady-of-clonfert. html). (For more information on Mary and Clonfert, see http://www.catholicireland.net/church-a-bible/ church/marian-spirituality/626-our-lady-of-clonfert.)

> According to an information plaque in front of the Clonfert Cathedral, "There is evidence that many pre-Christian religious sites in Ireland were subsumed into, or developed as places of Christian worship. Although no evidence of pre-Christian use has been found to date, it would not be surprising if such a site were chosen by Brendan to found his church circa 560 CE."

The area around Clonfert is a very powerful place. Over the millennia different religious and spiritual communities have been attracted to it because of something intrinsic to the location itself—as well as because of its growing reputation. Its power continues to resonate, drawing Eddie Stones, the Travelers, and Marian devotees, as it has drawn others pilgrims in the past.

Getting there

Clonfert Cathedral is 27 km (17 mi) northeast of Portumna by N65, R355, R356 via Eyrecourt and minor road E. Key available from the house to the right of the cathedral. Road signs point to "Emmanual House" and to Our Lady of Clonfert. (See map on p. 299.)

More to Experience

Croagh Patrick

Croagh Patrick, Co. Mayo, Ireland's holiest mountain, is located south of Westport. The conical, quartzite mountain rises 763 m (2503 ft) into the sky and dominates Clew Bay. Croagh (pronounced "Crohg," with a soft "g") Patrick was the home of the Mother Goddess and also associated with Lugh, god of light, and the Lughnasa festival at the end of July, and with Crom Cruach, a dark, underworld figure who received the last harvest sheaf. St Patrick "replaced" Lugh, and Croagh Patrick became the holiest mountain in Christian Ireland.

In honor of St Patrick, who supposedly fasted on the summit for 40 days, tens of thousands of pilgrims—some barefoot and fasting—climb the slippery slopes to the summit on the last Sunday in July, a date associated with Crom Cruach and close to Lugh's festival, Lughnasa (1 August). A pre-Christian pilgrimage route probably went from Crúachain in Roscommon to Croagh Patrick and ended in Caher Island (see Meehan, p. 657). On the summit are the remains of a pre-Christian hill fort, supplanted by an early Christian oratory and later by a chapel built in 1905. Begin at the Croagh Patrick Information Center for background information and useful tips—and perhaps a hiking staff. http://www.museumsofmayo.com/croaghpatrick.htm.

Connemara

Connemara, Co. Galway, is an isolated, stunning region, replete with mountains, lakes, fjords, bogs, beaches, and impressive views. It is a large *Gaeltacht* (Gaelic-Irish-speaking region) and it is worth spending a few days exploring the countryside and enjoying the local artisan crafts. For walking tours, check out http://www.walkingireland.com. A visit to Inishbofin (first mentioned in the seventh century, when St Colman established a monastery there) is another possibility. The ferry MV Island Discovery crosses to Inishbofin from Cleggan, 10 km (6 mi) northeast of Clifden. The island is famous for its traditional music (http://www.inishbofin.com).

Knockma

Knockma (or Knockmaa), Co. Galway, is the highest hill (552 feet) in the plains of North Galway and South Mayo. The great "Hill of Medb" is another legendary burial place of Queen Maeve/Medb. Knockma was also reported to be the home of Finnvara (Finnbheara), the King of Connacht faeries. The area contains many ancient remains, including cairns, underground passages, and forts. The region may have been inhabited 7000 years ago and has been associated with myth and magic for millennia (http://corofin.galway-ireland.ie/knockma.htm). It is 8 km (5 mi) west of Tuam, 29 km (18 mi) north of Galway City.

Afterword

Ireland is a very special country, full of sacred sites and friendly people, a land of mystery, magic, and music. We often say that *all* of Ireland is a powerful place, and the experiences we have had on the Emerald Isle continue to resonate in our lives.

After your journey around Ireland is completed, take time to contemplate what memories of Ireland you want to carry with you for the rest of your life. Is there a quintessential place that evokes Ireland to you? One particular experience that you will never, ever forget?

Why visit powerful places anyway? Is it in order to experience how our ancestors lived? To "remember" a more holistic way of living? For spiritual development? Is it a way to reconnect with an ancient way of "gnowing," a direct experience of truth and meaningfulness? Hopefully, it is not just a kind of "earth-mysteries tourism" where one collects sacred places like so many commodities.

Logically, we know that what we experience today at a reconstructed site like Newgrange is not the same as what our ancestors experienced 3000 or 4000 years ago. We carry flashlights and cell phones on our journeys; we "go online" via the internet for the latest weather report and to correspond with friends thousands of miles away. We understand the movement of the planets and can chart the passing seasons with elaborate computer programs. Nonetheless, it is clear that our ancestors knew things we have forgotten: for example, how to live in harmony with the earth. Without idealizing the ones who came before, we can learn from them.

We have much to gain from spending time at sacred sites. They are not simply anachronisms, quaint archaic monuments left at our disposal. As Tom Graves says (p. 206), "Whatever happens there, whatever it is that we are finding, it is happening not in some distant past, but here, now. The 'earth-mysteries' are becoming part of present-day reality, a present-day magical technology. And yet we must beware: we must preserve that sense of mystery, of wonder, or we will lose all sense of meaning with it, and possibly ourselves as well."

"Traditions are born and pass away; temples and structures erected at sacred places are built and destroyed.... That's the game of the universe: creation, preservation, and destruction. But the nature of what allows for all that to happen, that sacredness is always there. Remembering that sacred consciousness that permeates everything and everyone, without exception, is probably the healthiest point of view one can have, I believe. And that's what, for me, the art of the master builders is pointing to." Ferran Blasco Aguasca, Shen Dao Institute Barcelona

We have written this "Powerful Places Guidebook" to help you rediscover your connection with the sacredness of the land. Many of us are uprooted or rootless, detached from our environment. But we are of the land, part of the land, whether we realize it or not, and it is to our detriment—and the detriment of the planet—when we forget it. Our very bodies are made up of the same elements as the earth.

Mother Earth is not a commodity to be used and used up: she is vital for our existence at many levels, including the physical, emotional, and spiritual. We hope that by describing these powerful places and providing some suggestions for how to experience them, we are helping to foster a deeper relationship between you and the planet.

Glossary

alignment A row of standing stones (menhirs).

anima loci The "place-soul." The essential "personality" of a place. The sense of sacredness of a particular hill, spring, standing stone, etc.

axis mundi (world axis) A symbolic representation of the vertical "center" of the world; the cosmic axis or world pillar, where the heaven (sky) connects with the earth and access is possible between lower and higher realms. May be a tree, a pillar, etc.

BCE Before the Common Era (contemporary replacement for BC, which stands for Before Christ).

Beltane (or **Bealtaine**) The Celtic cross-quarter beginning-of-summer festival, often associated with fire, now celebrated as May Day (May 1).

Cailleach The ancient ancestral goddess, "divine hag," or "old lady of winter" in Celtic lands; associated with death and transformation.

cairn A man-made pile of stones, often in a conical form. Specifically refers to a megalithic tomb covered with a mound of small stones.

Candlemas Originally the Celtic cross-quarter day of Imbolc, which was Christianized to be St Brigid's Feastday (Feb. 1); Feb. 2 became Candlemas, the Christian feast commemorating the purification of the Virgin Mary and the presentation of the infant Jesus in the Temple.

CE Common Era (contemporary replacement for AD, which stands for Anno Domini—in the Year of the Lord).

Celt A nineteenth-century term used to describe any of the European peoples who spoke, or speak, a Celtic language. The term is also used in a wider sense to describe the modern descendants of those peoples, notably those who participate in a Celtic culture. The six territories recognized by the Celtic League and Celtic Congress as Celtic Nations are Brittany, Cornwall, Ireland, Isle of Man, Scotland, and Wales. Limiting the territories to these six is disputed by people from England, Asturias and Galicia in Spain, and several other European countries that also retain some Celtic cultural traits.

Celtic cross A religious symbol that combines a cross with a circle surrounding the intersection.

chrismon A Christian symbol representing aspects of Christ: a circle, inside of which are an "X" and super-imposed "P," standing for chi/rho, the first two letters in the Greek spelling of Christ; within the crossbars of the "X" are the alpha and omega, standing for Christ as "the beginning and the end."

corbelled A building technique where a piece of stone juts out of a wall to carry the weight of stones above.

cross-quarter days The four days falling approximately halfway between the solstices and the equinoxes: Samhain, Imbolc, Beltane, and Lughnasa. They were important feast days in traditional Celtic societies and are still celebrated today, though with different names.

Cup and ring marks Stone-picked designs of hollowed-out cups and rings, often concentric. Thought to date to late Neolithic or Bronze Age. Found on megaliths and also on slabs of bedrock. Purpose unknown.

dolmen A type of single-chamber megalithic (large stone) construction (tomb), usually consisting of three or more upright stones supporting a large flat horizontal capstone. Most Irish dolmens date from 4000-3000 BCE. Although often used for burials, they were also ceremonial or "power" centers. They were initially covered with earth or small stones to form a tumulus or cairn, but in many cases that covering has weathered away.

dowse To search for underground water, metal, etc., by the use of a divining rod or pendulum.

Druid A member of the Celtic priestly and learned class during the final centuries BCE if not before. They were suppressed by the Roman government from the 1st century CE and disappeared from the written record by the 2nd century, although there may have been later survivals in Britain and Ireland. Their teachings were passed down orally, so very little is verifiably known about them.

equinox The day (twice each year) when the tilt of the Earth's axis is inclined neither away from nor towards the sun; as a result, night and day are nearly equal in length.

faery A mythical being or spirit. Faeries are sometimes described as the wee folk, the good folk, or other euphemisms. We use the spelling "faery" to differentiate them from the cartoonish, trivialized "fairies" popularized by modern media.

fault Fractures in the rock strata of the earth, caused by relative movement.

fire line A dry fault under the surface of the earth. A term used by dowsers for perceived faults.

folly A building, usually in a garden or park, constructed primarily for decoration.

Gaeltacht Officially designated regions in Ireland, mainly in the west, where Irish is the predominant language.

hermitage A place where one can live in seclusion; a retreat; a kind of small church.

holy well A spring or other body of water revered either in a Pagan or Christian context. Commonly used to refer to any water source of limited size where healing qualities are attributed to the water through the numinous presence of a guardian spirit or saint.

Ice Age A geological period of long-term reduction in the temperature of the Earth's surface and atmosphere, resulting in an expansion of continental ice sheets, polar ice sheets, and alpine glaciers. The last Ice Age ended around 10,000 years ago in Europe.

Imbolc The Celtic cross-quarter day, now celebrated as the feast day of St Brigid on February 1 (and as Candlemas on February 2). Imbolc (from 'ewe-milk") marks the beginning growth cycle of the new year, the birth of lambs.

intervisibility Visible to each other. Megalithic sites were often constructed to be within sight of each other.

Iron Age The period during which tools and weapons were primarily made of iron or steel, replacing bronze. The period began in Ireland around 500 BCE. There is a paucity of evidence of burials but much evidence of defensive and domestic sites.

kerbstone A stone on the perimeter of a megalithic mound; for example, the carved boulders encircling the base of Newgrange.

labyrinth An intricate spiraling design with a single pathway leading to the center (unlike a maze, which has numerous paths).

Lughnasa or **Lughnasadh** A Celtic cross-quarter harvest festival held around August 1, Christianized as Lammas (loaf-mass day).

mantra A (sacred) verbal formula repeated in prayer, meditation, or incantation.

megalith A large stone which has been used to construct a structure or monument, either alone or together with other stones. Megalithic means structures made of such large stones, utilizing an interlocking system without the use of mortar or cement. They date from 4500-1500 BCE in Europe.

menhir An upright monumental stone standing either alone or with others, as in an alignment.

metamorphic A stone that has been changed in structure or composition as the result of intense heat and pressure.

Morrigan Celtic goddess of war, death, destruction, and sovereignty; one of the Celtic Mother Goddesses, also known as Morrigu, Modron, or Morgan. The mother of the goddess Brigid.

nave The central part of a church, extending from the narthex to the apse and flanked by aisles.

nemeton A sacred space utilized in Celtic religion. Nemetoi appear to have been primarily situated in natural areas, and often centered around trees; as such they are often described as sacred groves. Nemeton is related to the name of the Nemates tribe of what is now Germany and to the goddess Nemetona.

Neolithic The New Stone Age. A period in the development of human technology, beginning about 9500 BCE in the Middle East (and around 4500 BCE in Ireland), that is traditionally considered the last part of the Stone Age. The Neolithic people were farmers who domesticated plants and animals and created pottery and woven textiles. They built numerous constructions, including dolmens, stone circles, and earthen henges and erected many standing stones. The Neolithic begins with the rise of farming, which produced the ""Neolithic Revolution," and ends when metal tools became widespread in the Copper Age or Bronze Age, followed by the Iron Age. The Neolithic is not a specific chronological period, but rather a suite of behavioral and cultural characteristics, including the use of wild and domestic crops and the use of domesticated animals.

Ogham script An ancient form of writing, found exclusively in Ireland, Scotland, and Wales, dating around the 3rd to 6th century CE.

oracle A person, such as a priestess, who "relays" the response of a deity when consulted.

passage tomb A megalithic site usually dating to the Neolithic. Some have simple single chambers, while others have sub-chambers leading off from the main chamber. They were entered via a long, covered entryway. They are called tombs but also served other ceremonial purposes.

Pattern (or **Patron**) **Day** An outdoor assembly with religious practices, traders' stalls, etc. on the feast day of a patron saint; a day of special devotion at a holy well.

purgatory In the Roman Catholic Church, a place or condition of temporary punishment after death, meant to cleanse the souls of those destined for heaven but not quite ready for it.

rag (or clootie) A strip or piece of cloth, a rag or item of clothing, usually tied to a tree branch near a sacred well as an offering or prayer.

regalia Ceremonial clothing, finery.

reliquary A container for the physical remains of saints, Christ, or the Virgin Mary. The relics may be bones, pieces of clothing, or some object associated with the person.

ring fort A circular, oval, or d-shaped fortified settlement built during the Iron Age or Early Middle Ages. In Ireland, often called a *rath* (e.g. Rathcroghan).

ritual landscape A landscape in nature that has been modified (by addition of megaliths, holy wells, etc.) to be used for ritual purposes.

sacristy A room in a church used for keeping vestments and other church furnishings.

Samhain The Celtic cross-quarter day around October 31, now celebrated as Halloween.

sarcophagus A stone coffin, often inscribed or decorated with sculpture.

Sheela-na-gig Figurative carvings of (often skeletal) naked women displaying exaggerated genitalia. They are found on churches, castles, and other buildings, particularly in the British Isles, dating approximately from the 11th to 16th centuries.

Sidhe In Ireland, a supernatural race said to live underground in the faery mounds and in the *raths* or ruined ring forts. Also called "the people of the mounds."

solstice An astronomical event that happens twice each year, when the sun's apparent position in the sky reaches its northernmost (summer) or southernmost (winter) extreme. These correspond to the longest and shortest days of the year.

souterrain A type of underground passage or man-made cave associated mainly with the Atlantic Iron Age; purpose unknown, perhaps used for storage, refuge, or ceremony.

temenos A sacred enclosure; a piece of land dedicated to a god; a sanctuary, a holy grove, or a holy precinct.

"thin place" A place (in nature or in a human construction) where the veil between this world and other realms (faery, the Other World, etc.) is thin and passage between our normal consensual reality and a different kind of reality is more easily accomplished.

topo map A topographic map, characterized by large-scale detail and quantitative representation of relief, usually using contour lines.

torc A large, usually rigid neck ring, typically made from strands of metal twisted together.

tumulus A mound of earth and stones raised over a dolmen. Often referred to as a tomb, but served as more than a burial site. Tumuli are also known as barrows, burial mounds, *Hügelgrab* or *kurgans*, and can be found throughout much of the world.

Votive offering An object left in a sacred place (church, holy well, etc.) for broadly religious purposes such as the completion of a vow or to gain a favor from the deities.

wouivre An old Gaulish name given to snakes that glide, to rivers that snake through the landscape, to telluric currents that snake underground from the depths of the terrestrial strata, bringing life that fructifies Earth and Man.

zodiac A circle of twelve 30° divisions of celestial longitude which are centered upon the ecliptic: the apparent path of the sun across the celestial sphere over the course of the year. The twelve signs of the zodiac are used in astrology to cast horoscopes.

Bibliography

Annals of The Four Masters. Compiled in the seventeenth century. http://en.wikipedia.org/wiki/Annals_of_the_Four_Masters.

Boylan, Eamonn. "Tobernalt Holy Well – Sligo – History and Heritage." Publ. by Fr. Jim Murray, Curate of St. John's Parish, Carraroe, 2002.

Brennan, Martin. *The Stones of Time - Calendars, Sundials, and Stone Chambers of Ancient Ireland.* Vermont: Inner Traditions International, 1994.

Cooney, Gabriel. "The passage tomb phenomenon in Ireland," in *Brú Na Bóinne – Newgrange, Knowth, Dowth, and the River Boyne,* pp. 7-8. Originally published as a supplement to *Archaeology Ireland,* Vol. 11, no. 3; this edition published 2003. ISBN 0 9534426 3 2.

Clooney, Gabriel. *Landscapes of Neolithic Ireland.* London: Routledge, 2000.

Dames, Michael. *Mythic Ireland.* London: Thames & Hudson, 1992.

Delyth, Jen. *Celtic Folk Soul – Art, Myth & Symbol.* Portland, OR: Amber Lotus Publishing, 2008.

Devereux, Paul. *Stone Age Soundtracks: The Acoustic Archaeology of Ancient Sites.* London: Vega, 2001.

Eogan, George. "The passage tombs of Brú na Bóinne," in *Brú Na Bóinne – Newgrange, Knowth, Dowth, and the River Boyne,* pp. 9-11. Originally published as a supplement to *Archaeology Ireland,* Vol. 11, no. 3; this edition published 2003. ISBN 0 9534426 3 2.

Gilroy, John. *Tlachtga – Celtic Fire Festival.* Glanmire, Co. Cork: Pikefield Publications, 2000.

Graves, Tom. *Needles of Stone Revisited.* Glastonbury: Gothic Image Publications, 1986.

Hale, Susan Elizabeth. *Sacred Space, Sacred Sound – The Acoustic Mysteries of Holy Places.* Wheaton, IL: Quest Books, 2007.

Halpin, Andy, and Conor Newman. *Ireland – An Oxford Archaeological Guide.* Oxford: Oxford University Press, 2006.

Harbison, Peter. *Guide to National and Historic Monuments of Ireland,* 3rd edition. Dublin: Gill & Macmillan Ltd, 1992.

Healy, Elizabeth. *In Search of Ireland's Holy Wells.* Dublin: Wolfhound Press Ltd, 2001.

Herity, Michael. *Rathcroghan and Carnfree: Celtic Royal Sites in Roscommon.* Copyright 1991; available from Cruachan Aí Heritage Center.

Jerman, James, and Anthony Weir. *Images of Lust: Sexual Carvings on Medieval Churches.* London: Routledge, 1993.

Kelly, Eamonn P. *Sheela-na-Gigs – Origins and Functions.* Dublin: Country House, in association with National Museum of Ireland, 1996.

Knight, Peter. *West Kennet Long Barrow – Landscape, Shamans and the Cosmos.* Wiltshire, UK: Stone Seeker Publishing, 2011.

Lorenzo Villanueva, Joaquín. *Phoenician Ireland,* 2nd edition. Transl. Henry O'Brien. London: Joseph Robins, originally published 1833. http://openlibrary.org/works/OL12107736W/Phoenician_Ireland.

318

Macalister, R.A.S., "A Study of the Remains and Traditions of Tara." A talk given to the RIA in 1918.

Madden, Gerard. *Holy Island/Inis Cealtra.* Mountshannon: Holy Island Tours, 2008.

McMann, Jean. *Loughcrew – The Cairns – A Guide.* Oldcastle, Co. Meath: After Hours Books, new edition, 2005.

Meagher, Robert Emmet, and Elizabeth Parker Neave. *Ancient Ireland – An Explorer's Guide.* Gloucestershire, England: Arris Books, 2004.

Meehan, Cary. *The Traveller's Guide to Sacred Ireland,* revised and updated. Glastonbury: Gothic Image Publications, 2004.

Moroney, Anne-Marie. *Dowth – Winter Sunsets.* Drogheda, Co. Louth: Flax Mill Publications, 1999.

Murphy, Anthony and Richard Moore. *Island of the Setting Sun – In Search of Ireland's Ancient Astronomers.* Dublin: Liffey Press Ltd, 2006.

Ó Crualaoich, Gearóid. *The Book of the Cailleach – Stories of the Wise-Woman Healer.* Cork: Cork University Press, 2003.

O'Kelly, Claire. *Concise Guide to Newgrange.* Dublin: Eden Publications, 1996.

_____ "Dowth – Co. Meath, Ireland." Brochure, 1996.

Patten, Terry. "Finding Absolute Freedom in Any Moment: The Practice of Ever-Present Awareness." Session Four, in *Integral Spiritual Practice: The 8-Week Course,* 2011. Evolving Wisdom, San Rafael, CA (http://evolvingwisdom.com/integralspiritualpractice/online-course/).

Pennick, Nigel. *The Celtic Cross.* Cardiff: St David's Press, an imprint of Ashley Drake Publishing Ltd, 2007.

_____*Celtic Sacred Landscapes.* 1996/2000 paperback ed.

Ramo, Chet. *Climbing Brandon – Science and Faith on Ireland's Holy Mountain.* New York: Walker & Company, 2004.

_____*Honey from Stone.* First published by Dodd, Mead & Co., Inc, 1987. Paperback edition, Dingle: Brandon Book Publishers Ltd, 1997.

"Rathcroghan, Co. Roscommon: *Where the Táin Bó Cúailnge Began.*" Dublin: Archaeology Ireland, Heritage Guide No. 4, 2009.

Richardson, Alan. *Spirits of the Stones.* London: Virgin, 2001.

Roberts, Jack. *The Sheela-na-gigs of Ireland – An Illustrated Map & Guide,* Galway: Bandia Publishing, 2009. bandiajrr@yahoo.co.uk.

_____*The Sacred Mythological Centres of Ireland – An Illustrated Guide.* New Revised edition. Bandia Publishing, 2008.

Waddell, John. "Rathcroghan, Co. Roscommon: where *The Táin Bó Cúailnge* began." Archaeology Ireland Heritage Guide No. 44.

Zucchelli, Christine. *Stones of Adoration – Sacred Stones and Mystic Megaliths of Ireland.* Wilton, Cork: The Collins Press, 2007.

Index

CPSIA information can be obtained
at www.ICGtesting.com
Printed in the USA
BVOW09s0108121017
497366BV00001B/6/P